CW01261060

Katharine Briggs: Story-Teller

H.R. Ellis Davidson

Lutterworth Press
Cambridge

This book is dedicated to
Michael, Lord Marks,
a good friend to Katharine and to the
Folklore Society,
who made its publication possible

**Lutterworth Press
7 All Saints' Passage
Cambridge CB2 3LS**

British Library Cataloguing in Publication data

Davidson, Hilda Ellis
  Katharine Briggs.
  1. Briggs, Katharine M.   2. Folklorists —
  England — Biography
  I. Title
  398'.092'4   CR55.B7/

ISBN 0-7188-2659-0

Copyright © Hilda R. Ellis Davidson 1986

First published 1986

All rights reserved. No part of this publication may be
reproduced, stored in a retrieval system, or transmitted in any form or by any means,
electronic, mechanical, photocopying, recording, or otherwise, without the prior permission
in writing from the publisher.

Printed in Great Britain by
St. Edmundsbury Press

Contents

List of Illustrations   vii
List of Tables   viii
Acknowledgements   ix
Introduction   xiii

1 Yorkshire Heritage: The Family Background   1
2 An Artist's Daughter: Parents and Childhood   13
3 Growing Up and Making Out: The Imaginary World of the Briggs Sisters   46
4 Feats and Quests: The War Years   79
5 Search for the Hidden People: The Barn House, Burford   106
6 Tales and Traditions: Work in Folklore   137
7 Golden Harvest: The Last Years   156

Appendices

1 Her Account of Her Career   173
2 An Artist's Daughter   176
3 Eric Notes   179
4 Selected Poems   183
   1 A Handsome Sailor Came to Woo Me
   2 If You Eat of Fairy Fruit
   3 I Met a Fairy on the Hill
   4 I Waked or Slept, I Knew not Which
   5 The Sun Shines Warm upon My Limbs

6 Triolet: What a Lively Piece of Clay
7 Occupied Territory
8 Elspeth

Chapter Notes   188
Published Work   200

Index   205

List of Illustrations

Marianne Briggs	10
Catherine Briggs	10
Ernest Briggs with his brothers	15
Ernest Briggs	22
Katharine Briggs with her mother	24
Sketch of Mary Briggs by Ernest Briggs	26
Sketch of Katharine Briggs by Ernest Briggs	26
Sketch of Katharine Briggs by Ernest Briggs	26
Dalbeathie around 1911	41
Mary Briggs with her daughters	44
Katharine Briggs after taking her degree	63
Mary Briggs and her daughters	87
Katharine Briggs during the war	102
Katharine Briggs at Burford	115
The Barn House	118
Katharine Briggs at Burford, 1969	149
Katharine Briggs as Prospero	158
Katharine Briggs at Southolme	167

List of Tables

The Briggs Family	3
The Milnes Family	3
The Family of Henry Currer Briggs	12
The Family of Ernest Briggs	14

Acknowledgements

The writing of this book has been a pleasure and a privilege, because of the opportunity which it has given me to explore Katharine's past, to revisit Burford, to experience the serenity and beauty of Dalbeathie, and to see Southolme, where Katharine's happy last years were spent. It has also enabled me to make contact with many of those who knew and loved Katharine at various stages in her long life, and such was the force of the impression which she made on them that gathering information has been a joyful and enriching experience.

In expressing thanks to all who have helped with this work, I must first on my own behalf and on behalf of all Katharine's friends acknowledge the generous gift of Lord Marks to the Folklore Society towards its publication, making it possible to include a number of illustrations. Throughout the two years it took to write this book, I have owed a great deal to the help, cooperation and generosity of Katharine Law, Katharine's friend and literary executor. She has given me full access to Katharine's papers and notebooks, introduced me to many friends who met Katharine at Southolme and elsewhere, and laid the foundation for a biography by inviting a number of those who knew Katharine well to record their memories. I am particularly grateful to Evelyn Forbes, who was at school with Katharine, Evelyn Goshawk, who knew her at Dalbeathie and was in touch with her during the War years, Josephine Thompson, one of the Summer Players and secretary to Katharine at the Barn House, Faith Sharp, who worked with Katharine in play productions and in founding the Burford Guild of Arts, and Professor Margaret Hodges of Pittsburg, with whom Katharine stayed more than once on visits to the United States. These have all written lively accounts of their memories of Katharine, and given me much help and information; Evelyn Goshawk in particular has read chapters of the book and supplied much additional background, as well as passing on to me a manuscript book of poems which Katharine gave to her. I am most grateful also to two close friends of Katharine, Barbara Innes and Margaret Nash-Williams, who have read parts of the book and been unwearying in answering questions and drawing on their memories of Dalbeathie and Burford.

There are many others to whom I owe thanks for their help and interest. Isabel Hale knew Katharine at school, and gave me much information about Lansdowne House for which I am most grateful. Kathleen Lea told me something of Katharine's time at Oxford, and Jean Dalgleish and Catherine Hollingsworth, former members of the Summer Players, conjured up vivid memories of their activities, and of the fun and inspiration of those early performances. Tricia Atkinson has been most generous in showing me the house and grounds at Dalbeathie, and in supplying a number of photographs. The Reverend T. Fish Taylor has talked to me of Katharine's work on her thesis after the war. Letters from Brian Wood, who worked with Katharine while he was in the RAF, from Jim Rositter, Sister Ursula Blake, and Sister Mary Healey have helped to build up the picture of her life. I am most grateful to Isabel Templeton who unearthed and copied for me the records of Katharine's journey to Newfoundland in 1926. A talk with Peg Cooper, who met Katharine shortly before her death and is herself now no longer alive, gave me an unforgettable glimpse of Katharine's ability to make contacts with those whom she met on a deep level.

From Katharine's family, I must mention particularly Noel Currer Briggs, who gave me information about early family history, and encouragement, much appreciated, over the biography. Jean Melhuish, daughter of Donald Briggs, kindly let me use the family genealogy produced by her mother and some privately published material about the Briggs family. Karen Hardcastle gave me additional information about Katharine at Oxford, while Kathleen Laurie showed me some family treasures and allowed me to read an unpublished history of the Jackson family written by her mother, Edith Jackson. Others who have given help are David Ayerst of Burford, who knew Katharine as a neighbour, the Reverend V.D. Rogers, who supplied information about her confirmation; the Reverend Frank Walker of Cambridge and Mary Schroeder, who told me more about the Unitarian Church, and Dr Clyde Binfield of the University of Sheffield who gave me a new insight into the achievements of Unitarian families in the north of England in the nineteenth century. I have received help and encouragement also from members of the Folklore Society and friends of Katharine, particularly from Carmen Blacker and Michael Loewe, who read parts of the book in manuscript, Stewart Sanderson, Theo Brown and Neil Philip. I have had many helpful discussions with two

ACKNOWLEDGEMENTS

Japanese scholars, Mikiko Ishii and Reiko Yamanouchi, who are translating some of Katharine's books into Japanese. I am grateful also to Patrick Hardy for reading the manuscript at an earlier stage and giving me advice about it.

The number of names mentioned here gives some indication of the wide range of Katharine's friends, and the search for her past has taken me as far afield as Aberdeen in the north and Totnes in the south. Everywhere I have received a warm welcome, and found all her friends most anxious that her biography should be published. Study of the early letters and documents, many of which are now in the possession of the Brotherton Library in the University of Leeds, has made me realise how much interesting material exists concerning the Briggs family and their many connections. This I have regretfully been unable to include, but it has helped me to understand the qualities and ideals of Katharine which made her so outstanding a character. I extend thanks now to all who have helped me, allowed me to study family records and given me warm hospitality. I would like to conclude by thanking the Lutterworth Press for accepting the book for publication, and for making the production of it so easy and pleasant.

Hilda R. Ellis Davidson
Cambridge 1986

Introduction

*He who bends to himself a Joy
Doth the winged life destroy;
But he who kisses the joy as it flies
Lives in Eternity's sunrise.*

William Blake

The difficulty of describing Katharine Briggs to those who never came into contact with her or her work is that she fits into no obvious category. In an age of increasing specialisation she was not a specialist, although she became an undoubted authority in one particular field, in which she has no serious competitors. She received a doctorate from Oxford for her books on fairy lore and magic in sixteenth- and seventeenth-century literature, and lectured widely in England and America, but she never fully belonged to the academic world. She made a special study of the English Civil War, and wrote historical novels set in this period, together with two books for children which are likely to endure, *Hobberdy Dick* and *Kate Crackernuts*, but she was never recognised as a successful novelist and published no further work in children's fiction. She completed the enormous *Dictionary of British Folktales*, filling a serious gap and leaving something on which future students could build, but she was not a professional worker in the field of oral literature, and relied largely on literary sources. She devoted herself for years to dramatic work, acting, writing and producing plays, and organising a small travelling theatre, but was never a professional actress or serious dramatist. She proved an inspired teacher of Guides and Brownies, and was once sent to Newfoundland to win converts to the movement, but was never really accepted into the upper hierarchy of the organisation. When she joined the WAAF, her ability to provide entertainment won her many friends in what was at first an alien world, while she gained respect for her work as a medical orderly, but she never obtained a commission.

Yet she was far more than a gifted amateur with varied interests, who could afford to indulge in many activities because she was under no necessity to earn her own living. Her different interests and skills came together creatively in a manner all too rare in our time, rather in the tradition of the seventeenth century, that period in which she took such delight. Her energy and enjoyment in what she did brought inspiration into the discussions in which she took part. Katharine loved talking all her life, but never stayed at a superficial level; she constantly introduced a new element of perceptive enthusiasm, tempered by robust common sense and a puckish sense of humour. Carmen Blacker once referred to her 'quality of wisdom which would put you on the right touch, or light up with a kind of flashing dazzle a hitherto humdrum discussion.' Moreover Katharine's interests in different fields crystallised, as it were, in her outstanding gift, that of story-telling.

This is an art which belongs largely to a vanished world, although there are signs that it may be coming back into our lives, helped by an increasing preference among the young for hearing and watching rather than reading printed books. The value now put on story-telling sessions is at least partly due to the contribution of Katharine Briggs in keeping the art alive and making such rich material available. She excelled in the telling of tales, continually adding to her repertoire from ballads, folktales and robust fairy tales, until like some famous story-tellers of the past she had a vast treasury of tales stored in her memory to be recalled at will. She fought hard to save the fairy tale from the degradation it had suffered in children's books, transformed into a sugary, sentimental panacea instead of the disturbing tradition of a strange hidden race whose values differ from those of mankind. *The Penguin Dictionary of Fairies* gives some idea of the extent of her work in this field, bringing back much forgotten and neglected tradition. She made this available not only for imaginative children — and the effects of this are incalculable — but also for writers and thinkers to explore. Katharine believed that it was a good thing for the young to manufacture their own amusements, and also that they should be brought in touch from an early age with the traditions of the countryside and the homely wisdom of the folktale, part of the roots from which they sprang.

Her collection of tales and studies in fairy tradition will ensure that her name is remembered. She made another contribution, however, within her own wide circle by her rare personality and the extent of her influence. She made many friends, and in hospitality she was unrivalled, with a stock of vivid memories as well as stories to enrich her later years. She was an exquisite figure in her old age, elegant and gracious, with a low soft voice, and a gentle firmness

INTRODUCTION

which disarmed opposition. Unfailingly courteous, she could also be wholly unconventional, and she detested above all things insincerity and pretension. It is surprising that with all her warm and eager response to many people, men and women, Katharine never married. This may have been due to her great love and admiration for her father, the painter Ernest Briggs, who died when she was fourteen, and to the closeness of the tie with her sisters, particularly her younger sister Elspeth, whose gifts and interests were akin to her own. For years Katharine saw herself as the man of the family, planning for her mother and sisters, and throwing much energy into organising their lives in the house her father had built in Perthshire, set like an enchanted castle in woods beside the River Tay. In this isolated spot, the girls were cut off from others of their own age, and for years created their own imaginative world of art, literature and drama, gradually gathering a group of women friends around them and organising a travelling theatre. In their energetic and creative pursuits, the three sisters merit a place in the tradition of English eccentrics, and it is all the more astonishing that in later life Katharine was so fully at home in a wider, cosmopolitan world. Fame came to her late, and she enjoyed it greatly. In her journeys to the States, she charmed many audiences with her story-telling and personality, and made many new friends, until her visits were almost like royal progresses.

The life of Katharine Briggs is that of a most unusual person, whose gifts and way of life were unconventional ones, and whose influence ranged surprisingly far. Those who came into contact with her have been anxious to see an account of her life and development as a whole. Her activities were so varied that she came into touch with those from many different backgrounds, and even friends who knew her well were often ignorant of other facets of her life. This book is an attempt to fill the gap, and present a record of the background against which Katharine grew up, and her growth as a personality and writer. There may be something here of relevance for our perplexed and troubled times. Katharine refused to make a career for herself in the accepted way, or to live in accordance with the fashions of her time and class. She found her own way to enrich her life and the lives of others, to achieve good and lasting relationships, and to accept life as it came. To meet her was to encounter a serene and balanced mind, and it might be said of her in Blake's words that she was one of those who lived 'in Eternity's sunrise'.

1 Yorkshire Heritage: The Family Background

> *The whole world is an hour glass*
> *In the lean hands of Time;*
> *He turned it once, long long ago,*
> *And still the faltering sand slides slow,*
> *And still like a forgotten rhyme*
> *The generations pass.*
> K.M. Briggs, 'Lost Country'

In the early years of this century, a little girl, Katharine Mary Briggs, played in the garden of a corner house in Fellows Road, Hampstead, not far from where unceasing traffic now roars past Swiss Cottage. In 1902 she was four years old, the eldest of three sisters, and had already begun to play imaginary games with her adored father, based on the stories he told to her. The earliest of these, she believed, had been *The Water Babies*. By 1906, when she was allowed to stay up until eight, a whole world of literature was opening out before her, for her father read to her in the evening shortened versions of the immortal books of high adventure, *Treasure Island, Quentin Durward, Huckleberry Finn, Lorna Doone* and the like. The inspiration of these readings influenced the games played in the back garden of 102 Fellows Road, which survives much as Katharine describes it, with a straight path running between the two lawns from the billiardroom door to the toolshed, and a gate in the side wall leading into Kings College Road. This simple setting was the stage for many an exciting drama. It was, as Katharine wrote in 1980,

> a very good place for playing. There was a high wall between it and the road, over which you could only see the tops of people's heads, but there was one solid wooden gate rather lower than the road [?wall], and ill-bred people used to stand and look over ... to watch us playing. I used to stop and stare at them furiously, but they never took any notice, and I often wondered what kind of insensitive creatures they were.[1]

This was a sheltered existence for a sensitive, imaginative child, with a mother who ran the house with serenity and efficiency, and a father always ready to reveal to her a wonderful world of youthful heroes and inspiring exploits against dastardly foes, together with two younger sisters who grew up to follow her lead unquestioningly. But the larger family into which Katharine was born belonged to a different, harsher world, that which E.M. Forster in *Howard's End* called 'a life in which telegrams and anger count.' 'This other life', admitted one of his characters, 'though obviously horrid, often seems the real one — there's grit in it. It does breed character.' Ernest Briggs, Katharine's father, had been born into a wealthy Yorkshire family in 1866, intended by his parents to take his place in precisely that kind of world. He started his training in Leeds as a mining engineer, in order to enter the family business, a limited company founded by his father and grandfather to work several coal mines in the West Riding. The reason why he changed course was said to be the heart weakness left by an illness, but an even stronger force driving him could have been the absorbing passion which he felt for the world of mountains and rivers, and his two favourite occupations of water-colour painting and fly-fishing. His marriage in 1893 to a farmer's daughter was also outside the normal family pattern.

'I knew myself very lucky', Katharine remembered at the end of her life, 'to have an artist for a father.' She was amused and fascinated by the visits of her father's many artist friends to Fellows Road, and the endless technical discussions to which she sometimes listened, head bent over a book. This was clearly a most satisfying way of life to her; she remembered feeling sorry for 'little girls whose fathers went to offices in the morning and came home tired and cross at night.' But she respected the alien world of commerce, coal-mining and industry through which the Briggs had built up their fortune. Meetings with aunts, uncles and cousins, of whom there was a seemingly endless supply, must have made her familiar with it, although it never absorbed any of her immediate family group. Indeed in 1935, when she was living in Scotland, 'Miss K.M. Briggs, Great Grand-daughter of the Founder' was to write a short account of Henry Briggs, Son and Co. Ltd, Whitwood Collieries, Normanton, illustrated by photographs of mining shafts and lines of trucks bearing the family name.[2] She kept at a respectful distance from this demanding industrial world, and never herself went down a mine, but she was proud of the family achievement. These sharply defined contrasts in Katharine's background may account for what an Oxford

Table 1 **The Briggs Family**

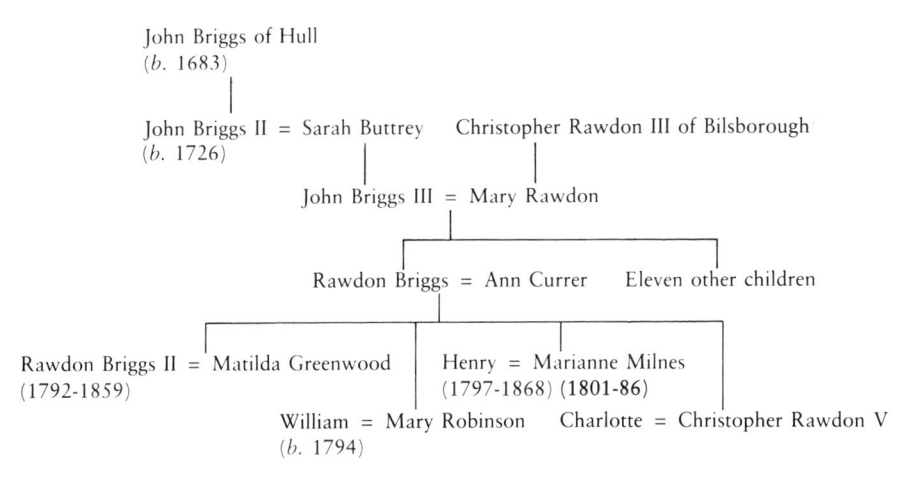

```
John Briggs of Hull
(b. 1683)
        |
John Briggs II = Sarah Buttrey    Christopher Rawdon III of Bilsborough
(b. 1726)            |                         |
              John Briggs III = Mary Rawdon
                           |
              ┌────────────┴────────────┐
         Rawdon Briggs = Ann Currer    Eleven other children
                     |
    ┌────────────────┴───────────────────┐
Rawdon Briggs II = Matilda Greenwood    Henry = Marianne Milnes
(1792-1859)                            (1797-1868) (1801-86)
                William = Mary Robinson   Charlotte = Christopher Rawdon V
                (b. 1794)
```

Table 2 **The Milnes Family**

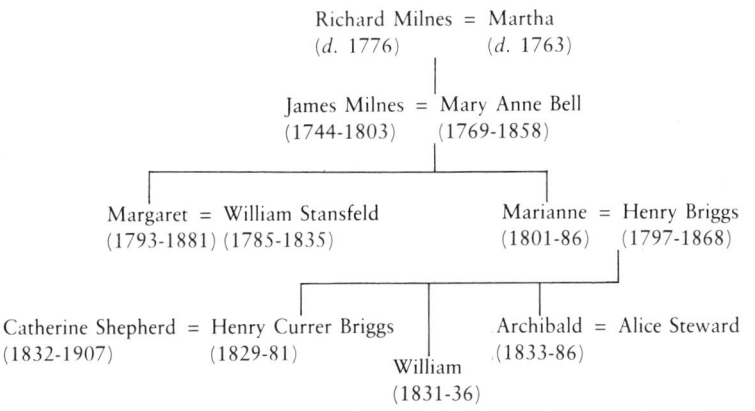

```
                Richard Milnes = Martha
                (d. 1776)        (d. 1763)
                          |
                James Milnes = Mary Anne Bell
                (1744-1803)    (1769-1858)
                          |
        ┌─────────────────┴──────────────────┐
  Margaret = William Stansfeld      Marianne = Henry Briggs
 (1793-1881) (1785-1835)            (1801-86)  (1797-1868)
                                         |
Catherine Shepherd = Henry Currer Briggs    Archibald = Alice Steward
(1832-1907)         (1829-81)               (1833-86)
                            William
                            (1831-36)
```

friend described as 'the admirable balance between her fine reason and gritty Yorkshire commonsense and a daring range of response to things beyond the ordinary experience.'[3]

Because of Katharine's pride and interest in the past achievements of her family, and the effect of this on her own development, it is necessary to spend some time on this Yorkshire background. The Currers, a name retained by many of the later Briggs, seem to have had little direct influence. Henry Currer took over Kildwick Manor, near Skipton, in the mid-sixteenth century, and built the beautiful manor house, which still stands today.[4] The main male line of the family came to an end in 1756, and the only direct link with the Briggs is the marriage of Rawdon Briggs to Anne Currer, daughter of William Currer, Vicar of Clapham in Craven, in 1791, resulting in the setting up of the firm of Currer, Briggs and Currer to run a mill producing woollen yarn and carpets at Luddendon Foot. Until recently, the first Briggs about which anything was known was John Briggs of Hull, born in 1683, but further work has now been done on the family genealogy by Noel Currer Briggs, Katharine's cousin,[5] and this John is found to be the son of an earlier John Briggs, a barber-surgeon and peruke-maker. The younger John married Sarah Buttrey in York Minster, and her ancestry has yielded some surprises: it can be traced back, mainly through the female line, to Cerdic, King of Wessex, in the sixth century, Arpad, King of Hungary who died in 907, and Erc, a fifth-century king of Dalriada, while one of her forbears, Isobel, was the illegitimate daughter of William the Lion of Scotland. There was thus a link between Sarah Briggs and the Macbeths, and this would assuredly have amused and delighted Katharine, with her love for Scotland and for Dalbeathie House not far from Birnam.

Sarah's husband, John Briggs, was a merchant in Yorkshire and a dissenter, who helped to build a small chapel in Bowl Alley Lane in Hull in 1725. Many such chapels were built in the years following the Toleration Act of 1689, to house congregations unwilling to accept everything in the Book of Common Prayer. Some of those which were fairly orthodox at the beginning came to adopt Unitarian opinions, and the Briggs were firm supporters of this movement, so that Katharine was brought up as a Unitarian. This did not mean deliberate opposition to the Church of England; the main principle of the Unitarians was refusal to limit their faith by creeds and written definitions, and to strive for religious tolerance. Many had their children baptized in the Church, and attended church services as well as their own chapels. The Unitarians had a strong sense of moral responsibility, and their religion was very much a practical affair; there is a constant record of the Briggs giving money and other forms of help where they felt it was needed. Family solidarity was strong, and the sons were loyal to their fathers and prepared to support the family business when their turn came. They were prompt to help fellow Unitarians, and also felt concern for their workpeople, taking part in all kinds of charitable and educational schemes. There was much interest in education and science, under the influence of leading men in the movement, like Joseph Priestley, the discoverer of oxygen, and they supported the new northern Universities, with their emphasis on science and technology and freedom from religious tests. Katharine's father and two of his brothers were sent down from Yorkshire to University College School in London, where teaching standards were high and there were no religious obligations on staff or pupils.[6] While their outlook might be serious, the Briggs and their friends were not puritanical, but enjoyed giving lavish hospitality and had an enthusiasm for amateur theatricals, while some were gifted musicians and artists. But for the leading men of the family, nothing was allowed to interfere with their ambitious business enterprises. They seemed possessed of untiring energy and determination, and were resourceful and adaptable, with a gift for running firms, factories and mines efficiently. They never shrank from taking on new projects, and it is hardly surprising that many of the Briggs men did not attain old age, but left wives to survive them for many years.

During the eighteenth century the family operated in the area around Wakefield and Halifax. The river Calder was a convenient route for sending manufactured goods to the coast, and later the Rochdale Canal provided a link with the Mersey. The Briggs were manufacturers, underwriters and bankers, with interests in shipping and the export trade. When a marriage took place, it usually meant an alliance with another hard-working Unitarian family, and a new business partnership. There were two such alliances with the Rawdon family, well-known in Yorkshire, who were manufacturers of woollen cloth at Hebdon Bridge near Halifax, which proved very profitable for both sides.[7]

The Briggs were ready to experiment in many different directions. In 1807 Rawdon Briggs took over the Halifax Commercial Bank, and ran it very successfully as a family concern.[8] His sons turned it into a joint stock bank, and Rawdon Briggs the second, a man 'of high and unimpeachable character' as a contemporary described him,[9] was the Chairman; he also stood for Parliament and represented Halifax for two years in the Reformed Parliament of 1832. His younger brother Henry was Katharine's great-grandfather, and it was he who embarked on the business of coal-mining in the

West Riding. This again was the result of a marriage, for Henry married Marianne Milnes of Flockton in 1824, and the Milnes family had worked the New Flockton mine on their land since 1774.[10] Henry, his mother-in-law Mrs Milnes, and Marianne's brother-in-law William Stansfeld formed a partnership to run the mine, and from that time the business expanded rapidly. Henry was soon owning and working new seams of coal south of the Calder, until in 1860 the company of Henry Briggs Son and Co Ltd was formed.[11]

Conditions in the mines of the West Riding at this time were appallingly bad. The coal seams round Flockton were thin, sometimes only ten or twelve inches, and small children were employed because they could get through the low gates when men and horses could not. The Report of 1842 on the employment of children in mines makes horrifying reading.[12] They worked barefoot in water, covered in dirt, and the men were often naked, while girls wore only a shift. Young children might be left alone for long periods in total darkness, waiting to open and shut the gates when the coal was brought through. Others had to push the flat baskets of coal through the gates and up steep inclines, thrusting them forward with their heads, and slow or stupid children were often ill-treated by the men. After describing such conditions in a 'wet' mine at Mirfield, not far from Flockton, the writer of the Report noted: 'This colliery belongs to a gentleman reputed for benevolence, but who knows nothing of his own pits.'[13]

It cannot however be said of Henry Briggs that he was ignorant of what was going on below ground, and when he gave evidence on conditions at Flockton Colliery on 3 May 1841, the Report reveals something of the kind of man he was.[14] He told them that children usually began work at nine years of age, but earlier 'where they are much distressed and there are large families', and described how they worked from six in the morning until about five in the afternoon, with an hour off for dinner. He did not leave them to open and shut gates, because he considered this a risky procedure, but they pushed the coal along the passages and through the gates, some no more than thirty inches high, moving about thirty 'corves' a day. On the whole he insisted that they were 'pretty well used', and resented the idea of Government interference:

As regards regulation of collieries, I object altogether to the right of Government to interfere as a principle. Supposing children were prevented from working in the pits till they were 10 years old, the best Flockton coal must cease to be worked, which is the best coal in Yorkshire. It would cost too much to increase the gates sufficiently.

Henry Briggs was a realist, and a man of his time, but he faced up to existing conditions with honesty and good sense, made it clear how the families depended on the employment of their children to keep them from starvation, and showed genuine concern for his employees. When the writers of the Report deplored the indifference of 'the higher orders of society' towards the workers, they singled out Flockton Colliery as an exception to this, because of the efforts made by the Stansfelds and the Briggs to help those who worked there.[15]

There is a detailed account in the Report of the classes held in a large schoolroom built on to the Stansfeld house. Here the children from the mine came on Sunday, and were also taken to services in church or chapel. There was school for the more intelligent on Monday, and various evening activities for old and young during the week: singing, indoor recreation, games and gymnastics outside, cricket for those who signed the temperance pledge, and allotments for the older men. The playground was run with great success by Miles Stansfeld and Henry Briggs, and the writer of the Report was much impressed by his visit there:[16]

> The attendance was excellent, and the zeal and delight with which the different games and exercises were pursued, generally in spite of a drizzling rain, were most delightful. ... As there are games and exercises adapted to both sexes and to each age, young men, lads, girls and children are mingled together, and nothing is more hopeful than the perfect good temper and decorum which pervades the whole party.... Nor is the kindly and grateful feeling which exists on the part of the work-people of Messrs Stansfeld and Briggs towards their employers by any means confined to the playground — it exists most warmly through the village.

This, he concludes, is due to the fact that 'the family themselves are the teachers and in great measure the companions of their workpeople.' Henry had great faith in education, and declared to the Commission that he believed that high wages were harmful if the men were uneducated, since they would then work for only three days a week and spend the rest of the time in the ale-house.

The picture of Henry Briggs which emerges from this Report, a man of toughness but also of integrity, and possessed of a strong sense of responsibility for those who worked for him, is characteristic of the Briggs family as a whole. Henry was a strong leader of industry in a ruthless, highly competitive age, and yet neither heartless nor wholly materialistic in his outlook. Many of his letters to Marianne survive, and it is clear that this was no marriage of convenience but a partnership of deep affection and respect on both sides. The letters reveal a man of tireless energy and resource, never sparing himself where business was concerned. He was continually travelling round the countryside on horseback or coach, and was prepared to walk miles through the streets of foreign cities in search of possible customers for his coal. He possessed an interest in science which was typical of the Unitarians, and gave papers to local societies, illustrated by chemical demonstrations.[17] He found time to be interested in music and art, and he remained a loyal Unitarian, conducting Sunday services and instructing his work-people after he moved to Overton with his family, while Marianne gave him able assistance. All that he touched seemed to prosper, and the only failure in which he was ever involved, that of the Stansfeld firm in Leeds, caused him much regret; he expressed the hope in his will that his sons could compensate those who had lost money through this.

As time went on, however, the good relationship noted at Flockton did not continue in the Briggs collieries. There were continual and bitter disputes, and antagonism against the mine-owners, while Henry, now president of an association of masters, became a target for hostility. 'All masters is devils, but our master is prince of devils', one collier was heard to say, and after a long strike, a letter came to Outwood Hall, where Henry and Marianne were then living, in 1863, threatening his life:[18]

> MR Briggs, I will tell you what i think by you. About this struggle you are getting an ould man and besides that you are a tyrant -ould B-G-R now sirs what do you think to that bit — we have stoped 13 weeks all redy but i have myself sw(orn) to take your Life and your son also. But you shlt not live 13 days ...

The same night a warning note came to Marianne: 'MRS Briggs do tell MR Briggs to mind for he is in danger.' As much as seventy-eight weeks of work was lost at the Collieries through strikes from 1855 onwards, and Henry and his two sons determined to find a way out of this impossible situation. In 1865 they introduced a new profit-sharing scheme, far ahead of its time. The workmen received a bonus on their yearly earnings, which could be used to buy shares. Surplus profits were divided between shareholders and workers, and about £34,000 was distributed among the workpeople during the next ten years. In 1869 one of them was elected by his fellow-workers to a seat on the Board, and this continued until ended by the trade unions in 1886. The Briggs experiment caused much interest at the time, both in England and France,[19] and worked very satisfactorily. Much of the organisation was carried out by Henry's son, Henry Currer Briggs,[20] but Henry remained an active Chairman until shortly before his death in 1868, while staying with his son in Dundee.

Marianne lived on until 1886, known to the family as Aye-Aye, a name said to originate from the cries of a small grandchild when she gave him rides on her foot: 'Igher! Igher!' She was a tall woman, nearly as tall as her husband, who was over six feet in height, and clearly a resolute character, but in her old age she was remembered as 'a very pretty old lady with a roundish smiling face and pink and white complexion',[21] constantly occupied with embroidery and exquisite paintings of flowers. The family business was carried on by Henry Currer Briggs, who expanded it in various ways and, like his father, never spared himself. He married Catherine Shepherd, daughter of the Governor of Wakefield Prison,[22] who was to have a strong influence on her youngest son Ernest, who was Katharine's father. Catherine was a gentle but courageous person, much loved by her children and grandchildren. Henry Currer Briggs died at the early age of fifty-three, while visiting a silver mine in Norway, and Catherine then lived for some years with her mother-in-law Marianne at Woodland House in Leeds. There the two widowed ladies lived in perfect harmony, while Catherine did much practical voluntary work, and organised a home for friendless girls in Leeds. When Marianne died in 1886 she moved to Pull Wyke, a house on Lake Windermere which her husband had built, and made a happy home there for her younger sons.

After Henry's sudden death, his eldest son Arthur became Managing Director at the early age of twenty-six, supported by Geoffrey Jackson, an engineer who had married Arthur's sister

(Left) Marianne Briggs, Katharine's great grandmother, in old age. She died in 1886.
(Right) Catherine Briggs, Katharine's grandmother.

Marion.[23] The two young men were able and hard-working, and complaints from elderly members of the Board that it was being run by 'babes and striplings' soon ceased. Arthur became Chairman in 1893, and weathered a difficult period when shares fell heavily in value; however Catherine had sufficient faith in the Company to buy up all she could for her grandchildren, and this policy was amply justified.

Arthur's wife, Helen Jones, supported him loyally in his busy life. She was Katharine's 'Aunt Nell', a vigorous and voluble character and a determined organiser. In later life she was a figure of tremendous size and considerable presence, wearing enormous hats and carrying large handbags. She loved music, and was a generous friend of Lawrence Schroeder, the minister of the Mill Hill Unitarian Church in Leeds, supporting the church loyally; she was also a shrewd business woman with a great talent for fund-raising. Arthur worked so hard that his family saw little of him at home, and in

1904 he took on more responsibilities as Lord Mayor of Leeds. His term of office ended in 1906, and he was able to spend some time in the family house in the Lake District, Broad Leys, designed by C.F. Voysey, not far from Catherine at Pull Wyke. However he left one afternoon to drive to Leeds for an important meeting, and next morning collapsed and died of a severe heart attack. Helen idealised her husband after his death in a way reminiscent of the widowed Queen Victoria; she lived on until 1938, a considerable force in the family, and a not altogether helpful one. Arthur's youngest son, Donald,[24] became Chairman in his turn at the end of the First World War, and it was he who had the task of bringing the work of the Company to a close when the Nationalisation Act became law in 1946 and the Briggs Collieries were taken over by the State.

Katharine and her sisters grew up with a lively interest in the family, delighting in tales of its more eccentric members, which they heard from parents and grandparents. It was particularly the women of the family, those formidable figures who survived their husbands for so long, who were repositories of the family legends. There were stories of Henry Briggs, parsimonious in his old age, rejoicing to save a few pence by getting his hair cut by a daughter-in-law or by refusing a deckchair on the promenade. There were many tales of Aunt Alice, who married Archibald, Henry Briggs' second son;[25] she came from Llandudno, was very musical, and extremely temperamental. She was said to lie on the floor kicking and screaming if she could not get her own way, and as she was thought to be consumptive, Archibald gave up his seat on the Board and moved to Italy, to a house on Lake Garda. In 1876 his clothes were found beside the lake, but there was no sign of his body; Alice suspected that he had deserted her, but if so the facts never came to light. Katharine's father Ernest remembered staying with his family at her house at Onslow in Cheshire when he was a small boy, and how one Christmas their nurse burst into the dining-room saying that she and a maid had seen an old man in a green skull-cap in Aunt Alice's dressing-room. His aunt took it quite calmly, remarking that he was often there. Katharine and her sisters knew Aunt Alice as a tall, thin old lady, who 'alarmed and amazed' Katharine, according to her sister Winifred, by addressing her in French when they met.

There was a vast number of relatives for the sisters to encounter, for the Jacksons, the Shepherds, the Stansfelds and many of the early Briggs had large families. Katharine and her sisters were conscious of the importance of their family tradition. They enjoyed the letters of Henry Briggs, Marianne and other members of the Milnes family, and it was intended that Katharine's sister Winifred should publish these together with a family history, but unhappily this was not completed before her death. There is no doubt that the qualities which stand out in the family records had a recognisable influence on the life and character of Katharine herself. She grew up in the firm belief that anything worth doing demanded hard work and unceasing effort, and she inherited a strong sense of responsibility towards those less fortunate than herself. She learned to admire outstanding characters who showed independence and determination. While a number of the Briggs family had undoubted gifts for building up new enterprises in business and running industrial concerns, there was also a strong strain of artistic and musical ability in the family, and here the Milnes, the Shepherds and even the troublesome Aunt Alice contributed much. Above all Katharine took for granted the value of integrity, both in business and in personal relationships; this was something which her father and grandmother Catherine Briggs had passed down to her, and it remained with her all her life.

As they grew up, the sisters spent much time discussing family folklore. When Winifred was a small child, her grandmother Catherine once told her that their great-grandmother had narrowly escaped being gored by a bull when she was young. Winifred at first thought this was Marianne, but later realised that it must have been Catherine's mother, Hélène O'Dwyer, who was brought up in France. The children solemnly discussed the story: 'We would speculate that we had had a narrow escape from never bring born, as if our Great-grandfather had married someone else, we should probably not be his great-grandchildren.' Here the little girls had some right on their side. It was indeed their family heritage which helped to make them what they were, and it is against this early background that we must trace the development of Katharine herself.

Table 3   **The Family of Henry Currer Briggs**

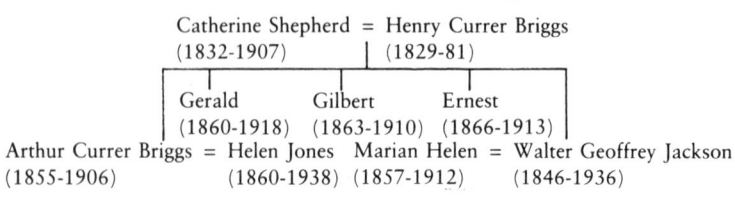

```
                  Catherine Shepherd = Henry Currer Briggs
                  (1832-1907)         (1829-81)
                  ┌─────────────┬─────────────┐
                  Gerald        Gilbert       Ernest
                  (1860-1918)   (1863-1910)   (1866-1913)
Arthur Currer Briggs = Helen Jones   Marian Helen = Walter Geoffrey Jackson
(1855-1906)            (1860-1938)   (1857-1912)    (1846-1936)
```

2 An Artist's Daughter: Parents and Childhood

> Most of us have been lucky enough to know a few people who were shiningly good, the best company in the world, with whom one was at once at ease because they were without malice.
>
> K.M. Briggs, 'Charlotte Yonge's Ethics'

When Katharine Briggs set out at the end of her life to describe her childhood, she remembered her family as a devoted one, a group of people who 'manufactured their own interests.'[1] Her father she described as an eminent water-colourist

> who had been early elected a member of the Royal Institute of Painters in Water-colours and was an active member of the St John's Wood Arts Club. ... With his wife and his three young daughters he spent his time between the Highlands of Scotland and his London studio ... a splendid big studio with a separate door for models and a corner where Mother's writing-desk and work-table stood.[2]

The studio was clearly the heart of the house in Fellows Road where Katharine lived until she was twelve. It stands much as Ernest Briggs left it, a high, square room built on to the side of the house, with a large window looking out on to the back garden and a fireplace with tiles in the Morris tradition. The atmosphere of the studio, according to the present occupant, is a peaceful, happy one, as might be expected. Katharine as a child used to slip quietly in here when her father was painting,

> and sit down in a far corner with a book, while Daddy went backwards and forwards to look at his picture and then put a few strokes on it. Sometimes he'd call me to see how it was getting on, and when we'd looked and talked about it perhaps he would lie on the sofa and we'd talk for a bit. He had a weak heart and sometimes he could not stand too long.[3]

Ernest Briggs, Katharine's father, was born in Dundee in 1866

Table 4 The Family of Ernest Briggs

Ernest Edward = Mary Cooper
(1866-1913)   (1867-1956)

Katharine Mary

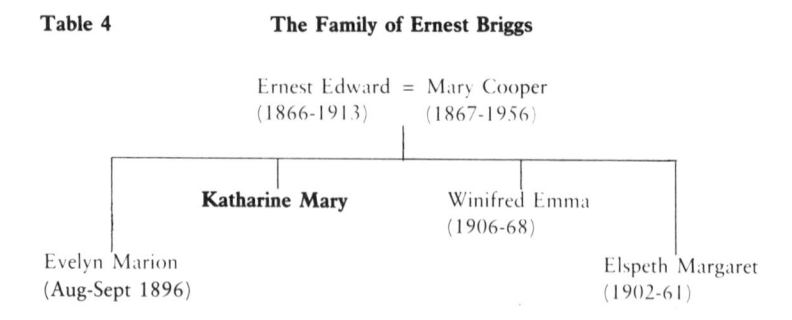

Winifred Emma
(1906-68)

Evelyn Marion
(Aug-Sept 1896)

Elspeth Margaret
(1902-61)

but moved to Yorkshire with his family when he was three. 'I was fortunate enough when very young', he says in his book *Angling and Art in Scotland*, 'to live in a country where trout fishing could be prosecuted to some advantage.'[4] His first attempts were in the Yorkshire rivers, but the years in Scotland had left an indelible mark on the family, and they loved to spend holidays there. When Ernest was at University College School in London, he used sometimes to slip into Euston Station:

> Watching the night expresses depart for the North and envy the ulster-clad sportsmen with their long rod-boxes. ... How in the spirit I journeyed with those rod-boxes northward through the night! Little thinking that it might ever become a common occurrence to make that journey in the flesh.[5]

Their mother clearly allowed the boys plenty of freedom. Although Ernest's health was not good, and his brother Gilbert was not strong and very accident-prone, they were allowed to go with their two elder brothers, Arthur and Gerald, into Galloway. The first of these fishing holidays on their own was to Dalry, when Ernest was thirteen. In his book, dedicated to Gilbert, 'the companion of my boyhood', he tells of walks of many miles over rough country until they arrived exhausted and famished at some lonely farm or little inn:

> In those early days we were not overburdened with luggage. Each had a large knapsack containing all his spare clothes, and a black glazy mackintosh, which was usually reduced to ribbons after a few severe scrambles up the burn-side on wet days, and became — like the carpet-bag — a thing of the past; while our angling

outfit consisted of a fishing rod, fishing basket, and lastly one landing-net — common property amongst the four of us.[6]

No doubt it was felt that the younger boys would be safe with the sensible cautious Arthur, eleven years Ernest's senior, who in the book is called 'the Skipper':

> He was exceedingly methodical, and had, moreover, a very level head; hence he always matured the plans on an elaborate scale, and carried them out with much discipline — nay, it was occasionally whispered amongst the other three, a wee bit over-fussily.[7]

It is illuminating to catch a glimpse of the future man of business and Chairman of the Company through the eyes of a young brother. The second son, Gerald, is 'the Duke': 'So-called because of his lordly, extravagant ways and ingratiating manners. ... Neither then, nor in after life, could his tackle be depended upon — nevertheless he

Katharine's father, Ernest Briggs (far right), with his three older brothers, Arthur, Gerald and Gilbert.

usually caught more fish than others, and lost even a larger proportion.' Gerald was a great practical joker, as the stories in the second part of the book reveal. He was to remain a slightly irresponsible character all his life, causing anxiety to the family by his rash business dealings. The third of the brothers, Gilbert, was Bert to his family but called John in Ernest's book. He was small and agile, but apt to lose his balance at crucial moments and arrive home soaking wet.

Ernest showed ability in drawing as a child. A card of 1876, when he was ten years old, is inscribed 'For Mamma from Ernest', and shows three characters from Tenniel's illustrations to *Alice in Wonderland,* copied very ably in indian ink. More examples of his early sketches are found in a home newspaper, the 'Belvidere Gazette', produced by Gilbert and Ernest in 1877 and 1878. Gilbert was Editor, and Ernest E. Briggs (FRS, FRCS, MA, LLD, L M N O P Q, etc) the sub-editor. The paper was written in various hands, with occasional help from their brother Gerald (General Geraldoff) who contributed 'spontaneous' poems. It contained family news; one item announced that Mr Archibald Briggs had slipped on the St Theodule Glacier and been in bed for some days, but was expected at Belvidere the following week. There are parodies of foreign news by special correspondents, and their father Henry Currer Briggs is referred to as His Majesty, Sultan of Belvidere, while an unpopular gardener is Leak Pasha:

> The step we have consistently urged upon his Majesty has at last been taken: Leak Pasha has been superseded. Far be it from us to express any petty feelings of spite. ... It is not because Leak Pasha unreasonably objected to the editors of this journal shooting at him with their bows and arrows, but a consideration for the public well-being.

There are many references to the family cat, Mrs Jupiter, and a detailed account of the rescue and subsequent death of a young peewit (Mr Perkin Peewit, aged thirteen days). Ernest delighted in producing advertisements in the style then popular: 'E.E.B.'s Pain Killer, the infallible! Prussic Acid! One teaspoonful only! Warranted to cure every possible ill that flesh is heir to in less than one second! No second dose ever required.' The paper was produced in 'The Smoke Room, Belvidere', which also housed the boys' library and Ernest's 'fine assortment of specimens ... collected from all parts of the United Kingdom'. In 1878, however, it was issued from the 'London Office' at 61 King Henry's Road, St John's Wood, after the brothers left in the autumn of 1877 for University College School, where Arthur had been earlier. The Belvidere Gazette affords vivid glimpses of a lively and not too restricted childhood, of Ernest's talents, his instinct for mischief, and his quick sense of humour.

We do not know how far his father encouraged his love for art. Possibly like the father of the hero in another book of Ernest's, *The Two Rivers,* he thought poorly of it as a career. That gentleman 'had a word of contempt for all who might be supposed to merit the generic name of artist. He conceived the whole pack of them dilettanti — creatures to be despised as incapable of any real work.'[8] Ernest went away to school in London at eleven, together with Gilbert. Gilbert left after two years, at fifteen, and Ernest also stayed away for a year, from 1879-80, perhaps on health grounds. He was back from 1880-2. The reputation of University College School at this time was high, and one advantage for Ernest was that art was taken seriously, so that at one time there were as many as sixteen drawing masters. The school was then beside University College, and the Slade School of Art was on the same site. In spite of trouble from what was said to be a weak heart, Ernest loved games and sport, and letters report him enjoying cricket, golf, tennis, bowls, shooting and billiards in later life. His great love, however, was for fishing, the skill of the fisherman being linked, as he saw it, with that of the landscape painter:

> They have much in common; each requires an observant eye, and a hand trained to obey that eye. ... Moreover there is one closely-connecting link for all time between them; it is that common though wonderful and ever-changing fluid which we call Water.[9]

Katharine claimed that it was as a painter of water that her father achieved his finest effects: 'His greatest talent, amounting almost to genius, was for running water. It is hard to find in the work of any other artist an equal knowledge of the anatomy of water.'[10]

Ernest was no lonely fisherman, escaping into solitude; he liked to go fishing with relatives and friends, enjoyed the company of other anglers he met, and delighted in unusual characters among the ghillies and country people. He had the ability to make and keep friends, and was clearly never a recluse. He particularly enjoyed the company of children. Arthur's younger son Donald described a visit to

Catherine Briggs' house at Pull Wyke when a small boy when Ernest was in charge of the children at breakfast, and coaxed him into trying cold ham, which Donald had not previously encountered and refused to eat.[11] Another of his cards survives from 1893, with two sketches of his own face in pen-and-ink, drawn when he was staying with his sister Marion and her husband Geoffry Jackson at Aberford. It is addressed to Edith (Madge) Jackson and her cousin Margery, who was brought up with her, and runs: 'Mr Little Thing has much pleasure in accepting the Misses Edith and Margery Jackson's kind invitation to take tea with them at 4.30 this afternoon at playroom house in honour of their sweet respective birthdays.' Edith's daughter still remembers what a wonderful playfellow Uncle Ernest used to be, somewhat disapproved of by Nannies because he excited the children so much with his imaginative games.

In 1882, when he was sixteen, Ernest left school after his father's death and worked in the Company's office at Whitwood, under his brother Arthur's supervision. He was being trained as a surveyor, no doubt with the idea of using his abilities in drawing, but according to Donald Briggs his plans were usually drawn freehand and did not meet with much approval. Donald tells the story of how one day Ernest found a smoke helmet with a length of corrugated hose, put it on, and emerged into the corridor on all fours, growling, to encounter Mrs Ibbetson, the cleaner: 'The result was successful beyond belief, she threw her apron over her head, uttered a loud scream and fainted on the spot. Help quickly came, and Ernest tactfully departed by another door.'[12] There were also tales of him sitting on the roof with a catapult and aiming at the bowler hats of gentlemen coming into the office. It is not very surprising that a young man with Ernest's gifts and temperament failed to interest himself in office work. Yet in later life he was to prove the member of the family to whom others turned in times of crisis. Although he chose to carve out his own life for himself, he was never entirely free from the responsibilities of the Briggs world on which he turned his back.

His first serious illness seems to have taken place when he was beginning a course in marine engineering at the Yorkshire College, afterwards to become the University of Leeds. It may have been rheumatic fever. From this time on, he had trouble with his health; letters refer to pains, indigestion, headaches, feverish attacks, and above all, weakness, suggesting some chronic ailment. Yet he never gave up physical exercise, and was amazingly energetic and hardworking. Relatives and friends lay stress on his courage and cheerfulness right up to the end. He achieved an impressive amount of work, and if not strong enough to paint, would turn to writing as an occupation. He kept his sense of fun all his life, and knew how to enjoy himself. His mother and elder brother must have finally agreed after his illness that he should go back to London in 1883 to work at the Slade School of Art, under Alphonse Legros, Slade Professor of Art in Unversity College; for he was there until 1887.

In his novel *The Two Rivers* he has left an impression of life as he knew it among young, enthusiastic art students. The hero, Andrew Maitland, went to the Slade and lodged in the non-existent Charlton Street,[13] in the vicinity of Tottenham Court Road. He occupied a small room at the top of Number 12, near to the 'Restaurant Français' where the students used to congregate, and this could be Bertorelli's in Charlotte Street, which corresponds to his description. He tells us that Andrew's attic room had a way out on to a parapet running along the front of the line of houses, so that occupants of the top floor could visit one another; two of them even set up studios in a couple of unlet rooms without the landlady far below being any the wiser. There is a spirited discussion in Chapter XVI on what makes a good picture, with various unfavourable remarks made about the Selection Committee of the Academy and the fashionable pictures of the time. Nevertheless Ernest at twenty-three had a large picture, 'Strawberry Gathering', exhibited at the Royal Academy in 1889, and from this time until 1904 his pictures were hung every year, with the exception of 1899. As a water-colourist he could not become a Royal Academician, but in May 1893 he received an invitation to stand for election to the Royal Society of British Artists. By this time he was evidently accepted as a successful painter. It was in the same year that he married, and his choice of a wife, like that of a profession, differed markedly from the traditions of the family.

Mary Cooper came from Yorkshire, but her background was not that of the prosperous industrial scene to which the Briggs family belonged. She was from Clayton, near Doncaster, and her father, Thomas Cooper, was a small farmer. He had eight children who survived infancy, of whom Mary was the third daughter. Since the farm was not doing well and money was scarce, she entered domestic service and came to Catherine Briggs' house at Pull Wyke to work as a housemaid. One can well imagine the excitement and perturbation in the family when Ernest fell in love with this beautiful girl, a few months younger than himself, and declared that he meant to marry her. This was a serious step in the society to which Ernest belonged, and his consciousness of this is shown by references in his novel to a character who secretly married a servant in his father's house, with tragic results.[14] The crisis over Mary must have taken place in 1891, since in a letter of 1893 Ernest refers to a time two years earlier when their happiness seemed far away.

But the principles by which his mother Catherine governed her life differed from the materialistic and conventional attitudes of many well-to-do families of the time. It was finally agreed that Ernest and Mary should marry after a period of waiting, possibly to test Ernest's determination, and that during this time Mary should be trained for her future position as a rich man's wife. She went to live with Ada Barmby, Catherine's sister, the widow of the Unitarian minister John Goodwyn Barmby, who was in Sidmouth with her two daughters Mabel and Beatrice. Much later, in 1944, Mabel wrote to Mary after she had met Katharine for the first time: 'I want to know more of you now that we have both grown old and we haven't met for about 50 years! And I think we were both rather shy in those old days — I know I was and I'm sure you were too.' She would, she said, after receiving a recent photograph, have recognised Mary at once: 'I hope she has kept her lovely complexion, she was such a pretty girl, and she looks a very pretty old lady.' The Barmbys were clearly an affectionate family; the younger daughter, Beatrice, was a gifted writer and Icelandic scholar, who was an invalid from childhood, and died in 1900.[15] Nevertheless the two years of waiting could not have been easy for Mary. At last the wedding took place, in September 1893, from Marion's house at Aberford, with her daughter Madge and niece Margery as bridesmaids.

The letters which Ernest wrote to his wife show that he remained devoted to her during the twenty years they spent together, while Mary was a dedicated, thoughtful and unselfish wife and mother. She was an untiring nurse to Ernest during many spells of illness, and was often left with the children while he went painting or fishing, visited relatives or dealt with family crises. She patiently despatched letters and parcels after him, and made long complicated journeys by train to meet him, for Ernest spent much time in trains. Many of Ernest's letters to her survive, but from her there is almost complete silence. Those who visited Dalbeathie, the house in Perthshire which she ran so efficiently after Ernest's death, remember her as a quiet, retiring person, an excellent hostess with every care for their comfort, but who remained a little aloof from the excitement involved in Katharine's various ploys. She had a natural charm and dignity, and was said to be a person with whom one could not take liberties. Perhaps after Ernest's death the springs of her life had run dry, although like many of the Briggs wives she lived on for many years after his death in 1913.

A picture of their honeymoon in Italy is given in a long letter from Ernest to his sister Marion, sent from the Albergo Bonciano in Florence on 20 November 1893. It is full of boyish enthusiasm about the journey and the wonderful time they were having together. Ernest had been ill after they left Paris, so they stopped in Basle for three days. In Milan and Venice it was cold and wet, but Mary was happy to spend time in churches and galleries:

> Mary takes a very great interest in all the pictures and is constantly finding out new places to visit. ... Mary couldn't fancy Italian cooking very much at first, she wanted to know too much how everything was done and what every dish consisted of, but she has got much more used to it & we get on capitally.

They found a hotel in Florence which was 'quite Italian but very good & excellent cooking & very cheap', and Ernest settled down to copy a picture and paint in one of the churches, while Mary worked at her Italian and enjoyed shopping expeditions. Here they spent their first Christmas together, and Ernest sent Mary a letter addressed to her in a strange Italian hand, as a surprise. The envelope was evidently opened hastily, and it contains a moving letter from Ernest, full of underlinings, which begins: 'My Own Darling Treasure.' This is very different from the sober love letters of Henry Briggs, sixty years earlier:

> You are *so* dear to me, so loving and kind, that I just love you more than everything on earth. It will be *terribly dear* having a home together always & it will be most awfully dear going back to Pull Wyke & taking you my own *precious darling* with me. ... It seems such a difference from what it was two years ago, our happiness seemed such a long way off then, & now it has all come true, & even *dearer* & *sweeter* to me than anything I dreamed of.

In 1895 they were settled in the comfortable, compact house in Hampstead, 102 Fellows Road. It stands out from the other gaunt Victorian houses with their three storeys and a basement, and has something of the air of a country villa. Ernest posted another letter to Mary to be delivered when he was at home, wishing Mary a happy birthday and telling her again of his great happiness with her. He was clearly devoted to his quiet, restful and beautiful wife. He painted her portrait more than once, and made sketches of her. The largest of his water-colour paintings, still at Dalbeathie, 'Mary Go and Call the Cattle Home', shows her crossing the Solway sands. She was rather small, with dark hair and eyes and a delicate complexion, and has the quality of repose in her face. He also designed clothes for her. A dress of grey, hand-woven silk with a beautiful neckline, made from silk produced in Kent, was one designed by him. It is now in the London Museum.

Ernest Briggs in about 1895, soon after his marriage.

They had been married nearly three years when their first child was born on 25 August 1896, a daughter, Evelyn Marion. 'Dear little Evelyn Marion', Mary wrote in her birthday book under a second date, three weeks later, when the baby was buried in Hampstead Cemetery. On 19 September Ernest sent Mary another letter on the anniversary of their wedding:

> My poor dear little one! I'm afraid you will only find it a sad wedding day this year. It would have been so joyous if we had had our darling little Baby with us still, but I will try darling with my great love for you to make up to you as much as possible for your sad loss ... I think that God will give us another dear Baby some day, which perhaps can never quite take the place of the dear little one we were so proud and happy to have, but which will make us feel *very* happy again. We have been married three years now, and I want to tell you, my own darling wife, how *very very* happy I have been with you — as the time passes on I only seem to get to love you & honour you more and more. ... And I only feel that the troubles which we have to bear together will only draw us together closer & closer — God was very good to me when he gave me your love.

This then was the background of love, devotion and loyalty into which Katharine Mary Briggs was born two years later, on 8 November 1898, and it is easy to understand why she was welcomed and cherished with special affection by both parents. The day after she was born, Ernest received a joyful letter from his mother at Pull Wyke:

> I was so delighted just now to have your wire & cried for joy — I think you will both be pleased that a little girl has come to you in place of the dear little one you lost, and now that your great anxiety for Mary is over, you will have a better chance of getting strong.

Evidently Ernest's health had not been good, and there are anxious references to this in letters from his mother and other relatives from this time. With the baby, however, all seems to have gone well, and at Christmas Ernest enclosed a note with a gift 'For my own darling Mary and her dear little Molly.' It was as Molly, a variation of her second name, that Katharine was known for the early part of her life. She had been named after her mother and grandmother.

Katharine as a baby with Mary Briggs, 1899.

A second daughter, Winifred Emma, was born 15 July 1900, when Katharine was nearly two. Emma was the name of Mary's mother and favourite sister. The grandmother wrote again from Leeds:

> She must be a fine little lassie to weigh so much & it is nice to have two girls not very far apart in age — they are such good companions. ... I want very much to hear what Mollie says and if she seems to like it.

The third daughter, Elspeth Margaret, known as Elsie, arrived on 8 June 1902. This time all must have gone well, for soon afterwards Ernest was with his mother at Pull Wyke, planning a holiday in Wales for the whole family at the end of July. It seems that at one time there were hopes of a fourth child, a son, but presumably the baby was still-born since the birth was not recorded. In a letter written to Mary after Ernest's death, Mabel Barmby refers to this:

er such a sweet beautiful letter he wrote to Mother (Ada
hen you lost your dear little boy saying that God had
d in giving you your three little girls that you must
ieve overmuch for the child he had taken.

Wh   ed is not clear, as there are no other references
in le   mentioned in Madge Jackson's family history.
   Wh   the only child, Katharine established a close
relatio.   father: 'Before Winnie was born I was my
Father's   we were playfellows and companions for all
the rest o   aying of imaginary games began very early.
By 1902,   e was four years old, she received a long
letter from   the Lake District, addressed 'My dear Old
Jim' and sign   loving Huck.' She had evidently been introduced to the   kleberry Finn at that early age. The letter
shows Ernest's   lding a child's interest without talking down
to his correspo   d indicates also that Katharine must have
been a precociou   ghtful child to have inspired such a letter:

My dear Old J
   I must just take up my pen to write you a few lines to tell you how much I miss you. I should have been so glad if you could have come with me, but it won't be long now before I get home again. I am now staying with Gran in a little house with the windows looking right out on to a great loch called Windermere. There is ever so much water, and then beyond the water are beautiful mountains as far as one can see. It would be a lovely place for sailing your boat, & when we all come here to see Gran later on you will be able to do so. The funny part of this house is that it is built right out of the water & underneath there is a boathouse where Gran keeps her two boats. Now I must tell you about our house in Wales where we are all going very soon ... (A long description follows).
   I expect you will be having it cooler in London now as it is very cold here & I hope Old fellow that you are feeling very well & jolly now & that you and your little girl Winnie are enjoying themselves. I must go now, as I have to walk to a little town, called Bowness (being Sunday) to post this letter.
   With very much love & kisses to yourself and Winnie and Baby Elsie from
                                    Your ever loving Huck

A sketch of Mary by Ernest soon after their marriage. This is possibly a preliminary study for one of his paintings.

(Left & Right) Two sketches of Katharine as a small child by Ernest.

Evidently Ernest encouraged his small daughter to act out parts from the stories he told to her. *The Water Babies* was an early game, when Katharine was three, and another was *As You Like It*. Katharine remembered:

> I loved all the bits about the wrestling with Charles. I was rather embarrassed at having to enter rudely into the polite exiled

company and demand food which they were perfectly ready to give me, but I very much liked killing the lion and the serpent. What I could not condone was Orlando's conduct in carving names on trees and sticking up bad rhymes about Rosalind all over the place. I remember the Duke coming up to me one day when I was Orlando, and saying: 'Orlando, who do you think can have been writing all these poems and sticking them on the trees?' And I blushed hotly and said 'Oh Daddy - out of the game - can we cross all that out? It's so silly.' It was obediently crossed out, and Orlando's follies were forgotten.

This reference to 'crossing out' suggests that Ernest wrote down a simple scenario for them to act. *Coral Island* was another book used in this way, since Katharine remembered being Jack while her father was the rest of the characters. When she was eight, she received a letter addressed to Quentin Durward:

Dear Quentin Durward,
   I hope that this will find your excellency in the best of health, & that since I last saw you you have been refraining from eating too many chocolates and peppermints,

It ends:
With heaps of love to Winnie & Elsie & your noble self,
   I am
                         Yours ever my dear Quentin,
                                E.E.B.

By July 1908 all three sisters had been brought into the game, and in a letter beginning 'My good Varlet', the children ('villain rascals') are rebuked for 'revelling in the delectable lunch which had been sumptuously prepared for your betters'. Ernest ends: 'By my halidome! Thou art an arrant knave & a springald gadzooks! Have a care sirrah! or thou wilt come to a bad end.'

Katharine was a determined little person with a strong sense of what ought to be done. She regarded herself as responsible for her little sisters when their parents were not there. Winifred tells a pleasant story of how they were visited by a distant relative by marriage, Mr Dixon, who lived at Pitlochry, while on a holiday in Scotland. She remembered him as a gentle old man with a small beard, wearing a kilt and a tweed jacket, of whom her father was very fond. When he came into the room where the children were playing, Katharine, who was about five at the time, introduced the others:

> 'This is Elsie, she can walk, and this is Winnie, she can run, and I'm Molly.' 'And I suppose you can fly', said Mr Dixon. 'No', said Molly, 'but I can climb.' He thought it typical of Molly to be always ready with an answer.

For the children the early years were made up of contrasting winters and summers. During the winter they were in London, with Ernest working hard at his painting for the spring exhibitions, constantly visited by artist friends. During the summer they usually took a house in Scotland, and Ernest sketched, painted and fished. 'The three children keenly enjoyed both aspects of life, felt themselves country children in Scotland and enjoyed the social winters in London.'[16] Their education was entrusted to governesses, who were obtained from Charlotte Mason's College at Ambleside, the 'House of Education', as it was called in its early days.[17] It was opened in 1891, and while there was a full training course for girls who wanted to become governesses, the college was also open to parents and those interested in the bringing up of children by the new methods. Charlotte Mason's schemes of education, later to be developed in PNEU schools (Parents' National Educational Union), was to train children in concentration and use of memory by reading to them from interesting books or telling them stories, and then encouraging them to repeat what they had heard. Much time was also spent out of doors learning about the countryside, and there was emphasis on art, music and drama. Such methods revolutionised schoolroom teaching, and Ernest evidently became interested while he was living at Pull Wyke, close to Ambleside. The games which he played with Katharine as a child were in accordance with the theories of Charlotte Mason, while the stories she and her sisters made up and acted out later could well have owed something to the kind of teaching which they received. Ernest was also a good story-teller, and Katharine later attributed her early interest in folktales to hearing stories of the Turkish fool and trickster known as the Khoja Nasr-ed-Deen: 'My father knew a lot of these stories and they were almost our favourite of all the tales he told us',[18] she wrote when she began recording some of these at the end of her life. Education as conducted by Ernest was evidently tremendous fun, but some of the later governesses seem to have been only moderately successful in working with the bright, imaginative children. There were serious gaps in their education, particularly in languages and mathematics. One of the most successful governesses was 'our dear nursery-governess' Kathleen Godfrey, who was with them for some years, and looked after Elspeth as a baby. She was presumably 'Gee', who afterwards married and lived at Sleaford, where Katharine used to visit her during her time in the WAAF.

A very early letter in large untidy handwriting was sent by Katharine to her mother on one occasion when Mary had to leave them, and when Edith, possibly Katharine's older cousin, the daughter of Marion Jackson, was staying with them:

Dear Mummy,
After you had driven away we went round the garden and played with the batteldoors and chutelcocks you gave us and as far as we could catch was six times. Then Miss Godfrey fetched out a little doll that haden any clothes and dressed it. but it was to hot to go out so we played in the garden all day long. When Winnie went to beb (sic) Edith and I played at a very nice game but we thouth it was bad (for) our batteldoors so we didn't play it any more. Then I went to bed. I sleped with Edith. I woke at six a.clock and waited till Edeth woke and then got up and dressed and played until it was time to breake our fast. Are you all well and hows Aunt Maryen and couson Margery.
                      Love and kisses for all
                              from M.

The expression 'break our fast' is no doubt derived from the various historical dramas in which Katharine had been taking part. Later on she is writing more fluently, although spelling and punctuation remain a little unreliable, as in a letter to her mother when both parents had been away, presumably because of some family crisis:

There are lots of things I want to tell you about I don't know where to begin. I miss you awfully badly.... Glen is getting on finely with his lessons, he is such a good dog, he does almost everything I tell him to.'

Opinions differed, however, on Glen's progress, since Elsie, in a letter written at the same time, declared:

We played with Glen last night, he is getting on very badly but Molly thinks he is getting on very well. Mr Forbes made a see-saw for us and Glen was very naughty and got underneath it. Molly thort he was very sweet. I don't know what Winnie thort because she did not tell me.

It was not long after this that they heard that their parents would be back in time for Elspeth's birthday on 8 June, and Katharine wrote with much enthusiasm:

Darling Mummy

I am sorry very sorry I have not written for such a long time but now I have a great deal to tell you. Thank you very much for the lovely letter you sent me, and for the children's encyclopaedia which you sent me. I was so pleased to get it I read it through and through. I am glad you liked the flowers we sent you.

On Saturday we went to the bicycle shop to get a bicycle, and to our joy the old thing we generally have was out, so Mr Russel gave us a beauty it was a 'swift'. One couldn't help going well on it, it simply flew along. One day we're going to hire two bicycles, and get Mrs Forbes to take care of the children for a bit and bicycle to the Pass; won't it be fun? Elsie gave me the sweetest little drinking cup today, wasn't it sweet of her? She told me that she wanted a doll with beautiful hair that she could comb and plait and some dolls clothes.

With love from your own little girl
Molly

P.S. I'm so glad you're coming back on Monday, Mummy darling.

Already there are faint indications that Winnie and Elsie were not as close as Elsie and Katharine. 'Winnie did not tell me what she thort', Elsie had observed in her letters, and in another, probably written in 1909 when she was seven, she declared that she never knew what Winnie thought. At first the two little sisters must have been much together, Katharine recollected some of 'the idle bedtime games that they used to play between milk and biscuits and being settled for the night', and mentions some of them:

There was a Mr E. Gray and Mr A. Gray, for instance, who lived underground to save taxes. Mr A. Gray's garden path was down the parting of Winifred's hair and Mr E. Gray down the parting of Elspeth's; but these were pure amusement games, like Miss MacTowel's Bathing Establishment kept by our dear nursery

Governess, Kathleen Godfrey, and attended by all kinds of eccentric characters such as Prince Ensor, who insisted on wearing a wide gray hat in the bath with an ostrich feather in it. I think Sir Arthur O'Bower, one of Winnie's knights, attended her sessions too.[18]

She remembered too how when Winnie was old enough to listen to the evening readings, she would 'wedge herself into the sofa between my father and the back and listen with eyes as big as saucers.' Winnie's special favourite was *Lorna Doone,* and she liked games about princes, two of whom were called Ensor and Charlesworth, after characters in the book. She was given a tricycle with real tyres, and used to ride up and down the garden path in the character of Sir James Stevenson, carrying despatches, or go for short rides with her father on his bicycle. Ernest wrote charming letters to 'My dear little Winnie' and 'Little Miss Winnipeg', and in January 1909 produced one of his special cards for her with a sketch of himself, addressed to Lilac Cottage, Nursery Avenue: 'Prof. Stunderhausen has much pleasure in accepting Miss Winnie's kind invitation to tea at 4.15 this afternoon.' It is to be presumed that Winnie early discovered a love for drawing and painting, and that this was encouraged by her father.

Elspeth had a serious illness in her early days, a bad attack of colitis, and was the least robust of the three, and her mother and older sisters used to shelter and protect her. As she grew older, it became clear that she had an imagination akin to Katharine's. When she was very small, she had two 'pretend' children, Biddy and Widdy:

> We used to hear her crooning to herself 'I am Biddy and Widdy', and once we saw her sitting on the stairs with a doll on each arm, rocking herself from side to side, and singing 'Go to seep, Biddy and Widdy'. The only thing that we ever heard about Biddy and Widdy afterwards is that they had a goat that they were very devoted to.[19]

But one evening Elspeth surprised her sisters greatly. In the night nursery she suddenly sat up in bed and 'with stiff dramatic gestures she recited the lament of an exiled man.' This was in verse:

> Loch Donna, Loch Donna,
> I love thee not.
> By thy waters I suffer

> By thy waters I'll die.
> With no friends around me
> But a waste of black water
> Between my loved ones and me.
> Loch Donna, Loch Donna,
> I love thy black waters not.

Katharine remembered the incident all her life:

> Unfortunately Winnie burst into a peal of laughter, really I think, of admiration, and Elspeth darted down under the bedclothes in tears, but Winnie coaxed her out and persuaded her to say the poem again. Then we wrote it out and both admired it immensely. I personally felt that I could never write anything so impresssive. We never heard who the exile was.

This could have been the point when she first recognised Elspeth as a kindred spirit, with a power over words such as Katharine herself longed to possess. All three sisters were evidently writing early. Ernest refers to a story by Elspeth, *Little Prince Ernest,* and to one by Winnie. Elspeth said of herself on the cover of one of her books 'She always intended to be a writer.' They were soon drawn into the imaginary world which Katharine had enjoyed, and began to play the game 'Eric' before they left Fellows Road. As they grew older, Katharine and Elspeth shared a room, and used to talk far into the night. Those who knew all three in later life were instinctively drawn to Winnie, who was kind and understanding, but felt that she remained the odd man out in the trio, not wholly in tune with the world which the other two so delighted to create.

During the winter months Ernest worked in his studio on the sketches made the previous summer, and prepared for the Royal Academy and the Royal Institute Exhibitions in May. Then there were the excitements of Show Sunday, when the studios were open to friends, and everyone went from house to house, 'drinking cups of tea and eating tiny sandwiches and looking at the pictures that were going to be adventured.' Another excitement was to see how the pictures which had been accepted were hung, and whether they were in the coveted position 'on the line', or had been 'skied' or 'sunk'. In 1904 Ernest wrote to his mother that he had been 'most fortunate' that year:

> I have had many congratulations upon my paintings. The two

on the line looked first rate and it is a great compliment apparently to place them side by side next each other, showing the great variety in the style of the two subjects.

The artists used to hold long discussions about their work, and Katharine found some of these puzzling:

> One didn't in those days join in with grown-ups' conversation but when they'd gone I'd say things like 'I don't know what all this fuss is about composition. Isn't Nature good enough for you?' My Father would try to explain to me that every scene is complex and in depth and that an artist had to take out of it the aspect which he wanted people to dwell on. But I still thought there was something artificial about it.

Among regular visitors Katharine remembered Norman Wilkinson, who painted seascapes and was a great jester, and another unnamed artist who liked to persuade his friends to touch in little bits of his pictures for him, so that they became a kind of mosaic, and people coming to his studio on Show Sunday would know who had been there lately. A frequent visitor was Niels Lund, a Danish artist, who lived close by at 169 Adelaide Road. In one of Ernest's letters he is referred to as 'the Parson', and presumably is the character of that name in *The Two Rivers,* a Yorkshire man 'free from guile and possessed of a nature both simple and sincere.'[20] In the novel the hero Andrew was much impressed by a painting by the Parson of a Norwegian river by moonlight and admired the older man. If this is a true account of Ernest's first meeting with Lund, certainly by 1910 the position was reversed, since Ernest was then offering him fatherly advice on how to succeed with his painting, and helping him with loans, scrupulously repaid, when times were difficult. Ernest was outstandingly generous, and clearly viewed his considerable wealth as something to be shared with others less fortunate. One pathetic little letter survives from an artist's daughter who after her father's death sent him a little sketch which she begged him to buy for a pound and let her buy it back later; she was in desperate need of the money to buy shoes. Ernest kept the sketch carefully labelled, and there is little doubt that she received help from him. This side of her father's character made a powerful impression on Katharine and she followed his example in the use of her own money.

Thus for the children the winters in London were full of excitement and the house was seldom empty of visitors. One of their friends wrote the music for 'Pinkie and the Fairies', in which they saw Ellen Terry perform, and Katharine loved the theatre from childhood:

> At my first play how my heart leapt,
> At e'en my last 'twill swifter go,

she wrote in a poem. By about 1908 she was attending a small school in Hampstead while her sisters remained at home with their governess. In the summer there were all kinds of outdoor pursuits: cycling, roller-skating, blackberrying (a favourite occupation of Mary's), and looking for birds' nests. Their mother was a good oarswoman and they enjoyed boating on Windermere and in Scotland. She also taught them domestic skills, and all three were capable of cooking, baking bread and making jam, while Winifred became expert. Mary invariably insisted on good manners and punctuality for her daughters, and they learned how to entertain visitors. They were encouraged to have pets; when they were small, there were love-birds at Fellows Road ('The new love bird is very noisy and they are both very fussy', wrote Winifred to her father), and later on there were doves and rabbits. Ernest wrote to Winifred: 'What dear little things the rabbits must be. I am looking forward to seeing them tomorrow. But surely we can't keep them all!!!! I don't know where on earth they live, all of them.' He wrote long letters to Winnie about the doings of Tom Kitten, a little Manx cat at Aunt Marion's, and promised that if another kitten arrived, he would see if she might have it. Ultimately there was a Tom Kitten at Dalbeathie, but the girls had to change the name to Thomasina, because she produced a family.[21]

But although for the children it was a delightful life, giving them security, affection and plenty of intellectual stimulus, even if their formal education was somewhat neglected, the years from 1906 onwards brought increasing strain on their parents. More and more black-edged letters pased between members of the Briggs family as time went on. Arthur Briggs' sudden death took place in the summer of 1906, and Ernest was immediately off to Leeds, doing his best to comfort the children and the distraught Helen, who tended to overwhelm those around her with her emotion. Before long there was trouble over her daughter Dorothy's engagement to Austyn Barren, and Ernest did what he could to calm down the emotional mother and encourage Dodie, who afterwards wrote with much affection to thank him for all he had done. In 1907 there was a serious financial crisis for the Company, and trouble between Gerald and the Copenhagen Bank, making it imperative that a large sum of money should be forthcoming to save the Company's reputation. This caused general consternation, and Helen took it upon herself to visit Catherine Briggs and to tell her about the affair. The old lady was greatly upset, and wanted to help by drawing on her own savings. Again Ernest had to play a leading part, and in the end there was a satisfactory settlement, which meant considerable strain on him, however, and some financial sacrifice on his part. His mother had been clearly shaken by the affair, and begged him to come to Ghyll Head, where she now lived, to talk things over. Ernest went for a short visit, and a month later his mother was dead of a heart attack. Ernest himself collapsed, and was too weak to attend the funeral at Whitwood, and his sister Marion too had to stay away because of illness.

Ernest had always been very close to his mother. His aunt Ada Barmby wrote after Catherine's death:

> She would say, I have heard her say, 'Ernest will manage that for me' or 'Ernest knows all about such & such a thing.' She relied on you, as you have all relied on her, so my dear boy you will have to take some of her burdens on your shoulders.

Her daughter Mabel wrote:

> How thankful Ernest must be that he came for that little visit to his Mother when I was there. She did so enjoy it — she was like a different person after he wrote that he was coming ... and when he did come it was such a comfort to have him to talk about all the worries — I am sure it did her a great deal of good.

At this time Ernest was in poor health, and this is probably the time Katharine refers to when he was not strong enough to paint; some of the letters give the impression that he had a heart atack after his mother's death. Before she died, he had been reading to her out of the book he was writing, *Angling and Art in Scotland,* and now he turned to work on this as a distraction. It was published in 1908 by Longman, and received many flattering reviews, which were carefully collected from an amazing range of newspapers and journals by the family.

Angling and Art was illustrated by excellent coloured plates of Ernest's paintings, and these were deservedly praised, as was the unusual combination of the two subjects as material for a book. The *Burlington Magazine* considered that 'an ugly binding and a commonplace frontispiece' were 'an unfortunate introduction to a book which is otherwise above the average.' Most of the critics, however, were more appreciative, and *The Daily Telegraph* pointed out that 'Not to many men is given in one week two such events as the publication of a book written and illustrated by themselves and a one-man picture show in Bond Street.' This referred to an exhibition 'Fishermen's Haunts in Scotland by Mr E. Briggs', which was held in the galleries of the Fine Arts Society in New Bond Street, and visited by the Queen on 8 December 1908. The frontispiece which aroused adverse criticism was thought by many to be a painting of Mary with a fishing rod, but Katharine declared that this had been painted from a model. The other plates are all Scottish scenes of mountains, lakes and rivers, with one of the little town of Dalry; and they show the range and variety of Ernest's art and rich use of colour. The drawings at the ends of chapters were done by Hugh Radcliffe Wilson, who was brought up with his sister Margery by Marion and Geoffrey Jackson after their parents died.

The early part of the book is taken up with accounts of Ernest's visits to Galloway with his brothers when a boy, and the second with fishing experiences in the Highlands. He leaves a vivid picture of the merry mischievous band of brothers, and the critic of *The Manchester Guardian* describes the book as 'bright and breezy and even ebullient.' Oddly enough, the same critic remarks that 'in the earlier part the aged author gives us a somewhat garrulous reminiscence of his piscatorial youth.' One wonders how the family reacted to this, since Ernest at the time was forty-two. In fact, it is emphatically no old man's book, and the liveliness of the writing suggests that most of it was done before Ernest suffered from illness and depression.

The financial situation gradually improved, but Ernest felt it wise to sell Ghyll Head, Catherine's small house on Windermere. He did not want to live in the Lake District, but the money left him by his mother made it possible to leave London, and he decided to build a house in Scotland. Gerald had retired from the Company in 1907, to take over the Shap Granite and Chalk Quarries. Ernest's adopted niece, Margery, wrote on Marion's behalf to tell him how splendid it was of him to do what he had done for Gerald, 'and of Mary to urge you to do it', so it seems that Ernest had managed to clear up the difficult situation. Meanwhile in 1908 Mary had her own troubles, since her mother died in July, and she had to leave the children and go to Yorkshire. Ernest wrote to her there:

> I feel the deepest sympathy for all your brothers & sisters in their dreadful loss — how I feel the loss of my Mother! I know that your Mother was just as dear & sweet to all of you as mine was to me. What a sweet comfort you have been to me in all my troubles my darling! You are so very very precious to me, and whatever sorrows we go through can only draw us closer to each other.

He added that Molly knew of her mother's loss, 'but, poor girl, she did not know what to say to console you, & was a good deal distressed because she did not know how to say it.'

In January 1909 Ernest became a member of the Board in place of Gerald, to represent the family interests, which meant more journeys to Leeds. He went on searching for a suitable site in the Highlands nevertheless, writing from Loch Awe that he felt much better in the Highland air, and evidently had great hopes that his health would benefit from the move. At first the search proved fruitless: 'I have looked for a site here & don't think there is anything on this side of the loch which would suit us & I think it is out of the question to build on the other side.' It was the Shepherds who in the end helped him to find what he wanted. Walter Shepherd now lived at Dunkeld, and his son Godfrey was an architect. The chosen place was close to Dunkeld above the River Tay, on the site of an earlier house which had been burnt down. In April he was able to report how the building was progressing: 'The country is awfully pretty just now, more so than in summertime, I think. I was charmed with our site, it is certainly the nicest about here & it will make a lovely home.' The house was built partly in imitation of one in Hampstead which Ernest had admired, and was an original and attractive building which fitted perfectly into its surroundings. It was not very large, but gave an impression of spaciousness; the main rooms faced south, and the large bay-windows with their window-seats were ideally placed to encourage talk and hospitality, two activities dear to Ernest. Evelyn Goshawk describes the house thus:

Designed largely by Ernest, it stood in a perfect setting near the Tay, with a variety of levels forming terraces in different directions, with long grass walks leading away through silver birches, azalias and rhododendrons — 'half-wild and wholly tame.' The house was long — facing south, the entrance hall light, spacious, with a wide stair having a large, light window of heraldic glass at the turn; from the hall a corridor led on the right to dining-room and library, on the left to drawing-room, billiard-room and studio.[22]

The children had their playroom, which afterwards became Katharine's study, and each chose tiles from Liberty's for her bedroom fireplace. The wide billiard-room, on two levels, became the main workroom of the house when the girls grew up, and the centre of dramatic activities; here Ernest's painting 'Mary Go and Call the Cattle Home' still hangs. There was ample provision in the hall and the large rooms for Ernest's huge pictures, which fitted perfectly into their setting. In front of the house was a wide terrace, on which all kinds of activities took place; there was a bowling green for Ernest, and many sheltered corners in which to sit, talk and read. The grounds were planned by landscape gardeners, and a stream ran down through the trees, so that the effect was one of natural beauty without formality. Pears ripened on the sunny wall at one end of the house, and the summerhouse, among the trees, looked out on the Tay beyond, and was used for picnics, and for the children's lessons with their governess in the summer. There was a swing on a great beech, and a donkey lived in a shed near the summerhouse. Dalbeathie was indeed an idyllic place, and several of those who visited it have used the word 'magic' to describe the effect it had upon them.

The name chosen for the house was that of an earlier Dalbeathie, which had stood on the hill above a now vanished village, Middleton. Later on Katharine was to record this in poems forming part of the collection 'Lost Country':

> Here in the centre, sheltered by the beeches,
> Lies Middleton, and in the trickling burn
> The flax rots, on the dyke the linen bleaches,
> In every house looms clack and spindles turn ...

> Eastward, diminished from its former glory,
> Stands old Dalbeathie on the Castle Hill;
> Who built it first is a forgotten story;
> And half a mile beyond lies Stendon Mill.

The family learned about the village from a very old woman living nearby, who could remember life as it was in the past, and this made a considerable impact on Katharine:

> Here, where our house stands by the deepening river,
> A village stood a hundred years ago;
> The hopes they had, the joys, the fears, the pleasures
> Nothing is left of Middleton to show.
>
> When first we built our house here, by the ferry
> An old, old woman lived, so very old
> A hundred years stretched out in view behind her;
> And what we know of Middleton she told.

This close encounter with the past history of the country people may well have quickened Katharine's interest in folklore and popular tradition. She had discovered already the delights of folk and fairy tales from volumes in her father's library. She read Hartland's *English Fairy and Folk Tales* when she was about nine, with the companion volumes by Douglas and Yeats for Scotland and Ireland, and also John Rhys' *Celtic Folklore*. 'They coloured my taste in Folk Narrative for the rest of my life', she wrote in the preface to *British Folk Tales*.[22] Her father took a great interest in the beliefs and legends of the Scottish countryside, and introduced them into *The Two Rivers*. One of the last things he wrote was a story, 'The Serpent of Loch Gannaich', dealing with the belief held by a Highlander in a fearsome serpent in the loch, who was 'the old lady of Soudean Mialach' in one of her many forms. Katharine and her father must often have discussed such local legends during their time at Dalbeathie.

In June 1910 the family stayed at Pitlochry while work on the house was completed. The initials E and MB are set over the door of the house, with the date 1910, and the family moved in on 10 April 1911. Ernest had to leave the family at Pitlochry while he went to visit Marion, now an invalid, and then he went fishing on Loch Awe, missing Elspeth's eighth birthday. However he wrote her a splendid letter in disguised handwriting from 'The Observatory,

Mars', signed 'The Clerk of the Weather', which informed her that her 'highly respected parent Ernest Briggs' had requested a fine day for her birthday, and promising that he would do what he could. In the event there was a fearful storm and flooding, so that Elsie's proposed visit to the circus had to be given up. Ernest wrote again to console his little daughter and explain what must have happened:

> Thunder comes you know when the Clerk of the Weather loses control of the clouds — I expect your request for a fine birthday rather put the poor gentleman about & probably indirectly, it caused the rain on Friday. No doubt the clouds that he held back & which ought to have sent rain down on Pitlochry on Wednesday slipped through his fingers against some other clouds which he was moving off from some other little girl's birthday — we will say perhaps at Loch Awe, for it was fine here — and hence the dreadful quarrel and grumbling at Pitlochry on Friday. Clouds, you must know, are very pugnacious things (that is they love fighting) & when two heavy ones meet they throw lightning at each other & the growling is tremendous.

After the family settled at Dalbeathie in the spring of the following year, the Fellows Road house was put up for sale, and Mary set about finding suitable servants. An attractive house was built for the gardener, although conditions even in this carefully planned residence were in 1911 surprisingly tough; the cottage had no bathroom, and Jimmy MacKillup the chauffeur had to cycle up from Dunkeld every day and eat his lunch outside. Ernest had bought a new car in March 1911, a Hillman Tourer, described as a green open car with a basketwork top. The little girls were able to add to their stock of animals; in due course they had a donkey, a dog called Geordie, said to be very intelligent, and a kitten from a neighbouring farm. Elspeth wrote a delightful account of this little tabby, Thomasina, and her family of four, called D'Artagnan, Cleopatra, Athos and Una, who must have caused chaos in the house:

> They were a handful. Tommy used to chastise them; she took them between her paws and kicked their heads with her back legs when they were really unruly; but all the same they were sometimes almost too much for her. They played over everything. We had a stuff-covered screen in the dining-room, and they were up and down this all day, and over all the chairs. The wastepaper

basket was a particularly favourite plaything. They knocked it over on its side; one kitten got inside, while another got on the top, and between them they rolled it backwards and forwards on the floor.

So life passed pleasantly for the children in the new surroundings, but Ernest was never left undisturbed for long or free from family anxieties. There was much concern over Marion's health, for she was gradually getting weaker, needed a lift to get upstairs, and was finding it difficult to eat. This must have caused much sadness to Ernest, who was very fond of his sister. One of her last letters congratulates him on the approaching publication of his book, *The Two Rivers*, which came out after her death in 1912. Their brother Gilbert had died in 1910, and Gerald was in poor health, and wrote gloomy letters, complaining of overwork and scarcity of money. Nevertheless Katharine remembered the first year in the new house as an idyllic one, 'filled with the visits of friends in the hot delightful summer which marked George V's coronation'.

Dalbeathie with Katharine at the door, about 1911.

The Two Rivers was published by John Long in October 1912, and many of Ernest's relatives wrote to congratulate him. Again reviews on the whole were good, although there was criticism of the long descriptive passages, and also of the sections describing Andrew's life as an art-student. Clearly some critics were puzzled by the symbolism of the two rivers, which is far from clear. They seem to represent two different ways of life, the serene River Ken standing for the open, friendly world of Andrew's family, and the dark, sinister Dule for the cruel, violent life of the M'Cloor family. Thus they emphasise the contrast between the two women Andrew loved, his stepsister Margaret and Jess M'Cloor; in the end Andrew saw Jess as an evil enchantress, a Lamia figure with the eyes of a serpent. Most of the book is on a lighter, more realistic level, however, and Andrew's foolish, talkative stepmother and his artist friends are presented with humorous observation. The book is clearly uneven, with overmuch melodrama in the part about the M'Cloors, and some loose ends to the plot, but it has liveliness and vigour, with good descriptive passages and skilful use of dialect. Above all it expresses that warm, humourous attitude to life typical of Ernest.

Ernest did not have long to enjoy his home in Scotland. He had planned it as the ideal house, a little palace of art and culture, where life could be lived pleasantly without vain ostentation, and good friends were always welcome. In 1912 there are references to his serious illness and to devoted nursing by Mary. His reputation as an artist was growing, and in the spring of that year he had a letter from a friend, A.T. Yewell, congratulating him on the sale of two large paintings exhibited in the Academy, exhorting him to 'Go on and prosper & do another big water piece with yet more *mystery, spray* and Turnerism in it, & you'll knock 'em!' The following year one of his pictures was bought for the nation, but he was not well enough to go to London to enjoy his success, and he only managed to attend one Board meeting in May. Yewell refers to Ernest losing confidence in his doctor, and urges him to seek another opinion. In October he was apparently recovering from pneumonia, and his niece Margery refers to a haemorrhage:

> You are so brave & full of pluck & cheerfulness, but oh I *am* so sorry for you, poor dear, and little Mary too in her anxiety. We do hope you will get on a little better & not have another attack.

In the spring of 1913 there was some improvement, but by July Ernest's condition was grave. One of his artist friends wrote:

> What a very sad communication I got — you poor dear man! So good and gentle and kind, it is cruel that you should suffer as you do. You always appear before my mind's eye as I used to see you at Tummel Bridge — your fine thoughtful face bending over your work.

Concerned although they were about him, those writing to Ernest were full of plans for future meetings and activities, and his letters must have been such as to encourage this. But throughout August he grew weaker, and the end came on 4 September 1913. His Aunt Jennie wrote to Mary: 'I know you had lost hope and were more or less prepared for the end, but it cannot make it any easier.... I think and hope that the end was peaceful, he must have become so weak.'

The letters which Mary received at her husband's death stress how closely bound together their lives had been. Mabel Barmby brings this out:

> You made each other very happy all the years you were together and the thought of that will be a help. In all his letters Ernest used always to say *we* — many men would have said *I* — but it was always *we*.

This is echoed by Aunt Jennie:

> I can realise what it means to you, knowing the perfect love and union between you and how your lives were so closely one, much more so than can often be the case — every little detail and moment of the day has been associated and in a manner guided by him, for you have always thought first of him & he leant on you for the happiness of his life.

There is little mention of the children in these letters, except for expressing the hope that they would prove a comfort to Mary. Her suffering must indeed have been extreme, and for Katharine the last illness and death of so beloved a father must have been a grievous burden for a girl of fourteen to bear. With the loss of her father, one section of her life came to an end and her time of childhood was over. The influence of Ernest remained with her all her life, in small things as well as great. She was unwilling, even after the house

Mary Briggs and her three daughters, (from right) Katharine, Winifred and Elspeth, at Dalbeathie about 1911|1|.

had been sold much later in her life, that anything which her father had done there should be changed. More importantly, those qualities which his friends had admired in Ernest were enduring values in her own life also. His warm hospitality and generosity, energy and devotion to his art, sense of fun, delight in human nature, and feeling of responsibility for others, were characteristic also of Katharine. She shared his love of reading, writing and story-telling, and in a different way was determined to carry on his work for art and culture. With the aid of Niels Lund, who did all he could to help Mary to carry on with the business of living, a cross of pale grey granite in the Celtic style was raised over Ernest's grave in the little cemetery of Caputh, on a piece of land encircled by the River Tay. Mary had chosen where he should be buried, and Niels commended her choice:

Dear Mary, I think you were right when you bade me go to Caputh, it is so much more private, your comings and goings to and from the grave can be done in peaceful journeying as compared with Dunkeld or Birnam, and I think this is all more in harmony with your character and with what he could have wished.

Here in this quiet place Mary now also rests. It seems a fitting memorial to Ernest Briggs, along with the splendid house which he built. But his finest memorial, surely, may be seen in the character of his eldest daughter, whom he had made his 'playfellow and companion' for nearly fifteen years.

3 Growing Up and Making Out: The Imaginary World of the Briggs Sisters

For as the sweet juice touched my tongue, the world flowed all away,
And I was light as thistledown with which the breezes play.
I saw the world outside me, I saw it through and through;
And I cared no more what happened, as mortal people do.
                K.M. Briggs, *Manuscript Book of Poems*

It is impossible not to be struck by resemblances between the three Briggs sisters and the Brontë children in their creation of an elaborate imaginary world which occupied them for many years. Like the young Brontës, Katharine and her sisters created their own amusements; they were to a large extent isolated from other children, and even more so after the move to Scotland. While they had little formal education, they had free access to a wide range of books, and encouraged one another to make up stories and produce paintings. They acted out stories which were based on something they had read or had read to them, and gradually developed the plots on lines of their own, or took the characters into dramas of their own invention. Winifred Gérin says of the young Brontës:

> They had only to read to identify themselves with the characters; from this to *acting* the parts in dramatized reconstruction of the stories was but a step (this they called 'establishing a play') and then to add to the original plots was a natural consequence of their tireless inventions.[1]

The Brontës called such activities 'making out'. Mary Taylor, Charlotte's friend, told Mrs Gaskell: 'This habit of "making out" interests for themselves, that most children get who have none in actual life, was very strong in her. The whole family used to "make out" histories, and invent characters and events.'[2] When Charlotte went to school at Roe Head she studied with desperate resolution, and took little part in games or amusements: 'She seemd to have no interest or pleasure beyond a feeling of duty, and when she could get the opportunity used to sit alone and "make out".[3] This for Charlotte was an indulgence and a delight, and to be forced to forego it for long was agony; it led on to the creative writing of her stories and novels.

Although with the Briggs sisters the internal world of invention and story-telling did not lead to creative novels of the calibre of those of the Brontës, the pastime was something of great importance for Katharine's intellectual development. It seems at times to have had greater reality for her than the world of everyday life. She drew a clear distinction between this kind of inventiveness and 'pure amusement games' of the kind which her little sisters played when small children. A further distinction is made by another writer who created an elaborate imaginary world in childhood. C.S. Lewis in *Surprised by Joy*[4] claims that the world which he built up with his brother from the time when he was about six years old was more real to him than anything else in boyhood. He insists that this was not a case of fantasy or day-dreaming; this indeed he might indulge in from time to time, but it was in quite a different category from the creation of Animal Land, his imaginary kingdom: 'In my daydreams I was training myself to be a fool; in mapping and chronicling Animal Land I was training myself to be a novelist.' Katharine herself declared in a letter to Robert Silvey, who was writing a book on imaginary worlds created by children:

> Ours was not a private dream but a social and dramatic exercise among the three of us.... We got a great deal of pleasure out of it and it was valuable experience for the two of us who wrote creative books.

On the other hand, it seems that children with plenty of freedom to indulge in such inventive games over long periods run the risk of becoming so engrossed in them that they miss out on normal social activities with their peers. An interesting example is Eleanor Farjeon, who as a child played the game of TAR (Tessa and Ralph) with her brilliant elder brother Harry, who organised and led their inventive efforts. In *A Nursery in the Nineties*[5] she describes it as 'the usual childish game of pretending to be somebody else, but extended to a degree of intensity, complexity and accomplishment never equalled.' 'I know of no case', she wrote, 'in which the game of two was continued for more than 20 years with increasing richness.' But here she appears to underestimate the achievements of other young players of such games. What we know of the imaginary worlds of the Brontës, Hartley Coleridge,[6] C.S. Lewis and the Briggs sisters proves that young children with creative gifts and plenty of time at their disposal can go to amazing lengths of ingenuity and detail in planning the geography, history and social life of their imaginary countries, and can carry this on for many years; those of the Brontës and Briggs were certainly continued into adult life. Eleanor looked back to this fascinating occupation with nostalgia, but in later life came to realise that it had kept her within a narrow circle of childhood just when her experience of life and human relationships should have been widening: 'All other calls remained green when they should have been fruitful, frustrated when they should have been fulfilled.'[7] At the same time, she believed that she owed to the playing of TAR 'the flow of ease which makes writing a delight'. Similar effects, for both good and ill, may be seen in the developments of the Briggs sisters, who continued to take part in the inventive game long after childhood was over. 'How could a game which satisfied *young* children hold the interest of growing teenagers and at least one graduate?' queried Sister Ursula Blake (SHCJ) after Katharine had given her a long account of the game 'Eric' on 4 September 1980.[8] She observed that as Katharine spoke of it 'she was sparkling and enthusiastic, and I noted that she used a child's language to describe the episodes and developments.' There is no doubt that this game played an important part in Katharine's mental growth.

'Eric' seems to have sprung out of a story made up by Winifred and Elspeth about 1907, when Katharine was nearly nine years old, in which she came to take part. She describes it as being about two little princes, Charlie and Ernest,[9]

> who for reasons which were never quite clear to me, were living in the care of two footmen in a large capital city of which neither was a native. The footmen were rather harsh and given to spanking them as a form of discipline.

Possibly a story of Elspeth's, called 'Little Prince Ernest', to which her father refers in a letter, was connected with this drama, while we know that Winnie had a favourite prince Charlesworth, taken from *Lorna Doone*. Katharine then invented 'a pleasant young king Robert', who invited the boys to stay at his palace in the kingdom of Astgal, where a cousin of the king called Eric took care of them:

He was an eccentric character, a tremendous reader and booklover, never without a large tome in hand, who was nevertheless a splendid athlete, who could leap straight up from the floor of the Hall on to one of the rafters.

This presumably was a character enacted by Katharine herself while her sisters were the princes. The boys were happy at Astgal until King Robert was killed by one of the Colour Strips, a 'nihilist gang' from Asia. The death of a main character after the play had been running for a considerable time so affected the players that they remained 'quite subdued' for several days.

The characters and their world expanded rapidly as the children grew older. At one time there were three main kings, one for each child, and every country involved was called Dash, in order, it seems, to provide a certain objectivity; it would have been unfair, they felt, for any one of them to have England. The kingdoms were somewhere in Europe — maps of Holland and Denmark survive, and Holland (called Onstadt) is divided up into a number of 'counties' with names like Rathmore, Estwick and Lubshire — while the period of action was set a thousand years in the future, so that they could never be proved wrong, and were not forced to do endless research into history to get their facts right. The towns where the action took place were equipped with many secret passages and tunnels, and peopled by complicated royal families, noble heroes, and praiseworthy companies of adventurers like the Quicksilvers and the Rosebudders. There were naturally many villains as well, as these provided much of the comedy. There was, for instance, Carrots Sawdust (Henry Jack), who talked in a strange dialect, was small and immensely broad, and had large flat feet, so that he could be heard approaching along the sandy floors of the passages: 'You could always tell his trap-doors because they were so large to let him in and out.' He was a great robber, and had piles of treasure stored away underground. Elspeth was particularly good at creating villains. Winifred, on the other hand, excelled at knights and heroes, such as Ensor and Charlesworth. She used to ride up and down the garden path on her tricycle, 'carrying private despatches from King Bruce Rutherford of Dash', as she was the head of the royal guard, a picked body of twelve knights mounted on tricycles. They were a splendid band of chivalrous heroes, who composed and sang songs in between their adventures, another of Winnie's accomplishments; she was more musical and less bookish than the other two.

As time went on, the method of playing appears to have developed into a kind of joint story-telling or the creation of an imaginary history of royal families. Each represented a particular character, or related the fortunes of a kingdom, while the others listened carefully, in order to remember what had happened. They agreed on the accepted form of the history as they went along, sometimes after prolonged discussion, and then Katharine recorded it, as her father seems to have written down the early games which she played with him. The acting out of the story as a vigorous game was presumably gradually given up as the girls grew older. As well as the record of the history, there was a vast amount of practical detail to build up. Wars, treaties and royal marriages linking up the separate dynasties were diligently worked out; and maps and coats of arms of the various families painted with the greatest care. There were huge family trees and even plans of the houses where the chief characters lived. 'We must have covered reams of paper', Katharine told Sister Ursula. There was indeed a vast pile of manuscripts on Eric, but these were mislaid during the move from Burford, and Katharine was unable to find them when she went back. The girls did not, like the Farjeons in their games of TAR, keep the Eric game as a strict secret; grown-ups could join in if they wished, but according to Katharine it was not easy to learn the accepted method of improvisation without considerable practice. Some of the earnest young governesses, in fact, disapproved, so that the girls had to evade them when they wanted to go on with the game. Katharine's friend, Evie Forbes, who was at school with her, remembers the girls playing it almost continuously at Dalbeathie when she came to stay there in the holidays:[10]

> They and I were all different people, in a different county, about which they had made maps, house plans and for us pedigrees and coats of arms. It was all so real that when I got back home it took some time to discover my real identity.

Indeed she remembers it as having been a little frightening.

Letters written by Katharine make this clear. One is supposed to be from Julia to Sir Lionel Erskin, Baronet, and is addressed: c/o H.H. Prince George Terry:

My *dear* Lionel,

How are you all? I'm having great difficulty in writing, everyone is talking at once. Jessica is arguing with Geraldine and Mary is scolding Isobel, and Georgie and Everad will interrupt. I wish Everad were with his regiment. Mary wishes it as much as anyone, and we all wish that Georgie had never been born, how horrid she is!

Francis is growing up a very naughty child. I believe that he must be three now, I'm very good at remembering the children's names and ages. Isobel's sister came to see her the other day. I don't like her at all; she's older than Isobel. Leslie has gone to school, he wanted to go very much, but I'm afraid that he may not like it, and I hope Lesbia won't be lonely.

Mrs Howarth has two children, little girls, one of them is a little over a year and the other one is about two months. Jessica found this out.

I wish that the king would not come in when I am writing it does interrupt my thoughts so having to stand up. I think that Jessica is by far the nicest of the wives; I wish that Everad would not laugh so loud.

I told Isobel that I wouldn't have such a person to see me as her sister, Jean, I think her name is, I'm rather good at remembering names. John must have repented of his folly now. I am sure that he is glad to be with his regiment. How is your child or is it children I'm getting a little mixed with yours and Marjorie's. I don't think that I quite like Lesbia's governess, but I think that I must write to Ralph about it before I dismiss her.

Isobel seems rather offended with me. I can't think why. Give my love to Susanna.

                      Yours affectionately,
                              Julia

This gives some idea of the family complications and the necessity of remembering what had already been said. It may be noted that this was one of the main features of education as worked out by Charlotte Mason and practised in the PNEU schools, and such a method must have been employed by the Briggs' governesses.

The letter seems to be an early one, written before the move from London. Two others dealing with Eric characters were sent to the sisters when Katharine was at school in Edinburgh, and was at least fourteen. She had referred in her letter to their governess, Miss Witherow, and then suddenly turned abruptly to events in their imaginary world:

> Godiva is very much amused about Leslie's socks and handkerchiefs, but poor Nitocris is having the time of her life with them quarrelling over her. But the worm will turn one day, and I expect she'll go and marry some one else from sheer desperation.
> How old is Nydia? I forget.
> Fiametta is very bored with William, because he's not at all poetic, and doesn't care at all about lovely scenery. Poor Hadrian is as restless and unhappy as ever. But he's not strong enough yet to leave his Mother and live among ordinary people. I think that when he does go he will live with them for only about six months, because of course Godiva won't want to spare him for long. Hadrian has just burnt a book which he has been working on for some time.
> Who was it that Eric was going to fall in love with? I forget.

Evidently she received replies to her questions, and her next letter home follows on from this:

> Thank you very much for your letters; I should have remembered about Eric and Billie. It was very silly of me. Nydia is a bit too old for my purpose, can you think of someone of about 14 or 15, a girl of mine whose character we don't know much. I'm thinking of her with regard to marrying.

She then goes on to other subjects unconnected with the world of Eric.

It seems from these brief glimpses that the imaginary world was at this time a fairly realistic one, without magic or fantasy; the model seems to be Ruritania rather than any land of enchantment, and Ruritania with a distinctly domestic flavour. There is much emphasis on family relationships, while at the same time Sister Ursula gained the impression that there was not much love interest in Eric. Perhaps the talk of aunts and grandmothers about the many members of the Briggs family had some influence on the Eric saga. The story-making was kept up by correspondence while the sisters were apart, and renewed with much enthusiasm in the holidays. When Evelyn Goshawk became Katharine's friend in the thirties, Katharine had taken her degree at Oxford, and been at home for some years, but the 'serial romance,' as Evelyn called it, was still going on.[11] By then it had taken up more romantic and heroic themes, no doubt influenced by Katharine's medieval studies and love for ballads. There were borrowings from Old Norse and Celtic literature, from Malory and the Border Ballads, and like the Brontë girls Katharine composed poems about the characters:

> There was William that came from the North,
> And John Leslie from the East,
> And Erik from the Robson Hills —
> It was him she loved the least.

Erik now is spelt in the Scandinavian form. The old kingdoms also had more impressive names — Bocla, Albrodadin under Leoff Ghynt, and the 'sea-girt land of Yestermorna.' A manuscript book of poems which Katharine wrote out during the war includes the National Anthem of Astgal and Yestermorna:

> Mark Telfer, Stefan, Ivan the bold
> (Low, low, they lie).
> Claud's hand is still, John's heart is cold
> (Low they lie and the hare goes over them).
> Hush! The ravens shall be fed,
> Here we swear for every head
> Shall be a heap of Pagan dead.
> *(Astgal's National Anthem)*

A poem which laments the death of Sigmund, slain in the feast hall of Rederrol, is modelled on Old English alliterative verse, with echoes of *Beowulf*:

> Still lies our lord, the Lord of Rederrol,
> The killer has taken him with crafty knife,
> Bright was the board, the red wine beamed,
> Crafty the king smiled, waiting the killing,
> Gay were the guests, but the brown spears glinted,
> Of murderers and marsh-stalkers, men in bright corselets.

When the sisters were parted during the War, Elspeth still thought about Eric when alone in London in 1942. Finding it hard to start another book, she wrote to Winifred: 'I have had to fall back to thinking about Eric, and as there doesn't seem any prospect of playing for a long time, it's not so profitable.' After the war, when the sisters moved to the Barn House, the game was taken up again: Elspeth in a letter to Winifred at Dalbeathie remarked that so far she and Katharine had had no time to play it, but clearly assumed that they would be going on as soon as they had the opportunity. In another letter she referred to the death of a Swedish prince in Dakota as the result of a plane crash, with the comment:

> They do seem to have a lot of accidents, and to royalty too. They do seem to have got aeroplanes safer in Eric times, though they haven't advanced much in science in other ways. I suppose they have concentrated on that kind of thing.

Indeed neither Katharine nor Elspeth had much interest in technology and it seems to have played no part in their picture of the future.

The playing of the game seems only to have ended with Elspeth's death. Katharine herself stressed the fact that it was not an escape from reality, but rather an intellectual exercise, which taught Elspeth and herself more about the art of story-telling. Certainly there was no question of Katharine or her sisters projecting themselves into stories of a wish-fulfilment type, and seeing themselves as heroes and heroines. The cast of Eric was enormous, and the tales were told, it seems, objectively, as one might recall happenings within one's own family. At the time of her father's last illness and death and the bleak period afterwards, the playing of the game may well have offered the children a relief from intolerable anxiety and depression. It was, however, not a form of day-dreaming, since it had its own disciplines, and needed co-operation with others; rather, it provided excitement and amusement, and an absorbing occupation which could be carried out anywhere the sisters might be together. It may possibly have acted as a restricting influence on the early novels of Katharine and Elspeth; while it trained them in the management of plots and the development of situations, it does not seem to have led to the creation of outstanding characters. In the days when Katharine was at school, the game formed a link with her sisters through letters, and it was one of the many bonds which continued to unite her to Elspeth, and related her to her past. It was, however, by no means the only inventive, imaginary world which Katharine helped to create, and into which she drew others.

When Ernest Briggs died in 1913, the full, satisfying life of visitors, amusements and expeditions which he had built up for his wife and daughters at Dalbeathie came to a sudden end. There had been many guests at the house in 1911 and 1912. In her *Folktales of England* (1965) Katharine included several tales heard at Dalbeathie about this time, told by guests from London. But when Mary and her daughters were left alone, the remoteness of the house became felt for the first time, increasingly so during the First World War. The local ladies tended to be conventional, and obsessed with long and boring investigations into family backgrounds. Katharine in 1980[12] gave a vivid sketch of one of their neighbours, 'a typical Scottish spinster of the small laird class, whose conversation was generally what you might call genealogical small talk', and gave an example of this:

> Do you remember my telling you about that very nice woman we met at Crieff Hydro last year, who turned out to be a second cousin once removed of the Thompsons of Invergarrity? Well, it was a very queer thing, but when we were staying at Drumnadrochit this May we met a couple, very nice people — she was his second wife — and it turned out that his first wife had been a *first* cousin of the girl we met at Crieff — and she ... and so on. When I was young and impatient, I found that kind of thing very boring.

It is easy to imagine such enthusiasts for family histories speculating as to Mary's antecedents, which might have been embarrassing for her. Katharine also found the local girls of her own age and class very dull in comparison with the company at home to which she had been accustomed. Ernest had been anxious that she should go away to school, so that she could go up to Oxford later to read English, and she decided that this plan must be carried out, painful although the break must be.

There is no doubt that after her father's death Katharine saw herself as the man of the family, looking after 'the children', as she called them. 'Next Saturday will be Winnie's birthday; how old the child grows', she remarked in a letter to her mother. She even signed herself 'your Uncle Katharine' when she wrote to Madge Jackson's small children. Mary seems to have increasingly relied on her for decisions, accustomed as she was to fall in with Ernest's plans and activities, while she concerned herself with the smooth running of the home and her daughters' health and welfare. When Katharine was away, she sent her flowers through the post, and useful objects like hairpins, or books needed at school, and constantly inquired about her health. Katharine's letters to her, while always considerate and affectionate, tend to be a little on the managing side. She gives her mother instructions about finding a cottage where she and her friends can stay, for instance, and persuades her to put off proposed guests:

> I quite see dearest that I should be at home and that I can't leave you slaving at Dalbeathie whilst I go and desport myself in the cottage. But don't you think you could postpone the Hannams a bit? Because after all we invited them for April and we can't be expected to keep the whole year unengaged because they postpone their visit to September.

At first Katharine's entry into the unfamiliar world of boarding school cannot have been easy. Lansdowne House was a small school in Edinburgh, run by Charlotte Fenton and her partner, Ellen Mary Hale.[13] Charlotte was the eldest of four daughters of a wealthy coal-owner in the North of England who lost all his money through the flooding of a mine. She gallantly set out to open a school 'for country-bred girls of good family', with her friend Anne Emerson, in order to provide for herself and her sisters, and made a success of it. Both women knew Birnam well, and were buried there, so they are likely to have been known to Ernest and Mary, which would account for the choice of school. In many ways it does not seem an ideal one, since the atmosphere was strongly Episcopalian, and the academic standard not high, although when Miss Hale succeeded Miss Emerson she did what she could to improve it. Miss Fenton aimed at keeping the school small, and creating a friendly atmosphere. She set much emphasis on character training and encouraged music, literature and art, together with a knowledge of current events. The girls tended to come from families connected with the Army, the Navy or the Church; they were taught good manners and social graces, and many of them married husbands in the diplomatic or colonial services. It was rare, if not unknown, for any to go on to Oxford or Cambridge. Discipline was intended to be easy, but some of the seniors had a good deal of authority, and fussed over rules in a way which Katharine was likely to find irksome. She did not feel much affection for Miss Fenton, who was a formidable person, tending to bully those not able to stand up for themselves, although she could be kind and generous on occasion. She did not expect her girls to be particularly intellectual, and while newspapers and suitable periodicals were provided and there were visits to concerts and the theatre, the school library was negligible.

Katharine must have been fifteen when she arrived at Lansdowne House, and according to Evie Hill (afterwards Evie Forbes) who was to become a lifelong friend, she looked older than she was, 'due to the good but old-fashioned clothes she wore.' She was in half-mourning for her father, and Evie at first thought her very plain. Miss Hale's niece Isabel, some years younger than Katharine, remembered her as a 'tall, quiet, very dignified girl':

> She was not a curly fresh-faced school girl. She was pale, had straight rather mousy hair, a slim figure, reasonably good features ... a calm expression, with a rare but peculiarly sweet smile. She moved and spoke quietly and with dignity — might have passed, and probably did, for a nonentity among more polished and superficially attractive girls.

By accepted school standards, she may have seemed a little peculiar. Her mother insisted on Aertex bedlinen and underclothes, and Evie Hill immediately sympathised, since her mother had compelled her to wear Liberty velveteens and caped coats, and she had been brought up a vegetarian. Thus they stood out from the conventional herd who wore neat navy suits, adored cricket and liked to sew and play cards in the drawing-room after the formal dinner. Katharine and Evie preferred reading poetry ('principally Browning'). But even the independent Evie was somewhat taken aback when she learned that Katharine was a Unitarian; she herself was the daughter of the Provost of Aberdeen Cathedral, and had never met such people. Indeed before long the headmistress was suggesting to her that it was undesirable that she should become very friendly with the new girl, and Isobel Hale received a similar warning from a member of the staff. Evie, however, was a resolute character and always stood up to Miss Fenton: 'I firmly, and I hope not too rudely, said that Katharine and I would continue to be friends', and so they did, although their lives followed very different paths. They found much in common in their love of literature, their sense of the absurd, and their scorn for feeble and conventional characters.

Although she missed home greatly at first, Katharine found compensations in school life. There were some good teachers, and Miss Hale evidently did all she could to see that Katharine was properly prepared for the Oxford entrance, writing to Mrs Briggs in the spring of 1916 to say that she should be ready for the examination in a year's time, if she worked hard at Latin prose and learned sufficient Greek for Responsions. There had been some suggestion that she should have private tuition, but Miss Hale pointed out that 'work among the other girls would be much better for a girl of Katharine's age than private coaching lessons.' Katharine's accounts of exams in letters home indicate that she did only moderately well, except in literature ('The Macbeth paper was very nice indeed. ... I didn't think I did it very well, but Miss Wynne told me afterwards that I had done a beautiful paper'). Evie remembers that Katharine always won the school essay prize, while she herself had the prize for the best poem. Katharine persevered with drawing and the history of art, and did fairly well; she used to say that according to her father she would have been good at painting if only she had been able to draw. She was not musical, which had its drawbacks, as she missed visits to the opera ('Some people are going to Tannhauser; but I'm afraid I shan't be sent, as I'm not musical'), but she enjoyed trips to the theatre and to historic buildings. Team games she did not find exciting; she used to say that when she played cricket she used to pray that the ball would come within her reach, and then regret it if her prayers were answered. She preferred tennis (later a tennis court was made at Dalbeathie), and she and Evie resolved to learn to swim.

One welcome opportunity which the school offered her was the chance of acting in plays, and she took the leading part in several productions. She played Christiana in a play founded on *Pilgrim's Progress,* and Olivia in *Twelfth Night,* while Evie was Maria. Isobel Hale remembers also a 'most spirited impromptu performance as a courageous Christian missionary tied up and about to be tortured and killed by African savages', and another occasion when Katharine played Dante's Beatrice, dying of a broken heart in the last act:

> I see her now, stretched upon her bier, robed in white and garlanded, with her hair flowing over her pillow, looking I (aged fourteen) thought, ineffably peaceful and beautiful. I was the Spirit of Love, in a red satin nightgown with a gold sash and pink wings, and had to lead the sorrowing Dante up to gaze upon her. The part, like most of those in the school plays in which she appeared, was by no means worthy of her talent.

Katharine, according to Evie, was disappointed in having to take female parts instead of the male ones she coveted. She would have much rather have been Christian than Christiana, although in the school play this was the leading role. She evidently found a way of using her own special gifts early in school life: 'Our room has got an awful craze for telling fairy stories, especially me' she wrote in an early letter home. As time went on, she clearly became increasingly popular with both girls and staff. Isobel Hale writes of her:

> She was always kind, attracted confidence, and was always ready with helpful advice, although by nature retired and reserved. ... Towards the end of my time, being beset with the usual problems of belief and practice common to adolescents, and knowing no surer adviser and helper, I did consult her about them. The interview took place at midnight, in the sick bay, where we were both having mumps! She helped me over my problems with a skill and integrity worthy of an experienced teacher, and a tact in evading what could have become controversial issues which I have always remembered. She must have been about seventeen at the time.

Isabel Hale saw the more serious side of Katharine, but the letters show her enjoying herself, having plenty of fun, and proving herself no fool. There is one little glimpse of all the mistresses and girls moving over the neglected war-time lawn at the beginning of the tennis season, searching for the sockets for the posts in order to put up the nets. Miss Hale had a three-pronged fork, Fenny (Miss Fenton) a stick, and Matron a poker. As for Katharine, 'I stamped my foot about until I found metal under the grass, and I said "Here it is", and they dug and there it was.' Another story is about her three special friends, Evie, Nan Kinston and Tommy Oliver:

> Fenny ... sprung on poor Evie a command that she should put her hair up. On Evie protesting that she hadn't sufficient practice Fenny demolished her arguments by saying that one of her room could do it for her. So before lunch Tommy did Evie's hair. However Evie grew bashful and tore it down, just at half past one; then she lost her clasps; then she broke her comb; then Tommy came into her cubicle & told her that every one had been in at dinner for five minutes (It gave us an awful shock for the moment, but of course she was stuffing us). And so it seemed a wonder that she should ever get into lunch at all let alone get in, in time. We've had a mad time today. I'm afraid we're going slowly insane, all four of us.

The war seems to have affected them little, although at one time there was a scare about Zeppelins, and Summertime was introduced by the Daylight Saving Bill: 'The clocks were changed at 1 p.m. yesterday, but we just pretended that they were an hour fast until this morning.'

Katharine and Evie had little patience with humbug. Katharine records with scorn the fuss made when some wretched girl was found to have ordered a copy of the song 'Gilbert the Filbert', and from then on all song titles had to be scrutinised by Miss Fenton or Miss Hale: ' "I saw the unspeakable name of Gilbert the Filbert", said Miss Hale, "It, well, it quite sent cold shivers down my back." Did you ever hear anything so oldmaidish?' Later on she and Evie became powers in the school, when Evie was Head Girl (an honour she attributed to her distinguished Episcopalian background) and Katharine Head Prefect. 'From there', Evie claimed, 'we ran the school, being kind but not too gentle with our stupid young schoolmistresses.' In the summer after she left, Katharine's closest friends stayed with her for a week in a Perthshire cottage which her mother had found for her.

As early as 1916, while still at school, Katharine had a small book published. The subject for the school prize poem one year had been 'The Legend of the Christmas Rose or any other Legend', and Katharine had asked her mother to send her *The Child's Book of Legends* and anything else which would provide material. This may have inspired *The Legend of Maidenhair,* which Katharine's mother paid to have published by Arthur H. Stockwell of Ludgate Hill, as a present for her daughter. The little known and rather sentimental German legend is told simply and with restraint. Katharine's picture of her heroine Ursula rejecting life at court, which she sees as a prison, and telling the king quietly that she has no desire whatever to marry his son, reads as if it were characteristic of her own attitude; just as the account of mountain scenery at the beginning and Ursula's love of walking over the hills was no doubt inspired by her own experiences in Scotland. The book is referred to once in her letters: 'You know Arthur Stockwell said that he'd send the book to papers to be reviewed. I do wish they would review it, it would be rather fun'. This enterprise shows Katharine again anxious to follow in her father's footsteps. The publisher, however, did nothing, and the book had little or no impact. It is mainly significant as a pointer to Katharine's ambitions at that time; like Elspeth she intended to be a writer, and her interest was aroused by legendary material to be retold rather than by any impulse to create a new plot of her own.

In 1918, just before the war ended and when Oxford was recovering from a terrible influenza epidemic, Katharine went up to Lady Margaret Hall to read English. Henrietta Jex-Blake was then Principal, and Janet Spens, a Scot who specialised in Spenser and Elizabethan drama, was Katharine's tutor. Vera Brittain paints a gloomy picture of Oxford at the end of the war, but Katharine, plunging with rapture into English literature and the joys of reading and endless discussions with gifted people, did not find it so. She was always very busy, with many activities outside her studies. Her letters are a breathless account of lectures and coachings, working in the Radcliffe, listening to the Choir on May morning, learning to punt and canoe and having riding lessons. She met members of the family when they came to Oxford ('Aunt Nell is bigger than ever, she is enormous'), as her cousin Donald had returned from war service to take a degree in engineering, and his fiancée Elizabeth Denniston (Biddy) was up at the same time. Katharine continued to act, for at that time every college had its own productions, the possibility of women joining the University Dramatic Societies being as yet non-existent. She and her friends produced poems and songs for amusement and for College entertainments. She went occasionally to College dances, but does not seem to have enjoyed these greatly ('It's a pity that I can't dance better; I really must try and get a few lessons some time.') She seems to have made no men friends, the women's colleges being then self-sufficient to a degree which appears incredible today. She sent cowslips and primroses home, all the family keeping up the pleasant custom of sending flowers by post. On her twenty-first birthday in her second year at Oxford, she received a pearl necklace from her mother, an attaché case, a chair and table from Bakers, lustre china, gloves, books and grapes, while Winnie sent a cake-stand and Elsie a stool: 'Stella and Elizabeth were simply shocked at me, they think there was never anyone so spoilt, and I'm inclined to agree.'

Winifred and Elspeth started a course of study at the Byam School of Art in London, and their mother was in London for a while with them. At one time she stayed in the country eight miles from Oxford, and Katharine was able to cycle over to see her. Winifred and Elspeth once stayed a few days in college, and Katharine wanted to take them to a lecture, but this was not permitted. In spite of all her new friends and various distractions, Katharine had not forgotten Eric. This is referred to, rather cryptically, in a letter to her sisters: 'It's rather awkward leaving off in the middle of a part. However we're not so much in the middle as sometimes.' In another letter, after an account of her doings, she ends: 'I wish I could find time to write something. We shall have a lot to play next vac, if I have any time for play, which doesn't seem likely at the moment.' References to work are usually to Elizabethan literature, and the influence of Janet Spens was probably partly responsible for Katharine's growing absorption in the early seventeenth century. She writes, for instance:

> I have a very nice essay for next week 'The Effect of Travel on Elizabethan Literature', and I have to read all kinds of interesting books for it, Lithgow's 'Full account of a thousand miles of painful peregrinations' and things of that sort.

She was clearly stimulated by her Tutor:

> Miss Spens is very interesting on drama. She has exciting ideas. Today in the class she told us how she had worked out the cast in King Lear & Othello and decided that Cordelia took the Clown's part as well.

In a brief account of her career, Katharine described the three years at Oxford as 'blissfully happy'. It must have been an exciting time for her when in 1920 women were at last granted degrees, after the long period of working and waiting. The new statute came into force in the first term of Katharine's final year; the principals of the women's colleges became Honorary MAs by Degree of Convocation, and women for the first time wore academic dress, 'part of their new and glamorous status', as Vera Brittain describes it.[14] All college lectures were now open to them without fees, and lectures by women included on the official faculties' lists. Katharine would have been one of those who matriculated in 1920, a crowd of about 1000 women, and must have been present also for the visit of Queen Mary to Lady Margaret Hall in March 1921, when she came to Oxford to receive an Honorary Degree.

It must have been a severe disappointment to Katharine, however, when she took her Finals in the summer of 1921 and was placed in the Second Class. She had hoped for a First, and one of her contemporaries in the College, Stella Pulling (later Stella Brewer) achieved one in English, but the rest of the English students from

Katharine after taking her degree at Oxford in 1921.

Lady Margaret Hall had Seconds. This must have been a blow to her pride and self-confidence, and made her all the more determined later on to gain a doctorate. There was a good deal of language work in the Oxford syllabus at this period, and this probably affected Katharine's result; she had not had a good grounding in languages, and at school they were never her strong point, her Latin always remaining unreliable. Her excellent memory, love of poetry, delight in the use of words and interest in the historical background enabled her to enjoy Old and Middle English texts, but she was lacking in the kind of disciplined and exact scholarship and critical ability likely to lead to a First. By what seems to have been an error of judgement on her tutor's part, Katharine was dissuaded from taking a new optional paper on Ballads.[15] Miss Spens thought it more likely to lead to a First if her students took the paper on Elizabethan Dramatists, the subject in which she herself specialised. Katharine seems to have been a little in awe of her tutor, a brilliant and inspiring woman, and one can but regret that she did not on this occasion insist on having her own way.

After she went down in 1921, the family united again at Dalbeathie, her sisters having studied for a while in the art school in London. They enjoyed a holiday together in Italy, where Katharine was supposed to be studying Italian, but without much result. She does not seem to have contemplated taking a post away from home; she no doubt felt that her family needed her: 'It seemed a bit priggish to go off and pursue a career', she is quoted as saying to Byron Rogers of *The Sunday Telegraph* in October 1976. At Dalbeathie, Winifred concentrated on drawing and painting, and Elspeth on both art and writing. Katharine read widely in the history, literature and folklore of the sixteenth and seventeenth centuries, and communicated her interest and excitement about the period to Elspeth. They began to build up a collection of books on the subject, and the old schoolroom at Dalbeathie was turned into a library in 1922. The sisters had always delighted in fine volumes, and had been encouraged by their father, who used to give them books illustrated by Rackham and Dulac in the early days in London. Now they sought out all they could find on the period of the Civil War, and came to possess some rare early works, which after Katharine's death were bequeathed to Lady Margaret Hall. When writing a brief outline of her life, Katharine mentions as activities of this period work with Guides and Brownies, producing of plays, and the running of an amateur dramatic touring company. These were far more than occasional hobbies; Katharine threw herself into them with enormous energy and enthusiasm. All three activities helped her to develop that capacity for 'making out' which had been so important in her early life.

Work with Guides and Brownies must have started soon after her return home. Elspeth took no direct share in this, but Winifred worked with the local Guides and continued to do so through the war years. Their mother provided a Guide Hall at Little Dunkeld to help the work. There was a family precedent: their relative, Mr Dixon of Pitlochry, had, according to Winifred, worked with the first group of unofficial Boy Scouts formed in Scotland, while the Jackson girls were also enthusiastic Guiders. The College at Ambleside, from which the Briggs obtained their governesses, had encouraged the movement from the start, and a friend of Lord Baden-

Powell, Mrs Low, started a Guide Company in Perthshire as early as 1911. The early Guide leaders were mostly unmarried women of means, with leisure and enthusiasm for the work. They did a little training, gained their diplomas, and if considered promising were put on record for future assignments.[16] In 1926 Katharine became an 'Eagle Owl', and received her Brown Cord, worn on the hat. She was soon called on for service, and in 1927 was sent on an exciting and demanding journey for two months in Newfoundland, then still a British Colony, to conduct training courses for Guides and Brownies, since the District Commissioner felt that many isolated new Companies were in great need of trained help.

The Report on Girl Guiding in Newfoundland for 1927 has recently come to light, and through the kindness of the Chairman of the Archives Committee, Isabel Templeton, it is possible to quote from it:

> Miss Briggs, an Eagle Owl and experienced Guide, chosen by Imperial Headquarters, came to us recently for two months. She visited Springdale, Greenspond, Angle Brook, Corner Brook, Bolwood, Grand Falls, Hants Harbour, Winterton, Carbonear, Harbour Grace. She taught us much in Guide and Ranger Company work, and as an Eagle Owl she has given us longed for advice and instruction. Her address at the Old Colony Club on 'Childhood through the eyes of an Eagle Owl' brought us new sympathy and understanding ...
>
> Miss Briggs set herself a heavy programme, and Guides of every grade are grateful to her for her excellent constructive work. She was asked by an Educationist here 'What do you think of our Guiding?' ... Her quiet reply was 'Some of it is as good as good guiding anywhere. Some of it requires leadership, and all of it, especially in the Outports, is plucky. I feel Guiding has come to stay'.

It had been hoped that all the Outport Companies would be visited, but some were already 'winterbound'. She visited those which 'weather conditions made it possible to reach', and the list of places mentioned show that she travelled widely over the island. As a result of her visit, a new Company at Angle Bank, new Brownie packs at Carbonear and Harbour Grace, and a Ranger Company at Greenspond were formed.

This was not a particularly easy assignment. Much of the travelling was by boat, and Katharine was not a good sailor, and on one occasion she injured her leg arriving at a small harbour in the dark. However it must have been a stimulating and challenging experience, and she seems to have made a great success of it. When she was conducting Brownie Revels before an invited audience, the writer of the Report remembered the effect she created: 'Every little girl in the audience wanted to become a Brownie.' She continued to work for Brownies and take sessions on Brownie training after her return to England, and made what must have been her first broadcast on the BBC giving a talk about the Brownie movement.

Katharine was attracted to the work with Brownies because of the combination of the imaginative and practical in their training, as well as the emphasis on initiative and on open-air life. She also became interested in English folk dancing, advocated as part of Guide training as early as 1912, and this was something in which the sisters soon became expert. Katharine came into contact with Rita Cowan Douglas, who was also working with Brownies, and they prepared a booklet on 'Traditional Singing Games from Scotland and the Border'[17] for the children to use. Rita, whom Katharine at first found a little alarming, became a good friend, although she could not persuade Katharine to go to London and establish herself in the literary circle there. It was while working with the Brownies that Katharine developed her natural gift for telling stories, making use of folk and fairy tales in particular. The children, aged between seven and ten, made a splendid captive audience, and were on the whole very appreciative, although there were occasional dissenters. She used to tell the story of how after she visited a Brownie meeting, their Brown Owl asked the little girls: 'Wasn't it lovely having Miss Briggs to visit you, and didn't she tell you the most marvellous stories?' to which one small Brownie replied stolidly: 'Aye, but she's an awfu' leear.' Katharine and Rita both objected strongly to the unsatisfactory fairy lore and muddled thinking behind the names used for Brownies — Imps, Pixies, Elves and the like — and protested against it. Apparently they approached Lord Baden-Powell himself, but without success. It was partly as a result of their crusade that Katharine began to delve more deeply into traditional fairy beliefs, and became interested in the work of the Folklore Society.

About 1930 Katharine began to train Brownie leaders in the use of mime. A little booklet, *Mime for Guides and Brownies* was published by the Girl Guides Association, a second edition of which appeared in 1956. She claims in this that dramatic work trains the imagination, teaches unselfishness and cooperation by encouraging children to work in a team, gives opportunity for disciplined self-expression (of particular value to teenagers), and satisfies the aesthetic sense. She concludes characteristically:

> Acting teaches people to work for their own enjoyment, instead of sitting in the passively receptive attitude that is all too common nowadays. If dramatic work can do all this, it is worth the trouble we must take over it.

For Guides and Brownies, she argues, mime has some advantages over drama. It is easier to get good results from a group of mixed abilities, and it is more difficult for one promising actor to outshine the rest. She suggests beginning with a folksong, miming the action, and planning costumes and simple staging to indicate the period to which it belongs. Then a spoken ballad might be mimed, and finally a story, which is more difficult to present effectively; here folk and fairy tales offer the greatest possibilities. She gives as an example 'The Golden Goose', with the narrative divided into numbered stages, and action for each suggested, arranged for a narrator and fifteen performers.[18]

Katharine brought out three little books, each with a story arranged for mime in this way. In the period after Katharine came down from Oxford, Winifred had been trained as a printer, and the sisters obtained their own printing press, set up in a room behind the gardener's cottage at Dalbeathie, to celebrate the Coronation in 1937. Winifred did skilful and excellent work on this, and produced the three books on Mime, sold at 6d each, printed by the Capricornus Press. The first is 'The Golden Goose', as in the Guide booklet, the tale of the youngest brother who seemed a failure but won the hand of the princess by making her laugh when all others had failed; he did this with a magic goose, since those who touched it were unable to let go, and in the end he led a ludicrous line of victims behind him. The second was the Scottish tale 'Whuppity-Stoorie', belonging to the same type as 'Tom Tit Tot' and 'Rumpelstilzkin', in which the 'Gude Wife' had to find the name of the Strange Lady who restored her pig to life, or else sacrifice her baby to the sinister woman. This was arranged for two characters and the pig, and was a great favourite in Scotland. The third, 'Jesper who herded Hares', is the tale of a trickster, which in its Norwegian and Russian forms is distinctly bawdy, but which Katharine neatly turned into an entertaining but innocent tale suitable for Brownies. This has four main characters: trickster Hero, King, Queen and Princess, while a number of children could be used as hares. In her retelling of the second story, Katharine makes effective use of Scots dialect:

> 'What'll ye gie me, gudewife', says the lady, 'gin Ah cure yir muckle fat grumphy?' 'Oh, Ay'm shair, Yir leddyship,' says she, 'Ah wud gie onything that a pair body like masel' cud gie.' With that, the Strange Lady stretched out her long, thin aristocratical finger, and laid it upon the pig's nose. And the pig gave a great frumph, and jumped up and ran into the sty again, as lively as a calf in a thunderstorm.

Here once more she was following her father's example, since he had made great use of dialect in his books.

Evelyn Goshawk, one of Katharine's lifelong friends, first met her in 1934, when she attended one of the training courses. She worked with Guides, and had been one of the first 'Girl Scouts' in 1909. She was already interested in mime, but found Katharine's methods new and surprising:

> I first met Katharine in 1934 when she was conducting a training course for Guide Leaders. Apart from the usual subjects — signalling, woodcraft, first aid and so on — there was a special emphasis on drama, particularly mime.
>
> She looked us over consideringly. 'You can be a Knight of Scotland Born', she said to me. 'Go over there and practise riding.' I had never ridden anything except the nursery rocking-horse, but I went. We learnt how to make masks — a death's head was one of the most successful. We found how a Guide's uniform could form the basis of a medieval tunic by the simple addition of a pair of wide coloured sleeves and a hood with scalloped edges, covering the shoulders.

Katharine continued to work with Guides and Brownies until 1941, when she resigned her position as Scottish Commissioner for Brownie Training in order to join the Services. It must have been disappointing for her never to have been elected 'Chief Brown Owl', an annual office for which she would appear to have been well qualified. Possibly some of those at Headquarters mistrusted her brilliant but unconventional methods. There is no doubt that her work on mime had enormous influence on training methods of that period, and those who used it found it helped tongue-tied or awkward children to gain confidence and awake to new interests. Katharine gave a good deal of thought to methods of teaching, and used to go into the village school at Caputh and experiment with the children there from time to time, with the full approval of the headmaster. At some time in the thirties she wrote an excellent little booklet on the history of Wellshill School, founded in 1840 for destitute girls in Perth, in which she had evidently taken an interest.[19]

The delight which Katharine found in introducing others to the folk literature which she loved, and producing mimes and plays with simple costumes and stage effects was not satisfied, however, by work with young children. She was determined to take it to a wider public. The touring company known as the Summer Players was formed in the years after she came down from Oxford, and rehearsals were held at Dalbeathie from 1932 onwards. Before this a small hotel or village hall would be booked for two weeks for rehearsals, and the performance given there at the end of the period. Nine tours in all are recorded between August 1928 and April 1939. The idea of plays presented by a touring company was already familiar in Scotland, and Katharine used to attend performances given by the Arts League of Service at Dunkeld every year. These were supported by well-known actors and actresses, such as Flora Robson, and the profits made covered the expenses. Katharine's idea, however, was to visit small places where no theatre existed, and to provide an evening of varied entertainment. Her booklet on *Mime for Guides and Brownies* shows that she had become interested in the tradition of the Commedia del Arte:

> travelling companies ... emerged in early Renaissance days as the Commedia del Arte. ... The early characters were not silent. The plot of the play was stuck up in the wings, and the players improvised and adapted traditional speeches with great skill. The tradition of the silent mime must have been lurking among them, however, for it reappeared at intervals, as, for instance, in the silent Harlequin and Columbine of the English stage.[20]

The Summer Players attempted both improvisation and dumb show at various times. Katharine was also attracted by the idea of the ballad play, 'half way between mime and straight drama', when the words might be recited by one person or in unison. The programme presented by the Summer Players was a mixture of mime, ballad-plays and short one-act plays, some of these written by Katharine and Elspeth. They made no charge for performances, although hospitality was accepted if offered, and any money made went to a local charity.

Katharine and her sisters organised their own little travelling theatre, using a car and a van to transport a company of eight performers; the van held a portable stage, curtains, props and costumes, as well as a dulcitone to provide the music. 'Dulcie' was afterwards brought to the Barn House, where it took up less room than a piano; it was an instrument with a pleasant, tinkling tone, although it tended to sway giddily when the player used the pedal. In the early days it was played by Katharine's cousin Georgie Jackson, Madge Jackson's eldest daughter. The players had to be prepared for all kinds of conditions on their tours; sometimes they were invited into comfortable homes, or stayed in hotels, and sometimes they slept in a school or village hall. They took food with them and ate picnic meals on the way. Winifred had the onerous task of planning their trips each summer and writing to suitable contacts. During the winter Katharine worked with the Dunkeld Amateur Dramatic Society, and regularly produced plays, while the family supported the excellent Repertory Theatre at Perth.

Some of those who became established Summer Players came to know Katharine through her work with the Guides as did Barbara Innes, who became such a close friend of the family that she has been called the fourth daughter. Others were the children of friends, like Rita Cowan-Douglas' daughter Jennifer, and Jane Moore, whose mother, Una Moore, had been at Lady Margaret Hall. In the early days Katharine looked for students of music and drama who would join the company. One of these was Catherine Hollingsworth, known to the Players as Pelican Snelson (a name seen over a shop at Shrewsbury on one of their tours). She came from Brechin in Angus, and was to become widely known throughout Aberdeen and indeed Scotland for her brilliant and original work in drama and speech-training and her creation of the Aberdeen Children's Theatre. She was awarded an OBE for her achievements.[21] Catherine declared that her brief stay with the Summer Players opened a completely new world for her, and that it was Katharine, who, without knowing it, started her on a new course. After a conventional training in elocution she suddenly became aware of the importance of using the right material, and the possibilities of ballads and tales and traditional drama such as Katharine had selected. This is a striking example of how the inspiration from a small amateur group was passed on to countless children and adults, long after the Summer Players had ceased their performances.

The first trip made by the Players was to Devon and Somerset, and they visited many regions in England and Scotland. The fun and excitement of the expeditions to the unknown proved a great bond between them. Some still treasure the little open-work brooches, made from sections of a silver belt with a pattern of flowers and dragonflies, which they wore as safety-pins in their costumes. Their performances were made up of mimed songs, ballads and short plays. In 1933, for instance, there were three sessions of 'Mimes and Songs', including the ballads 'The Two Magicians', 'The Farmer's Old Wife', and 'When Good King Arthur ruled the land', together with three short plays: Sheridan's *The Scheming Lieutenant,* W.S. Gilbert's *Creatures of Impulse,* and Katharine's own play, *The Peacemaker.* The ballads were sung, and from about 1936 the main singer was Jean Dalgleish from Edinburgh, who could sing, in Evelyn Goshawk's words, 'in a cool, impersonal style, reminiscent of boys' voices in a cathedral choir.' Though the performance was an amateur one, the costumes and properties were well and imaginatively planned, and Katharine possessed the gift of finding suitable accompaniments for the ballads. She often took the principal male part herself. She had a beautiful speaking voice, and while her sisters were not such good speakers, all three moved well and were talented actors.

Evelyn Goshawk was not a regular Summer Player, because of home commitments, but in 1936 she came to Dalbeathie for the first time to take part in a Mime Week, open to prospective Eagle Owls and Guide Instructors. Katharine ran the week as a house party, and Evelyn's memories of what to her was an outstanding experience give a glimpse of the Briggs' way of life in the period between the wars. On arrival, the guests sat down to a splendid tea ('scones, flapjacks, pancakes — the lot'), while there was talk of 'local affairs, Highland Games, historic houses, Holyrood and Royalty.' To this Evelyn, knowing little of Scotland, listened fascinated, feeling very ignorant. Then the activities of the week began:

After tea we all went along to the billiard-room which was a sort of centre of activity and sociability, with a grand piano, striking paintings, the work of Ernest Briggs, Katharine's father, and a slightly raised dais at one end, with an enormous fireplace behind. We began discussing our programme, and were allotted parts. I began to thaw. Suddenly we all went up to the attic — 'to try on costumes' — where row upon row of dresses and theatrical equipment were displayed ... By the next day I was beginning to find my feet. ... We spent the morning in the studio, making properties, practising, and adapting costumes. I was given a roll of black velvet with orders to 'make a bodice', and settled at an electric sewing machine, an unknown quantity until then, but somehow it worked and I finished my garment without further loss of face. We learned our parts and rehearsed in the garden, where different levels, terraces, vistas, made a background of timeless beauty; the sun shone and the magic of Dalbeathie took hold of us all unawares, and after half a lifetime is still memorable.

There were many such gatherings at Dalbeathie, when Katharine not only organised entertainments or rehearsals for the Summer Players, but introduced other artistic or creative activities. One autumn they all made woodcuts, Katharine producing one of two duellists, since she and Elspeth had recently taken up fencing and used to practice on the terrace: 'her woodcut was repeated more than once, because somehow the figures invariably turned out to be left-handed in the printing, but Katharine was never deterred by mere details.' The blocks were printed by Winifred on her press, and used for illustrations for books or for Christmas cards. Sometimes Katharine read aloud, told stories or recited ballads. They might all sit down and write verses, after Katharine had given them a theme or a first line. The sisters were well practised in this, and could produce nearly spontaneous poems. One scribbled down by Katharine one evening, 'The Fairy Thorn', was copied out by Evelyn next day; she remembers it being written 'practically on the spot':

>Fair Annie sat at her bower door
>Upon Midsummer's Een,
>When by there came three merry maids
>With kirtles of the green.

> 'Oh leave the rock, Fair Annie', they cried,
> 'Oh cast the reel aside,
> Come up and dance at the Fairy Thorn
> That stands by Rowan's Ride.'
>
> 'If I should dance at the Fairy Thorn
> That were an unco' thing,
> For it's there that dwell the Fairy Court,
> But and the Fairy King' ...

leading to the inevitable close:

> They hid their eyes, they stopped their ears,
> They did not move nor cry,
> But like a rush of winter's wind
> Fair Annie passed them by.

Katharine was always the centre of the group, inspiring and organising, urging on the others and suggesting new games and competitions, in which she herself always shone, although she was generous in encouraging the talents of others. She used at times to show off, and

> casually pick a handful of nettles without blenching, or swallow a toadstool with nonchalent ease, hit out wildly at tennis, exclaiming 'Dotard' each time the ball went wide, or if we turned to archery for a change. 'Dotard' to the popinjay who never stirred from his perch.

Evelyn remembers one of the group declaring on such an occasion: 'She's a perfect darling and an utter fool!' Her sisters supported her enthusiastically in all that she did, while her mother remained slightly withdrawn, a gracious and unobtrusive hostess, always insisting on punctuality for meals. They used to change every evening into 'decorous garb for the conventional dinner, rooted in Edwardian tradition'. Mary Briggs concentrated on the smooth running of the house, and her domain was the drawing-room, while guests came and went, and wild and merry doings went on in the billiard-room and garden. There were always animals at Dalbeathie, cats and kittens, a much-loved, irresponsible Bedlington called Martin Pippin, and later on two Chinese geese and a little patrol of ducks named Petrum, Partum, Perry, Merry and Dixie (from an old jingle used by the Mime group). The varying characters and the rituals of the ducks amused the sisters, and they were particularly devoted to Winnie, looking for her continually and greeting her with loud quackings if she appeared at a window. Dalbeathie, for those who knew it at this time, possessed something of a fairytale aspect, a fitting background for Katharine's unending stock of tales and ballads.

By the 1930s Katharine was caught up in another imaginary world, that of the Civil War. She and Elspeth were working on novels based on events of this period, and read widely on the subject. Elspeth's *Borrowed Names* came out in 1932, and *Restoration* in 1935, the year in which Katharine published her first novel, *The Lisles of Ellingham*. There are many escapes, disguises and pursuits in these novels, and this may have prompted the playing of 'the Game', which linked up Guide Training, the Eric game, and Katharine's interest in the Civil War.[22] It was first tried out at Foxlease, the Guide Training Centre in Hampshire, as a test of initiative, and according to Barbara Innes, Katharine had been hoping to enact the story for a long time. It was set in the imaginary world of the future, like the Eric game in its early days, but not so far ahead. It was supposed to take place in 1974 when Princess Elizabeth had become Queen but been forced to leave for Greece on account of a rebellion. One faction wanted to bring her back, and another to put her son Arthur on the throne, and two opposed groups were the Sealed Knot, a loyalist secret society, and the Young Englanders. While they were negotiating, one of the Sealed Knot was accidentally killed, and a man called Tressillian was held to be responsible and condemned to death by the President. Two young men on the Council, Peter Rodney and Andrew Kerr, thought this unjust, and Andrew quietly removed the President's Seal. The two were left tied up in an upstairs room while the Council debated what to do, but they escaped out of a window disguised as women, and set off for the house of another Council member to deliver the Seal to him so that he could save Tressillian from execution. They had to reach him before one o'clock on the third day, with only a map, compass and six shillings to help them to make the journey of nearly a hundred miles.

When Katharine produced this as an initiative test, the result was disappointing. The Guides chosen refused to travel at night, and when they set off they simply hired a taxi and lay on the floor, reaching their goal without difficulty, much to Katharine's annoyance. She wanted it to be a real test of ingenuity and endurance, and so she staged it in New Galloway in 1939, with a select company of friends. The fugitives were herself as Peter Rodney and Barbara Innes as Andrew Kerr, and Barbara wrote a detailed account of the long journey in a letter to her brother shortly after it took place.

The members of the Sealed Knot Council had a number of cars, and were led by Elspeth as President. Evelyn Goshawk was Dick (Richard Rodney Dannett), Edith and Kitty, two of the Jackson cousins, were Lady Petronelle and Doctor George, an elderly lepidopterist. Jean Dalgleish was Richard Perrett, and 'Peter' Duff (a woman friend of Barbara's) and a police girl, Mary Bailey, also took part. They all stayed at a hotel in New Galloway posing as a walking club, and it afterwards transpired that people there had been alarmed by their strange behaviour and suspected that they might be German spies. The fugitives duly escaped and set out with an hour's start. They spent four shillings on a supply of cheese, sultanas, chocolate, MacVita biscuits and a small bottle of Horlicks at the village store, and then walked three miles along the road without getting a lift, hiding in a quarry while the pursuing cars passed. They then caught a bus for Carsphairn, but had not enough money left for the whole fare; however the kindly conductor agreed that they should send it later, and they reached their destination and set out into the hills.

They were soon soaked through in a rainstorm, but went on with brief rests and stops for food, missed the path in the dark and went as much as ten miles out of their way. They slept under a hawthorn till dawn and then got a lift on a lorry carrying wood; Barbara was so sleepy that she narrowly escaped falling off. After Sanquhar, a farmer gave them another lift of about seven miles, and at Crawfordjohn they bought twopennyworth of milk and got leave to sleep in a barn. At five in the morning they were off again, over the main road and across the moor to Tinto, just escaping discovery by 'Peter' Duff, stationed on a nearby hill with binoculars. They were half frozen and very weary as they approached Thankerton to cross the Clyde at about midnight. Barbara hid with the Seal in case the enemy was waiting by the bridge, and Katharine went over alone, but there was no sign of pursuit. It was too cold to sleep, so they went on:

> We talked in whispers for a long time afterwards, and leapt behind trees and into hollows and long grass and nettles and what not whenever a car was heard. We went on walking and we were very

stiff ... Peter had blisters between his pads and toes and my left knee went wonky. I also got the chitters and couldn't stop. We saw some interesting sights too. A large lime tree curtseyed quite distinctly and there was an entertaining Turkey carpet pattern on the road, and coloured lights in the tree tops, and Peter saw a giant in the wood. Light was first coming as we came to a farm beside the road.

There they got some milk and were allowed to sleep in a stable until about 9.30, when they were turned out into a glorious morning, with only ten more miles to cover. At last they saw their goal, the bungalow where Tressillian was supposed to be held. But the Sealed Knot were on the watch, and there was no shelter; they just avoided meeting the President by ducking down into a bed of nettles. Then a small girl came by with a herd of cows, and Katharine gave her the Seal in a biscuit carton and offered her their last three pennies if she would deliver it at the cottage. The child set off after doing the milking, but the President intercepted her at the gate and took the packet. So the fugitives failed at the last moment, after walking about ninety miles in eighty-four hours.

A Court of Inquiry took place next morning, with Elspeth as Court Marshal. It soon became evident to those who knew her well that while most of the players took the affair as a game and were casual, even flippant, about the result, Katharine took it far more seriously. Evelyn even suspected that she was on the point of breaking down, partly from tiredness, but also from 'reaction, a sense of failure and perhaps disappointment that the others had no identification with the story.' Evelyn in her character of Dick Danett, argued that the fugitives had had an honest desire to help and should not be treated with severity, and the meeting ended with the Game declared a Draw. This episode indicates how real it had been for Katharine, and how fully she had been able to identify with the fugitives and enter into the experience of a desperate flight to evade capture. The later part of her novel *The Castilians,* probably written before this, is taken up with the pursuit, capture and final execution of two fugitives who are the central characters of the book. Her interest in such situations may be seen as a natural development from the inventions of the Eric game, while part of the attraction of the records of the Civil War was that she could for a time merge her identity with those who had really lived and suffered such experiences. Something of this is expressed in one of the poems in the MS book:

> Dead people, long ago,
> Dear to my heart,
> We never met, I know;
> How can we part?
>
> In scattered dusty books,
> Now here, now there,
> I've traced your lives and looks,
> And found them fair.
>
> The griefs you had to meet
> Made my heart bow;
> The joys you felt most sweet
> I still feel now.
>
> Strange life, shining through death,
> Fancy can give;
> Sepulchres quiver with breath
> And dry bones live.

After the Game, Katharine soon recovered her composure, and indeed wrote a light-hearted *ballade* on their onerous journey. 'The Ballade of the Well-Fed Fugitives', which begins:

> Our stock of food is adequate and neat,
> Lucellus' shelf could hardly wish for more;
> Horlicks and cheese, sultanas, vita-wheat,
> A slab of chocolate to complete the store.
> Look, it's beginning suddenly to pour;
> Let's take two more sultanas for a treat.
> That should revive our hearts, our zest restore.
> We really don't need very much to eat.

It is perhaps surprising to realise that this enterprise took place just before the outbreak of war, when Katharine was forty years old. The war, when it came in 1939, was to cause a jagged break in her serene, energetic and independent life. Her excursions into an imaginary world of adventures and hardships, begun as a child, had continued for many years as a background to living, and the games and drama enacted with her sisters, the Guides, her troop of Players and band of friends, had been of great significance for her. In a sense she had not yet fully grown up, however, or found the creative work she needed to do, although she had helped and inspired many on the way. She had become increasingly conscious of her own powers, but she had also suffered disappointments and frustrations; neither the academic world, nor the Guide movement, nor her dramatic work, nor her study of the historic past had proved wholly satisfying. She wanted to write books and have them accepted, but so far had paid for all her works to be published. She needed a wider audience, but her work was not really appreciated or sought after except by a small group of friends, and she had not yet found the right medium in which to work. The world of imagination in which she had found such riches, and that of work and study, into which she had put much effort, had not yet come together in successful fusion. She was still seeking a challenge worthy of her.

4 Feats and Quests: The War Years

> *With all my might I slackened pace,*
> *Courage sprang in me like a flame.*
> *I halted at the dark bridge-head,*
> *And looked back by the way I came.*
> *The evil thing stared in my face —*
> *Stared and stood still; my heart beat high,*
> *I braced my knees and kept my place.*
> *It moved more near, and then passed by*
> *With faltering and broken pace.*
>   K.M. Briggs, MS *Book of Poems.*

The games of the three sisters had led on to creative work. Winifred turned to art, which had always been one facet of the games. Katharine and Elspeth were determined to be writers, and for some years concentrated on the period of the Great Civil War in England. They were both saddened and fascinated by the loyalties and cruelties which that war engendered, and made it the theme of their first books. Yet although they put much work and energy into these novels, they remain productions of an unreal world, never really relating to the human condition and the life of adult men and women caught up in war. The link which the Brontës found between their imaginary world and the material fed into it by their father's tales and human dramas among their Yorkshire neighbours was lacking here, and study of history did not supply it.

 Katharine wrote two books, *The Lisles of Ellingham* and *The Castilians.* The first, published for her by the Alden Press in 1935, was based on the early history of a courageous old lady, Dame Alice Lisle, whom Judge Jeffreys condemned to be burnt alive (and who, in the end, was beheaded) for sheltering fugitives after Monmouth's rebellion. Katharine reconstructed her early life; married to John Lisle, a fanatical Parliamentarian, and watching her loved husband gradually grow more intolerant and unreasonable as the war progressed. Alice was torn between loyalty to him and her love for her son, who favoured the Royalist cause, and by the end of the book she had seen John Lisle become alienated from the rest of the family.

This is an adult theme, the failure of human relationships and the breaking of family ties and affections because of the pursuit of an idea. Alice herself is presented as a woman after Katharine's own heart, warm, generous and tolerant, impatient of humbug and with a ready sympathy for young people. Arguments are put forward on both sides, and it becomes clear that while Parliamentarians could be stubborn and bigoted, Royalists could be arrogant, self-indulgent and brutal. Unfortunately the book does not succeed as a novel because the characters, even Alice herself, do not come to life as individuals, but remain mouthpieces for different points of view.

The same is true of Katharine's second novel, *The Castilians,* sent to various publishers without success. In 1942, when she was in the WAAF, she wrote to Elspeth: 'It's a pity they don't like the Castilians. I think we might try one of the American publishers for luck, don't you?' But in the end it was brought back for the Alden Press to publish in 1951. It is based on the records of the siege of Pontefract Castle, recaptured by the Royalists in 1648 and held for some time until they were finally forced to surrender. The main characters are Colonel John Marris, who twice changed sides, finally rejoined the Royalists, and held command of the Castle, and a young yeoman farmer, Michael Blackthorn. These two became close friends, escaped when the castle was given up, and tried to reach the Lancashire coast to find a ship; but in the end they were captured and condemned to death for treason. Again the theme is serious, but there is no central figure this time to win sympathy, and the characters remain superficial. The careful use of records results in many minor characters and complexities, resembling those in the Eric game, and the narrative never breaks loose from its framework.

Elspeth's first two books, *Borrowed Names* (1932) and *Restoration* (1935) deal respectively with the escape of Prince Charles in the Civil War and the problems caused by the return of a father to his family in 1660. She was much under the influence of Jane Austen, but the stories are neither good comedies nor exciting narratives, and lack human interest. *The Rhyme for Porringer,* published by Peter Davies in 1939, is an attempt to answer the question of what would have happened had Mary survived her husband William III instead of dying in 1694. It contains a good deal of politics, and it is a dull book. *The White King,* printed by Winifred on the Capricornus Press, and brought out in 1949 by the Munro Press in Perth to commemorate the tercentenary of the death of Charles I, was on a subject about which Elspeth felt strongly. It deals with the last period of the king's life, leading up to his execution. Even so, it does not escape from the blight of the previous ones, inferior in interest and vigour to the straightforward accounts of the king's journey towards death in her sources. Elspeth was a careful and accurate student of history, but unable to produce creative novels until she came to rely more on her imagination and to deal with people of lesser importance. *Service is None Heritage* (1948), *Another Unicorn* (1954), and above all, *Squire's Fairing,* published just before her death in 1961, aim at entertainment for younger readers rather than treatment of an impressive theme. Here her knowledge of the historic background serves her well; politics are less important than people, and Elspeth writes with a lightness of touch which holds the interest. *Squire's Fairing* was published by Frederick Warne, the other two printed by the Alden Press, and they included her own wood-engravings. There is some resemblance between *Squire's Fairing,* the tale of a young girl working at the Manor House, and Katharine's *Hobberdy Dick,* where Elspeth also used her detailed knowledge of seventeenth-century customs and beliefs to produce a children's story which convinces and holds the reader as the earlier novels never did. But before Katharine herself could achieve this, she had to change her mode of life.

Successful within their limited scope are the little one-act plays which Katharine and Elspeth wrote to be acted by Guides and Summer Players, most of which have a seventeenth century setting. The first was Katharine's little comedy, *The Garrulous Lady,* which she had published by the Golden Vista Press, Fetter Lane, in 1931. This is on one of her favourite themes, the hunt for a Royalist fugitive, but now treated very lightly. The daughter tries to warn her mother that they are sheltering a young man, but can never get out more than a word or two before her mother overwhelms her with an unquenchable flow of talk. Fortunately the Colonel searching for the fugitive is similarly defeated by the lady's relentless tongue. Katharine herself often took the part of the mother, who is a little reminiscent of the stepmother in her father's novel, *The Two Rivers.* Both may well have been inspired by a notorious garrulous lady in the family, the strong-minded Aunt Nell. After the first of their plays had been printed, Winifred produced the others on her press in similar style. All were set in the seventeenth or eighteenth century. *The Peacemaker,* first performed in March 1933, is about a well-meaning lady trying to reconcile her warring sisters-in-law, who finally make up their quarrel and combine against her. *Lady in the Dark,* performed in 1937, is a family comedy in which a group of young people upset their elders' plan for their marriages. *The Fugitive,* acted on the tour of 1938, is set in the time of the 1715 Rebellion, when a brother and sister help a fugitive to escape after the defeat of the Pretender, and come to regret it. The plays are all slight, designed to provide effective material for amateur actors, and pleasantly written. One by Elspeth, acted along with *The Fugitive* in 1938, is *The Constant Gardener,* an amusing picture of an apparently guileless gentleman fighting on the side of the Royalists in the Civil War, who, like the Scarlet Pimpernel, is not as simple as he seems. It has the same warmth and light-hearted sense of comedy as *Squire's Fairing,* and shows the livelier side of Elspeth which was too often swamped in her endeavours to be a serious historian.

During the years preceding the War, the sisters were all working hard, concentrating on the activities of the Players and on their books and plays. In 1936, however, there came the interruption of Winifred's breakdown and that year the annual tour of the Players had to be cancelled, while Katharine arranged the Mime Week at Dalbeathie instead. Winifred had had an earlier collapse after the death of her father, but this one was more serious, and she was sent away for treatment to a mental home. From early days Winifred was the one of the trio who seems to have remained a little apart; at one time she apparently believed that she was adopted, and the close sympathy between Katharine and Elspeth must have increased her sense of isolation. Those who knew Winifred found her warm-hearted and generous, and it was to her that members of the Summer Players group who found themselves 'overwhelmed and depressed' by the drive and activity at Dalbeathie would turn for comfort.[1] Winifred was dark, like her mother, but without Mary's good looks, and she was more feminine and domesticated than the other two, with considerable practical ability. It was she who did much of the organisation necessary for the tours of the Summer Players, while she did excellent work on the printing press, and later on proved capable of running Dalbeathie practically single-handed during the war years.

More than one person who came into contact with Winifred felt that she should have broken away from her family and planned her own life, but the isolation of Dalbeathie and her concentration on family activities gave her little chance to make outside contacts. Apart from these, her chief interest was in working for the Guides, to whom she gave devoted service. She was the only one of the sisters who painted seriously, using both water-colours and oils, and she had a number of small exhibitions. Her favourite subjects were flowers, landscapes and buildings. She had sketching trips abroad, one with Katharine, Cousin Violet Shepherd and Aunt Nell to Algiers, which was not a great success because Aunt Nell proved an exacting and difficult travelling companion, and happier ones with Katharine or Barbara to Switzerland and Austria. As wardrobe mistress she was largely responsible for the effective costumes of the Summer Players, and she was a competent actress, specialising in character parts, and a good country dancer.

In January 1939 the final decision was made to buy a house in the Cotswolds, after the sisters had explored the country round Oxford to find a suitable place which would be more accessible than Dalbeathie. Katharine felt that her mother, now in her seventies, was finding the strain of continual visitors and parties too great, and that they must have a centre where the housekeeping could be run in a less ambitious way. At last they came upon the Barn House in Burford, a small, attractive building in Cotswold stone, parts of which had originally been a barn and were of considerable age. Before it was rebuilt as a house, Cecil Sharp and his friends had visited it for country dancing, and this gave it an immediate attraction in Katharine's eyes. A long sloping garden ran up from the house to a lane behind, and this promised to provide a splendid setting for dramatic performances. The house itself, 'draughty but beautiful', as one visitor described it, was not very conveniently planned, but certainly of great character, with one large room opening on to the garden which would replace the billiard room at Dalbeathie as a centre of activity. When she was living there after the War, Katharine was able to sleep on the upstairs verandah on summer nights, and meals could be taken outside on the terrace. There was a great deal of building and decoration to be done, and in due course Katharine was to build a library on one side of the house, but before it could be adapted the War began, and the sisters hastily returned home to face evacuees and other problems.

It was in the same year, 1939, that Katharine formed the Secret Society of the Companions of the Order of the Rose. Its nucleus was the group which had so often gathered at Dalbeathie: the sisters, Evelyn, Barbara, Jean, 'Peter' Duff and Kitty Jackson, and there were plans for contacting various friends and inviting them to join. The Companions' badge was a rose, and Katharine again used links from a silver belt, together with a set of heraldic emblems painted on ivory counters from a game. The aim of the Order was to support the Arts by creative work and service, which might be seen as an endeavour to continue the work and ideals which Ernest had had in mind when he built Dalbeathie. Reading and discussion groups were planned, and the first works suggested for study give some idea of the interests of Katharine at this time: they included works of Chesterton, T.H. White's *The Sword in the Stone,* and Sir Thomas Malory's *Tale of King Arthur,* and Jane Austen's early novel *Love and Freindship.* The patron saint of the Order was St Hugh, and religion played some part in the activities of the members.

Perhaps the most important feature of the Companions and a clue to Katharine's development at this period was the insistence that prospective members of the society had to undertake 'feats' of some kind, or enter on a 'quest'. One of Katharine's own feats was to spend forty-eight hours camping in the grounds of Dalbeathie blindfolded, with guide ropes to help her to find her way about; she was anxious to know what it was like to be without sight. Her mother knew nothing of what was going on, and the sisters and Evelyn would slip down through the trees from time to time to see if all was well. A poem which she wrote later must be based on this experience, as she imagines herself clinging to past memories of the visible world when her sight fails (*App. 4, v*):

> On my dark screen I still can see
> All the sweet sights
> That once gave glory to the day
> Joy to the nights ...
>
> Though a mist is breathing on the screen
> I can see them yet.
> Oh hold the details clear, my heart!
> Do not forget.

Katharine's interest in the Order continued into the first years of the War, although it never seems to have been received with the same enthusiasm by her friends as was the Summer Players organisation.

In 1942 'Peter' Duff's married sister, 'Jim' was hoping to join, and she wrote to report a feat of going without food for eighteen hours, and to suggest some other feats which could be attempted:

> I want to keep silence for 24 hours as well — it should be easy after the holidays as I shall be alone. I'm also hoping to do an all-night-walk then too, when there's no one there to be inconvenienced in any way. It sounds incredible — but since Barbara first gave me a list of the feats I've tried steadily to do a month's *really* regular private devotions, but I don't believe I've brought off even one week, certainly not two consecutive ones.

Three months later 'Jim' wrote to give a vivid account of her walk, which she had begun at four in the morning, describing the sunrise and the dawn chorus of birds. She also reported that she had read some of the books recommended and was about to begin *The Sword in the Stone*.

Katharine at one time scribbled down a form of words for the admission of a candidate, apparently Winifred. She named as President the County Secretary for Guides in Durham, Alex Dalymple Smith, although it would seem that Alex never joined the Order in the end. According to this preliminary plan, Winifred was to be received first as a Companion and then as a Knight:

> Winifred, you have duly performed your feats to the satisfaction of us all. It is time that you should be received as a Companion of the Most Noble Order of the Rose.
> Do you intend to do some sterling work for Art in your own place or in the world at large?
>
> R. I will do it to the best of my ability.
>
> Will you guard our secrets and follow our usages?
>
> R. I will.
>
> And will you live in good fellowship with all the Companions?
>
> R. I will.
>
> Have here your Rose, and wear it with joy and honour for the

rest of your life. Having been received as a Companion it has been thought that you have qualities that will make you valuable to us as a Knight. Will you use your best wisdom in our counsels and spend thought upon the good of the Companionship?

R. I will.

You are duly elected as Knight Companion of the Most Noble Order of the Rose, and we welcome you with joy and gratitude to our counsels.

Thus Winnie, once the leader of the intrepid Knights of Dash, was now to enter into a new allegiance, still part of the legendary world of make-believe which Katharine was creating with the help of her sisters.

Part of the symbolism was clearly based on the traditional fellowship of King Arthur and of medieval knights, while there seems to have been a religious side to the discipline which the members imposed on themselves. It was as if Katharine was seeking a replacement for the Game which would offer the little group both an ideal and a challenge. As the fellowship which she valued so much was threatened by the War, she may have seen the Companions as a way of holding it together. She wrote a poem in August 1941, before leaving home to join the WAAF, which throws light on her intentions. It is called 'Rosa Hugonis' (Rose of St Hugh), and the writer imagines herself in old age looking back to the Companions and their ideals as something which endured through all the horrors of wartime:

> 'Rosa Hugonis', and the years retire
> And once again my tired pulse races free
> As I remember all the merry choir
> Secrets and quests and singing revelry,
> And of our faith, that gay humility
> Could still withstand the worst of human ire,
> Though the sky darkened with men's cruelty
> Rosa Hugonis blossomed on his Briar.
>
> Then I shall laugh to think we could conspire
> To be companions although solitary,
> Walking the night, and watching against fire,

> And when we met, even by two or three
> How few were needed to make up a choir
> Which sang against all odds triumphantly
> 'Rosa Hugonis blossoms on his Briar'.

But with the outbreak of war it seems that there was little time for such imaginative activities and games in which the group could take part. The sisters became occupied with evacuees at Dalbeathie, with local Guide and Brownie work, and, for Katharine, with helping in a school for Polish refugee children at Castlemains, Douglas. The evacuees arrived from Glasgow when war was declared, and there were at first thirteen children of school age, but the numbers varied constantly, as parents were apt to take their children home again when there seemed no immediate threat of air raids. At one time there were as many as thirty at Dalbeathie, some accompanied by their mothers, and eight of the children stayed for some years. A

Katharine (left) with her mother, Elspeth (standing) and Winifred in the Period before the war.

few of the small ones were found to be sewn into their clothes for the winter, and some of the arrivals were noisy, dirty, and hard to control, including a pair of terrible twins, always in mischief. They were put in the servants' part of the house, but the work of feeding and organising them must have taken up much of the sisters' time, and the main part seems to have fallen on Winifred's shoulders. The little evacuees, from a class of society with which hitherto Katharine had had little contact, were bewildered by their glimpses of what to them was an extraordinary way of life. 'Will you be putting on your nightgowns tonight?' one of them is said to have enquired as dinner-time approached one evening, for Mary and her daughters still regularly changed for dinner. They had elaborate evening gowns, made in medieval style, and in the late thirties possessed three in honey, apricot and mushroom velvet, while a dress worn by Katharine in violet shot taffeta is now in the museum at Leeds.

One of the boys at Dalbeathie who did well later on was Richard (Dick) Keith, who sent Winifred a long letter in 1949 when he was serving in the Palestine Mounted Police, telling her all his news and describing the girl he hoped to marry. He refers to the arrival of the noisy hordes from Glasgow:

> I wonder if they (i.e. the various neighbours) remember the crowd of noisy children who used to break through the peaceful tranquillity of the neighbourhood with piercing screams and shouts. I suppose some are still feeling the effects of our rowdy invasion from Glasgow. How often I long to walk along that beautiful road from Caputh to Dalbeathie House.

Dick sends respectful messages to Mrs Briggs and the other two sisters, but it is obviously 'Miss Winnie' whom he remembers with affection and gratitude. Katharine was probably away for much of this period, although she used to tell the children stories, and she and Winifred encouraged them to act. Dick refers to his sister Rena, also one of the evacuees, continuing 'the acting which you taught her' after she went back to Glasgow. Katharine was busy with Brownies and with the Polish School at Castlemains, where the workers were shorthanded, and under constant stress; she helped with the teaching there and produced plays. In the end Winifred was left to continue the work at Dalbeathie as best she could, and seems to have been very successful with the Guides, to judge from a series of letters from one of them, Margaret Thomson, who later went to work in Red Cross camps for displaced persons in Europe. Dick too appreciated Winnie's efforts at Dalbeathie: 'It always amazes me when I think of how you Miss Winnie manage in a place the size of Dalbeathie so capably without the slightest help while your sisters are called elsewhere.'

When Katharine gave up these various voluntary activities to join the forces in the summer of 1941, she did not choose the WRNS, according to the usual practice of Guide leaders, who usually got their commissions straight away, but deliberately turned to the Women's Auxiliary Air Force. The idea of choosing something demanding had been haunting her for some time, and she had a strong sense of patriotism which must have been intensified by the Battle of Britain. She told Evelyn in confidence that she wanted to learn humility; possibly also she realised that it was her last opportunity to join up as an ordinary recruit before she became too old, and she was always eager for new experience. The sisters decided that Winifred was the one to remain at home, and Elspeth left for London to be trained as a draughtsman, so that she could apply for work near Dalbeathie when her time came to be called up. It surprised many people that Katharine made no attempt to find some kind of work for which she was specially suited, but entered the ranks, and accepted training as a medical orderly. Her friends reacted to the news in various ways. One of those with whom she had worked at the Polish School wrote in October 1941:

> Well, you certainly took my breath away when you told me that you are going to the WAAF. I admire you, my dear, and I know that you will adapt yourself and probably like it very well, although you're such a rascal for *making* yourself do things you don't like. I know that good humour of yours will always stand you in good stead.

Her school friend, Evie Hill, was now Evie Forbes, married and back from India with her husband and two children. She had been working as fashion editor of *Vogue,* and then became chief copywriter for the Ministry of Food. Evie was horrified to learn of Katharine's action; she could so easily, she felt, have found some interesting work for her in London:

> Katharine, of all people, with all her gifts and skills became a woman soldier in the ranks! I couldn't get over it ... expostulated,

made a dozen other suggestions. It seemed ridiculous that Katharine with all her brilliance should be scrubbing floors and doing a dozen other menial tasks.[2]

It was assumed by many of her friends, by her mother and sisters and almost certainly by Katharine herself, that she would get her commission before long; she would prove herself by doing things the hard way and then pass on to more interesting work. But as Evie, accustomed to the ways of Government departments, had, no doubt, foreseen, it did not work out like that.

Katharine wrote many letters home to her mother and sisters from the various places where she was stationed, often on odd scraps of paper with inadequate pens (on one occasion she asked Winnie if she could buy her a new pen somewhere), usually undated, with no address beyond SSQ (Station Sick Quarters) or 'The Waffery', and the day of the week. She wrote with determined courage and cheerfulness, but is is not difficult to see how trying she found life in the ranks, crowded into noisy huts with much younger girls with whom she had little in common. A revealing paragraph in her interview for *The Sunday Telegraph* in October 1976 recalls this isolation:[3] 'I remember sitting in a canteen with a tablecloth in front of me spattered with other people's spillings, and watching them stir their teas and put the spoons back in the sugar bowl.' A brief outburst at the time when she was moved to Padgate indicates how much she was missing the conversation of her own kind. She had met a Visiting Sister during one of the interminable periods of waiting, and wrote of her: 'She's an educated woman, & the first equal kind of talk I've had with anyone since I joined the Service.' One of the most trying features of the new life must have been the almost complete lack of privacy and quiet in which to read and write. She wrote from Padgate in February 1942:

> There are quite a lot of nice girls, and some who are really tiresome. There are about twenty-six of us, or so I think, they are not really noisy, but my bed is near the stove, which is nice of course ... but rather near to all the conversation which is going. That's why I'm glad of the room in the NAAFI to write in. There wasn't a fire there this evening, but I'm writing in another room, which is nearly as quiet ... as there is a dance in the Gym which is calling people away.

Another source of frustration was the apparent waste of ability, since as soon as anyone settled down to do useful work, he or she was liable to be moved elsewhere. Expeditions were limited to visits to local cafes (which deteriorated as the war went on), to the cinema, or to concerts; one of Katharine's letters was written 'through the duller items' of a concert, since she was trapped in the middle of a row. Travelling still filled a good deal of her life, since she tried to make the most of her periods of leave, but was an ordeal under wartime conditions, with crowded trains often hours late.

Katharine was first sent to Morecombe with other new recruits in November 1941, to go through the various preliminaries. She did her first PT ('We spend a lot of time marching about turn, swinging our arms as high as possible ... till we are almost strutting'), and had her trade interview, when she was put down as Nursing Orderly. She was made senior aircraftswoman of their billet, to enforce general discipline ('It's lucky that they're a nice, easy lot'). She was then posted to Harrogate to do her medical training, and then to Padgate near Warrington. The actual training course she found quite enjoyable:

> I am enjoying the training very much & getting quite excited about it. We have been getting on well as a class & I do a certain amount of coaching of the others. I really hurry downstairs quite eagerly to get to the classroom in the morning ... I rather hope they will give me an interesting job if I should get a commission.

As Evie foresaw, however, there was a good deal of menial work to be done by the orderlies, not only scrubbing floors but also dealing with the many needs of the patients in wards which were often severely understaffed. Katharine's hands were soon in a sorry state, although she made light of this in her letters home. On the medical side she had few problems, for she had very high marks in her final examination at Padgate, and was at the top of the list. She even took a liking to the hospital there, although it seems to have had a bad reputation, and she started there in the gloomy winter months:

> We are lucky to have landed in this hospital; it is the only one so far which has given special facilities to the people under training. Everyone had told us that this was such a frightful place; our hearts quite sank coming here; but really it is much nicer than the one Mary Streeter is at, for instance ... there is a friendly feeling about the whole place. There's something to be said for starting in this kind of weather. We are seeing the place at its worst.

All the same, it must have been frustrating to be an orderly, dependent on the whims of Ward Sisters and unable to take real responsibility. Once more Katharine made the best of it:

> This has been a busy week, but I have enjoyed it, because I'm beginning to feel at home in the ward. The Sisters are very nice & make me feel almost like an assistant Sister. I shall be very sorry to go on to Ward III on Monday. I like the men very much too & get on with them very well. Poor Simms, the quietest Orderly, has been moved to Ward I. I don't know how I'd get on there, for the Sister is a Tartar. She was away on leave when we were there. We were lucky to miss her.

Katharine spent a good deal of energy planning how to use her free time most profitably, and visited friends and relatives within reach; she found the huge Briggs family a useful asset here. When she was in Lincolnshire she was able to get over from Syerston to stay with Gee, who had once been the nursery governess at the London home of the Briggs, and also to visit Evelyn, whose vicarage at Horbling, near Sleaford, was about forty miles away. At Winthorpe she was even nearer, and used to get a lift there or borrow a cycle for the fifteen mile ride, leaving some of her civilian clothes with Evelyn. Evelyn remembers one desperate attempt to get back to camp in time:

> One evening we started off along the Grantham Rampa expecting to be overtaken by some passing vehicle. But it was in the days of petrol rationing, and transport was limited. By the time it was dark, and we had covered half of the fifteen miles, not a car had passed us, and I had to turn back while she went on alone. She arrived back in camp just in time to escape the charge of AWOL (absent without leave).[4]

While at Winthorpe, Katharine was allotted a bicycle, as she was billeted outside the camp, and later on when back at Syerston she brought her own bicycle back from home after going on leave. One of her most desolate letters chronicles its disappearance during the journey and her attempts to trace it; it clearly meant a great deal to her, and happily it was recovered after a day or two from some distant railway station.

Katharine looked forward to her rare trips home for a long while beforehand, and planned the difficult journey, sometimes stopping with friends on the way. She tried to arrange occasional visits from her mother and Winifred, but her plans might be defeated by wintry weather or cancellation of leave. She sought out pleasant little hotels where they could stay, and outlined their journey in a way reminiscent of Ernest's arrangements for Mary and the children on summer holidays in the past. Her excitement over possible meetings and counting of the days until a long leave was due echoes her longing for the school holidays when she was at Lansdowne House, waiting for her mother to come and take her home. Writing to her sisters whenever she had a moment to spare, she managed to keep old interests alive: 'I want to show you a triangular bandage which makes a perfect foundation for a medieval wimple', she wrote to Winnie from Padgate in 1942; 'remind me to show it to you when we meet.' Her family supported her nobly, and letter after letter acknowledges something received from home; precious luxuries, some of them in short supply — cakes, biscuits, jam, chocolate, apples, pears, plums (she had to ask them to stop sending these, since they seldom survived the journey), clotted cream, and occasionally even oranges. She pleaded 'Don't give me everything you've got. I am afraid you will run yourself short of sugar with all the lovely things you send to me.' She shared these goodies with other people at parties and picnics whenever possible. She kept up the tradition of birthday presents as well as she could, but now it was not easy. 'Here's a little brooch, not much from me, I'm afraid, only a token of birthday wishes, the best thing I could get you in Warrington', she wrote to her mother.

Meanwhile Elspeth was in London, training as a draughtsman, and was also the recipient of frequent parcels from Winnie and her mother in 1942. It must have been something of an ordeal for the shy Elspeth, but she endured it gallantly. When bombing began again, her mother wanted her to come home, but Katharine wrote firmly against this, and had her way. At first Elspeth worked at typing, and then at drawing and tracing, though understanding nothing, she told her sisters, about the objects she drew. There were various old friends in London she could visit, including Evie, Jane Moore, Evelyn's daughter Bridget and her cousin Violet Shepherd, and she explored London with a map and sometimes managed a theatre or exhibition. She stayed at first at a private hotel, then at a hotel in Lancaster Gate, and finally in a guesthouse in Queensborough Terrace, where she had a room at the top of the house, and an extra bed for Katharine if she came to London. She wrote home:

> Tell Mummy I am really very comfortable here. I come in in the evening & light my gas fire & draw up an easy chair & settle down to write, & don't need to go out or downstairs again. It's a famous way to get on with writing. I'm getting quite excited about my story.

She and Katharine both managed to get home for Christmas 1942, and some time in the following year Elspeth finished her training, and after some waiting was given a job with the Admiralty at Almondbank, not far from Dalbeathie.

Katharine in 1942 had been preparing to apply for a commission, urged on by her mother, who must have worried continually about both her daughters. In February the Wing Commander in charge at Padgate told Katharine that it was absurd for her to be a Nursing Orderly, and that he would do what he could: 'But tell Mother not to be too hopeful, for these things take ages. I must say it would be rather nice to have a Commission for lots of little reasons, but chiefly for the chance of congenial company.' Later in the year she took an examination, doing very well in the medical section, and at last was called up to London for an interview with the Board. She decided to stay with Evie, 'to cheer myself up' in case the interview went badly. She had expected it might be something of an ordeal, but in the end it was not particularly alarming:

> They were very nice & chatted with me rather than questioned me. The waiting was the most alarming part. They warned me at the end that if I did pass I should probably have a long time to wait before my Commission came through. But they were so nice to me that I think probably they have passed me. We musn't be disappointed if they do turn me down.

After this it must have been depressing to hear that she had been turned down after all, to the indignation of those who knew her at the Station. A possible reason may have been Katharine's lack of respect for 'red tape'; for instance, she admitted she had never studied the regulations until she read them up in the train on her way to the interview. But she bore the disappointment with fortitude, and in the end was to say of herself, looking back: 'She was very fortunate in never rising beyond the rank of Corporal.' To her mother she wrote:

I do hope you won't be very disappointed, but they seem to have turned down my Commission. Mrs Hall sent for me today to Syerston to tell me about it. She was very nice & said she was furious about it and so was Mrs Spinks, who was going to make enquiries & make a fuss about it. ... I am afraid you will be sorry and disappointed about it, but as I say it's really for your sake that I'm disappointed, because I probably shall have more ease of heart as I am.

All this had taken a considerable time, because of the inevitable delays, and fortunately for Katharine by the time the decision was made she was far more contented with her lot.

Syerston had clearly been bearable, since she found friendly people there, enjoyed much of the work, and was becoming valued by those in authority. But in the spring of 1942 she suddenly heard that she might, if she chose, be transferred to Winthorpe, where there was a satellite station at Coddington Hall, two miles from Newark. There were only thirteen of the WAAF there, and one other orderly, with no officers, so there would be considerable freedom. The Hall was a large manor house in a well-wooded park, used as an Officers' Mess in 1940, when Polish Bomber Squadrons flew from Swinderby for raids on Germany and invasion forces across the Channel, and Winthorpe was used as a satellite. In February 1942 it was made a satellite of the station at Syerston, and new runways were constructed, destroying much of the park. There is now an Air Force Museum on the site. Katharine and the other Orderly, Brian Wood, were to run the Sick Quarters, referring serious cases to Syerston, from which the MO came over once a week. Brian Wood occupied the hut at Sick Quarters, so Katharine was billeted in a private house at Coddington, where she and a young girl, Betty, to whom she took an instant liking, were with the Wallers, 'kind hospitable people'. Katharine remarked characteristically in her letter home giving this news: 'Mother will be pleased to think of my having a room of my own.' Thus with what she would no doubt have described as her 'luck', but which had something to do with the impression made on those among whom she had worked, she had at last a congenial and fairly responsible job in a small corner of the RAF, away from the frustrating organised turmoil of a large station. Above all she was working with someone with whom she could have real conversation, whose company was stimulating, and who shared her interest in books and art.

Brian Wood was an architect of thirty-four, nine years younger than Katharine, a hardworking, responsible person with a good sense of humour. He was a Cambridge man who afterwards trained as an architect, and she found him good company from the outset: 'I had a most interesting evening with Brian Wood', she wrote home after their first meeting. As her letters continue, her enthusiasm for having such a colleague increased:

> You would like Brian Wood. He is an educated man, with ideas on art and music — tremendously keen on his work here. The MI hut is in the shade of a yew avenue — the park must have been lovely before these huts were dumped all over it. Brian has really made it from nothing, & has I think a tremendous reputation in the Camp ... Brian Wood does the garden very enthusiastically & has a little black & white half-Persian kitten called Shookie & reads his medical books and doctors his patients from morning to night ... I shall rather enjoy working with a man. Brian is very kind and friendly, and does everything he can to show me the ropes. Also he'd let me off any time I liked, only I musn't trespass on his kindness.

'I enjoy working with him immensely, and we can choose our time for things. We are extraordinarily free', she wrote to her mother, and in another letter home: 'I am as happy as ever here, & Brian is one of the most delightful people possible to work with. ... In fact I am frightfully lucky, and wake up every morning looking forward to the day's work.'

Here for a while the two were left in comparative peace, yet with the feeling that their work was important and necessary. They created a friendly, pleasant little world on the Station. Brian refers to time spent polishing the new lino in Sick Quarters, marking medicines, tidying up the rough ground, growing Arctic Giant lettuces, sweet peas and other flowers, 'while reminiscing about Oxford and Cambridge.' Katharine much enjoyed the gardening: 'Evelyn gave me a lot of plants for our garden on which Brian has been dumping heroic loads of earth. I'm not allowed to help him carry it.' Brian found her a glutton for work; he remembered her 'thorough and careful medical treatment' of patients under her care, and how he had to make a determined effort 'not to be elbowed out of any unpleasant jobs.' They found challenging and amusing tasks to do, such as sweeping the chimney, and in the evenings they could sit reading, writing or chatting. One result of all this was that Katharine clearly achieved a new ease in approaching and understanding others. Brian mentions that she was often in demand as a listener and adviser to those with personal problems. She was ready to help anyone who needed teaching, and spent a good deal of time with one of the medical orderlies at Syerston who was learning Latin. There was no organised entertainment laid on at Winthorpe, and before long she had introduced play-readings in the evenings, which she describes as 'hilarious and very popular.' She also started 'games evenings' for the girls, which were received with enthusiasm:

> Only five came — our numbers are always small — but they enjoyed it so much that we couldn't get them to go to the NAAFI at nine & I finally had to drive them out at half-past ten. We played silly things like Poor Pussy and the Burlesque Band and Dumb Crambo.

Such evenings sound like echoes of the old days at Dalbeathie. There is mention of reading *The Garrulous Lady* as well as *Twelfth Night, Macbeth, The Scheming Lieutenant* and *The School for Scandal*. Katharine felt a new zest for living: 'There's a kind of blossoming feeling about it that is very stimulating', she wrote. The influence of Brian, who was a good mixer and whose capacity for hard work matched her own, was of great importance for her at this stage. It meant an escape from the predominantly female society in which so much of her youth had been spent, and now she had found someone with whom to co-operate instead of a group of admiring companions to dominate. She wrote a poem about life with Brian on the Station:

> Inside the house the world's askew,
> For all contrariwise we work;
> With cunning turns each seeks to foil
> The other's appetite for toil,
> Leisure the only thing we shirk.
>
> The world may find a wiser way
> Yet something may be said for this
> That gives to labour double zest,
> And makes work more desired than rest,
> Perhaps our plan is not amiss

She felt at last that she was accepted within the little community. When Brian was away on leave, she slept at Sick Quarters:

> It will be quite nice to be sleeping in my own little house. I am afraid a lot of people will drop in to cheer up my solitude in the evenings, but I must not discourage them because one does want to keep in touch with people.

Inevitably, however, this happy time could not last very long. In the late summer Brian was moved back to Syerston, waiting to be posted overseas and applying for a Commission. Tiny, whom Katharine liked and who wanted to keep everything as Brian had had it, took his place for a while, but he too was moved elsewhere. Katharine wondered what she should do with Brian's little cat, which he had to leave behind:

> I rather wonder sometimes about bringing our dear little Shookie back with me. I must consult Brian about it. Bill is very devoted to her, but he may be posted overseas & it would be dreadful if someone took over the place who did not like cats. Shookie has had such special attention. But we should miss her from here very much and no other cat would quite take her place.

That autumn Shookie had kittens, named Blondie, George Moore (after one of the men) and Euclid, 'the winsomest of them all.' A home was found for the charming Euclid, but the other two grew up with their mother, and Katharine chronicled their development in letters home and praised Shookie's abilities as a mother. But this too came to a sudden end.

In October Katharine heard that she was to go back to Syerston, since Winthorpe was returned to the control of Swinderby. It was at this point that she wrote to her mother with final news of Shookie. The cat had gone off with her kittens while Katharine was out, and although the kittens were afterwards found, Shookie never returned:

> Some people saw her yesterday, but she never came home, & this afternoon, walking back from Newark, I found her body by the roadside. She must have been run over, though there was no wound anywhere. I think it must have been very quick, because she looked so tranquil. I carried her back and Bill (?) buried her for me. I am going to take the kittens to Syerston ... They are devoted to each other and always like to sleep in each other's arms.

You should have seen Blondie's joy when little Georgie turned up again. They're darlings, but I'm very sad about Shookie, both for her own sake & because Brian was fond of her.

This is a controlled account of what must have been a most painful experience, a cruel ending to the happy period at Winthorpe. Katharine evidently took the kittens back to Dalbeathie on her next leave, since Winifred later refers to them in a letter, and there is a photograph of Katharine and Elspeth holding them.

The same year Katharine passed a test for the rank of LAC (Lance Air Corporal), and the news came through in September, earlier than she had expected. 'I am pleased about it', she wrote. 'I really did want my LAC'. Back at Syerston she was in the same hut as before, about a mile and a half out of camp, but now she found the quarters comfortable and the food good. It seems that after taking the kittens home she had other cats for company, since she mentions Mrs Tabbs and her kitten who were distracting her from writing letters. She found herself now on a much more friendly footing with those among whom she worked at the Sick Quarters. She told Byron Rogers in an interview for *The Sunday Telegraph* years later: 'In the WAAF ... they called me 'Old Katie'. I think they thought me rather odd, but nobody ever took advantage of me.' In a letter to her mother she is more explicit:

> You mustn't bother about the work for me. I generally have much less hard work than the others. I suppose it is because I am older that people generally come & help me when I'm alone. The men are much more helpful when I'm duty orderly than when the others are & I am never allowed to do extra duties. Also I am lucky & find that accidents don't happen when I'm about. So that though I sometimes get fed up like everybody else, I really haven't anything to grumble at, and should probably get equally fed up with any steady work I had to do. I'm lucky to live with such a nice set of people.

She now did a little lecturing ('on a dull subject though — FFA's admission to hospital & that sort of thing'), and more importantly, she found that her knowledge of stories, poetry and rhymes could be used to help men under stress. She wrote from Syerston: 'The men have developed a passion for having Shakespeare recited to them. They also like repetitive rhymes. Bert is quite enraptured by the Old Woman and the Pig.' 'They were always asking me to tell them stories', she recalls in her *Sunday Telegraph* interview, and in another with Sylvia Sachs of the Pittsburgh Press (15 November 1977) she remembered: 'When I was in the Air Force in World War II the men would come back to their barracks late at night and say "Give us the one about ...", whatever their favourite story was, and I'd tell it.'

Her letters contain little or nothing about the suffering and personal tragedies which she must have encountered. It was at Syerston that she had the experience of helping a doctor to deliver a baby, which arrived without any preparation being made, as the mother had succeeded in concealing her condition. Katharine for a time seriously considered adopting the child, whose mother did not want to keep it. She makes one telling reference to life on the Station in *The Sunday Telegraph* interview:

> What was tragic was life on the operational station. You got so anxious for the men as they neared the end of their 200-hour tours of duty. You saw the strain on their faces. They were doomed men.

However life had its lighter side. She had the cycle she had brought back from Dalbeathie, which made expeditions further afield possible. She wrote a long account to Winifred of the ballet of *Twelfth Night* at Nottingham, which she greatly enjoyed, and was excited by the possibility of examining some papers at Coddington Hall relating to the Gunpowder Plot. It was at this point that she began to write *Kate Crackernuts,* perhaps the most powerful of her books. A little manuscript book of poems afterwards given to Evelyn seems also to have been compiled at this time, and illustrated with miniature paintings.

Katharine made three further moves during her time in the Service. She must have been delighted to hear that she was to go to Errol in Perthshire, not far from home. There she celebrated her second anniversary of war service by a visit to the familiar theatre at Perth to see *Love in a Mist* on 14 November 1943. At Errol she was in charge of the Station Sick Quarters, and also dramatic producer for the station, so that play-readings and productions formed part of her duties. She was still faced with the risk of losing her best actors at a moment's notice, an unavoidable hazard in the RAF, but she found the dramatic work very satisfying. In the spring of 1944 she was down at Sidmouth for a short period, and there met Cousin

Maisie, a daughter of Frank Shepherd, and Mabel Barmby for the first time. Mabel and Katharine got on very well, and made plans for bringing her mother and sisters down to Sidmouth after the War was over.

Clearly it could not last much longer now, and Katharine's last move was to Ternhill, a pleasant spot near Market Drayton in Shropshire. The WAAF from Errol were moved down in a body, and at first there was some grumbling because the RAF had left some rooms very dirty. Katharine had little patience with their complaints: 'Of course, being sillies, they moaned, & the Ternhill people didn't like it naturally enough ... I do hope I shall be left here until I am demobilised, since I have the Dramatic Society got going again.' She took a liking to Ternhill from the start, and delighted in her own room in the Old Married Quarters, with seven or eight WAAFs to each house, and the houses grouped round a green, 'like a dear little village.' Her description of her room shows how she must have been longing for a place of her own during these unsettled years living under Service conditions:

> My room is deep cream with very pale green paint, and I have a nice long window seat with a view over the regular Shropshire country. It could not be nicer. There is a picture rail, and I'll get one picture I think to hang over the mantel piece and one nice vase to arrange flowers in.

Winnie at once sent off one of her paintings and Katharine put it up in her room.

Now that there was less sense of urgency and a need to keep those manning the Station occupied, play productions were in demand. There were successful readings of popular modern plays: *Rebecca* and *Dear Brutus* are mentioned, and the last play which Katharine produced was *Blithe Spirit,* in which she herself played the part of the Medium. She had a valuable addition to her group, a boy called Reg, who had been at John Gielgud's Dramatic School, and she remarks on the number of good friends made in the short time at Ternhill. It is clear that many of the barriers which had separated her from those of different ages and backgrounds had now come down. She had won general respect, gained her confidence, found that she could get on with both men and women, and that her special gifts were appreciated in a very different setting from the protected realm of Dalbeathie. Life still held much that was good, for all the

Katharine in the WAAF, with her cast as producer
near the end of her wartime service.

grim background of war and its aftermath, and the deprivation of much that had enriched her earlier life. The fact that she makes no reference in letters of the tragedies and losses which she must have witnessed during her years in the Service does not mean that they did not leave a mark on her. One of her best poems, in a collection of poetry by members of the Forces,[5] comments on the depths of sorrow round us from which we shield ourselves instinctively:

> So casual and light are the sorrows we do not know,
> Striking the heart with a touch like a butterfly's blow.

In letting herself become exposed to a wider, less sheltered world, Katharine had broadened her whole range of experience and become a fully mature person.

It was while the rehearsals for *Blithe Spirit* were going on that Katharine received the news that she would soon be released, since there were now too many Corporals in the Women's Air Force. She wrote eagerly to Winifred, telling her how they were waiting impatiently for each news bulletin, hoping to hear that Japan had surrendered:

It's difficult to believe until it really happens. I shall be digging the borders this Autumn all right. Isn't it grand. We might plant some nut trees and fruit trees as a victory celebration. I keep thinking of all kinds of things we can do. How lovely it is!

On the day when the long-awaited news came through, she also learned that she had been put on the list of those to be released as soon as it was decided that they did not need replacements. This meant that she would be at home in a few weeks:

I can hardly believe it; I am going about in a daze ... I'm so happy & excited I hardly know what to do ... We can begin making plans for all sorts of things again. And isn't it lovely that my War Service has lasted right to the end of the Japanese War? ... I'm almost too excited to write. Lots of love to all of you until I come home again.

The years of the War were clearly of great importance for Katharine's development as a writer. They enabled her to escape from home at last. She had known hardships, frustrations and disappointments, and one of her darkest hours was symbolised by the discovery of the body of the cherished little cat Shookie lying beside the road, a humble example of the losses which war brings with it. Katharine had never been unaware of the wider world outside the protective fence of home and family, nor had she been hostile to it, as her work with Guides and Brownies showed. But when she first joined up, there was little real communication between her and her companions when she had no privileged position from which to make approaches to them. In the end, although in no position of authority, the situation was very different, and she was respected and liked for herself. This no doubt is why she counted herself fortunate in 'never rising above the rank of a Corporal.'

Something of this difference can be seen when the early poems in the collection called 'Whispers', printed by the Capricornus Press in 1941 and written and illustrated by the sisters, is compared with later poems in the manuscript book written in the War years. The poems of 'Whispers' are pleasing and musical, but somewhat precious, belonging to an artificial world of medieval fantasy like that conjured up by the Summer Players:

> The Princess Melisande stole out
> To dance beneath the orange tree,

> Her grave small feet slid round about
> And circled it with wizardry ...

Some of these early verses are repeated in the manuscript book, including the merry rhyme 'A handsome sailor came to woo me', which Katharine delighted to recite in her old age. There are also, however, poems of a different type. One of the most powerful is a description of a dream or vision which must relate to her relationship with her family at Dalbeathie, beginning 'I waked or slept I know not which':

> I knelt upon the window seat
> And looked out at the terraced lawn,
> Upon the road was tramp of feet,
> And on the terrace stood my dears.
>
> They glowed with joy, and I leant out
> And called to them, they made reply
> Clear sweet and distant to my shout,
> I heard gay music in my head.
> I was afraid, I knew not why.
> The truth came sudden to my mind —
> All those I saw outside were dead.

Another short poem deals with the necessity to be free from possessiveness if true happiness is to be achieved:

> And if in wealth that can be told
> You find your only joy and pride,
> Then like the miser's fairy gold
> Whose lustre by the morning died
> And turned to leaves withered and dried,
> Will fade the wealth your hand can hold,
> And leave your heart unsatisfied.

Katharine was faced with the special problems and temptations which come to those who never have to worry overmuch about money, but it is not only material goods which she had in mind in writing this poem. She knew that she had to be prepared to surrender her most cherished privileges of independence and freedom to create. One other short poignant poem is a cry for the renewal of inspiration. Throughout the war years she had been unable to write when inspiration came to her, and must have often been faced with the fear that her creative powers would be lost for good in the relentless, practical world which she had chosen to enter:

> Across the page my pencil moves
> Because my head has willed it so;
> But the creator's pulse and glow
> The happy stirring breath that proves
> That life has come where all was still,
> Alas, that springs not at my will.

The war service had brought her valuable experience in human relationships and also in self-knowledge, but while submitting to it, Katharine had not turned her back on the Other World of fairy tradition which had meant so much to her in her story-telling and her work with the Summer Players. In some of the poems of the manuscript book, this seems to be springing up to new life, as it was to do in *Kate Crackernuts* and *Hobberdy Dick,* books in which that 'happy stirring breath' of inspiration was indeed present. The collection includes poems on witches, on a changling child and a fairy wife, while in one poem she describes an encounter with a creature of the fairy world:

> An alien mind, whose strangeness mocks
> The thought that human beings call wise.

These new figures of the Other World are more potent creatures than the fairies of the earlier rhymes. At the close of the War, Katharine was conscious of new discoveries about herself and others, and of a new stirring of energy and creative ideas. She returned to the fair, sheltered world of Dalbeathie, but now she had achieved freedom from it. She had escaped from the shackles of her past, and although she never wholly renounced the ties of loyalty which bound her to it, she was now in a position to begin afresh and discover where her true interests lay.

5 Search for the Hidden People: The Barn House, Burford

> *The folklorist who specializes in fairy-lore is often asked if he believes in fairies — that is, in fairies as a subjective reality ... For myself, I am an agnostic. Some of the fairy anecdotes have a curiously convincing air of truth, but at the same time we must make allowances for the constructive power of the imagination in recalling old memories, and for the likelihood that people see what they expect to see.*
>
> (K.M. Briggs, Preface to 'A Dictionary of Fairies')

It was not very long after the happy reunion at Dalbeathie at the close of the war that Katharine was off on her travels again. She never settled for long at Dalbeathie now, but kept the Oxford terms at Burford, and often extended her stay there beyond them. For the next ten years until their mother's death in 1956, her sisters were constantly on the move between Scotland and the Cotswolds. Sometimes they were trapped at one end or the other by bad weather, as in the bitter winter of 1947, and sometimes they made short trips abroad, but for the most part their world was divided between Dalbeathie and the Barn House. Katharine was at Burford in 1946, as soon as she could contrive it, making the house habitable and writing a happy account of settling in to console her mother, who worried about her being alone there:

> I am enjoying myself so much. Of course it will be nicer still when you come down, and I hope you will find it warm and comfortable; but it's lovely to be studying again, and I love the little bustle round the house to put things in order before I go, & finding it nice and friendly when I arrive back.

In the early days she stayed at the Bay Tree Hotel, not far away, and continued over the years to make use of it for meals and for entertaining visitors, but comfortable and friendly as it was, she assured her mother, 'there's nothing like being in a home of your own.'

She had made arrangements to work for the degree of B. Litt. at Lady Margaret Hall, and had as her supervisor Ethel Seaton, Tutor in English Literature at St Hugh's College. Miss Seaton worked on somewhat obscure subjects, but found fascinating material in them. She had published her main work, *Literary Relations of England and Scandinavia in the Seventeenth Century,* in 1935, and at the time when Katharine first came into contact with her was working on the life of the poet Sir Richard Roos. She must have been a stimulating person with whom to work, and she was able to put Katharine in touch with many important and little-known sources. Katharine had evidently now made up her mind about her subject, and wanted to work on fairy lore, witchcraft and other aspects of popular beliefs in the supernatural world in the seventeenth century. The final title of her thesis was 'Some aspects of folk-lore in early seventeenth-century literature', since the amount of material was so great that she had to limit it to some extent. Certain alterations had also to be made when her supervisor recommended that she should work for a D.Phil. rather than a B.Litt.

It would seem that by this time she had written *Kate Crackernuts,* a story of witchcraft set in seventeenth-century Scotland, and had finished *The Personnel of Fairyland,* since she took this with her when she went to see Miss Seaton for the first time:

> I went into Oxford in the afternoon to see Miss Seaton. She's elderly, as you'd expect, with a very, very gentle voice, and very learned. I feel rather nervous; I left the Personnel of Fairyland with her, and I'm afraid she may think it very unscholarly.

These two books contain the key to Katharine's new line of work and future development. She had moved away from the historical figures of the seventeenth century to those of the fairy world and of men's contacts with it, although her knowledge of the historical background was necessary and invaluable. She had always been interested in folk and fairy tales; her father had introduced her to them, as to so much else. She had devoured all the collections in his library at an early age, and later shared his enthusiasm for Scottish tales and legends. Her work with Guides and Summer Players had set her on a continual search for tales, rhymes and ballads suitable for mimes and story-telling. The lonely period in the WAAF must have given her time to let her mind dwell further on traditional literature, and she had found that it might appeal to most unlikely audiences, such as the airmen in the RAF. She had also become increasingly inquisitive about the different types of fairies after her instinctive reaction against the confusing hotchpotch of fairy lore presented to the Brownies. Years of story-telling to children had taught her that the old tales from our own popular tradition were the most successful in holding their interest. Much of the sophisticated material from France, elegant narratives of Cinderella or Bluebeard, and the flimsy, sentimental figures which flitted through contemporary stories for children, were, she realised, far inferior to the native material on creatures of the Other World, which was little known and yet well within our reach.

In *Kate Crackernuts* she takes an old folktale and expands it into a book. It has echoes of a short story she wrote before the war, *The Witches' Ride,* which was printed by Winifred on their own press.[1] This was the tale of a young girl, Sally, who discovered that the old woman she worked for was a witch, but through innocence and good luck she was saved from harm and found a crock of gold. It is a slight story, simply told, but the atmosphere of evil and terror investing the witches is effectively conveyed. In *Kate Crackernuts,* a similar theme of evil witchcraft is played out in seventeenth-century Scotland. The book was not published by the Alden Press until 1963, after *Hobberdy Dick* had appeared, but a reference in one of Katharine's letters shows that she began it at Syerston in 1943, and it was evidently the first of the two to be written. She may have altered it during the years, but it does not give the impression of revision; it has a vividness and power marking it out from her other writings. Parts of it have the quality of a memorable dream, and there is deep emotion expressed in it. It seems as though much of Katharine's inner experience went into this book, transmuted though it may have been into a tale of enchantment which she took over ready-made.

The tale is a strange one, of how one half-sister freed the other from a spell, and finally married a prince whom she rescued from the power of the fairies. It was sent to Andrew Lang by a reader of *Longman's Magazine* in 1889,[2] and was said to have been contributed by a lady whose name is not given, but who claimed that it was told 'by an ancient lady of an old family in Angus' to her descendants. In 1890 Lang published it in the journal *Folk-Lore,* and Joseph Jacobs retold it in his collection of folktales in the same year.[3] Katharine told the tale in her own words in *The Anatomy* of *Puck*,[4] and used Lang's version in her *Dictionary of Folktales*.[5] In this the fair sister who is bewitched is not given a name, although Jacobs names her Anne; however it is implied in Lang's version that both girls are called Kate, although this point could be easily missed: 'The king had a dochter, Kate, and the queen had one.' Katharine evidently interpreted it in this way, since in her summary she refers to 'the king's Kate' and 'the queen's Kate.' The mother of the dark girl, Kate Crackernuts, marries the father of the fair one, and the new queen, resenting the beauty of her stepdaughter, puts her under a spell and sets a sheep's head on her shoulders. The other Kate takes her half-sister away to a neighbouring kingdom and works in the palace kitchen while the bewitched Kate hides herself in an attic and is seen by none. Kate Crackernuts then rescues the king's son from enchantment after entering a fairy mound, and discovers also how to free her sister from the evil spell. She marries the king's son, while her sister marries his brother, and they live happily ever after.

Katharine keeps faithfully to the outline of the tale, only making some slight alterations, such as marrying the fair Kate to an older man, a friend of her father. She places the tale in Galloway, a part of Scotland she knew well, at the time of the Civil War, and changes it from a story of kings and queens to one of minor landed gentry in Scotland and Yorkshire. She states in her introduction: 'It may be that the real Katharine Crackernuts had a homelier setting, and had to be contented with a laird for her stepfather and a dame for her mother, and a rough-hewn Galloway keep for a royal palace.' She makes the father of 'the laird's Kate' Andrew Lindsay of Ackenskeoch, who fought under Gustavus Adolphus and brought a Swedish wife back to Galloway. When the tale opens, his wife and his sons had died, and little Katharine was his only surviving child. When she was twelve, he married a widow called Grizel Maxwell, a handsome but sinister woman, thought to have dealings with the local witches. Grizel also had a daughter called Kate, who loved to roam wild over the hills and collect nuts and berries, so that she was called Kate Crackernuts. But in contrast to this realistic setting, the little girls, who became friends at an early age, are introduced as figures resembling creatures of the Other World. The small Katharine was dressed in white, a fashion of mourning which came from her Swedish nurse, and she had pale-gold hair and 'eyes of deep misty blue':

Kate's heart turned over at the sight, for it seemed that she was one of the white fays, those high and rarely seen fairies that haunt old majestic ruins and places of which great stories are told, or who glimmer through the mist beside tall, old rocks high up in the hills. They are more than mortal in stature, and this little creature seemed like one of their children, which might sometimes stray into mortal haunts.

In her turn, Kate Crackernuts 'seemed no less a creature of fairy to Katharine', since her mother, in spite of the minister's disapproval, insisted on dressing her in green, the fairy colour:

So Katharine saw before her the very image of a fairy, one of the People of Peace who swarm about the hills — a lean, tall child with her green kirtle kilted high and dark elf-locks hanging about her narrow face, who looked at her out of shining dark-green eyes.

But neither was afraid; they loved one another from their first meeting, and their affection and loyalty is the main thread running through the story. Later on the fairy association is emphasised again. Katharine, hiding away in a farmhouse while her sister works, does housework by night like a Brownie, while Kate finds her way into the fairy hill and is able to hold her own there and make friends with a fairy boy.

The picture of the witches' gathering, to which Grizel takes her daughter Kate, is a superb evocation of the mingled nastiness and heady attraction of witchcraft. Kate feels the pull, and is strongly tempted, but is saved from giving away to it by the goodness and innocence of her step-sister. Grizel's increasing mental desperation and destructive hatred, as 'the cloud surrounding her mind came closer and darkened', are powerfully conveyed. The highlight of the book is the terrifying scene where Grizel apparently triumphs, and through her contrivance the evil old henwife Mallie sets a sheep's head on the fair Katharine. This is baldly stated in the original story, but here it takes on a new, hideous and convincing reality:

The fire was burning up and she could see the pot above it, clear in the light from the smoke-hole. She went quickly to it and lifted the lid, intent on getting her errand over.

'What's in the pot? What's in the pot?' sang out Mallie Gross behind her.

'A sheep's head', said Katharine.

'Look well at it, look closely, peer in and make siccar.'
'It is a sheep's head, but it is no way to dress it for the pot.'
'Is it woolly? Is it hairy? Has it goggling een?' sang Mallie.
'It is hairy, it's woolly and rolls its eyes on me,' said Katharine, shrinking back.
'Is it in the pot? Is it out of the pot? Is it in the pot? Is it out of the pot?
'It is rising,' said Katharine in a whisper.
'Aye it is rising sure enough. Look up, it is hanging in the reek above you. It is hanging, it is floating, it is gliding down fast. Ha, ha!' said Mallie with a scream of laughter. 'Your bonny face is hidden in an old sheep's head. Best take your kerchar and hide yourself from sight.' ...
Katharine ... kept her head down, with the dirty cloth drawn tight over it, for she was convinced in her heart that if she lifted her hands they would touch a long, woolly snout, and she seemed to see double out of golden eyes, set at each side of her head.

The question is skilfully left open as to whether this is merely an hallucination on Katharine's part. When Kate persuades her to show her face, it appears to be still human but cruelly disfigured:

The face was so altered that she felt that she might hardly have known her Katherine. The face was pale and swollen with the lips strangely thrust forward, and the eyes were so wandering and starting that they seemed hardly the same.

The fear and torment in Katharine's mind, from which she is delivered by the devotion and courage of Kate and finally cured by the blessed white stones dropped into the Lady's Well, are convincingly conveyed. The account of the healing of Katharine, and also that of Will Frankland, who was drawn by the Seven Whistlers into the Fairy Hill, and left in a state of depression which would have ended in death had it not been for Kate, are as moving as anything which Katharine Briggs ever wrote. Moving and exciting also is the description of the drowning of the evil witches, Grizel and Mallie. Kate's suffering at the end because she knows her mother to have been evil and laments her loss while she cannot regret it, is poignantly expressed, even while allayed, in true fairy-tale fashion, by her new love for the laird's son: 'Oh Mother! Mother!' she said weeping, 'You loved me well in your way and I just couldna love you again.'

It is to be supposed that much reading and thinking went into the detailed and effective treatment of the old tale in its seventeenth-century setting, and to the presentation of the witch's curse, the Seely Rade of the fairies, and the visit to the Fairy Hill. It may have been some years before Katharine had the book as she wanted it, but the story must have been chosen at the beginning because it had some special significance for her. 'This little obscure tale happens to be dear to me', she said at the International Helsinki Conference on Folk-Narrative Research in 1974, when she read a short paper on this story, called 'An Untypified Tale.'[6] The opposed figures of the two sisters, both essentially loyal and good, are given the names of 'the King's Kate' and 'the Queen's Kate' in her account of the story. They may perhaps have represented for her the two sides of her own nature — her father's Katharine, the adventurous, brave, boyish Kate Crackernuts, and her mother's Katharine, the quiet, truly feminine Katharine Lindsay.

Katharine's mother Mary Briggs was herself good and innocent, with no suggestion of the wicked witch, and yet in some ways she posed a problem and a torment for Katharine, in her continual anxiety and over-protectiveness. Although she never attempted to keep Katharine with her, any more than she had done to Ernest, she threatened by her very devotion to deny her daughter the kind of life she wanted to lead, by keeping her safe, protected and unfulfilled. This aspect of her mother became increasingly apparent as she grew older, as is indicated by the letters which passed between Dalbeathie and the Barn House. Katharine frequently wrote to her mother, seeking to interest and amuse her by accounts of her doings, but she had to reassure her continually that she was not cold, or lonely, or working too hard, or failing to get proper meals, or without domestic help, or driving to Oxford in bad weather. Her various feats before the War, such as walking ninety-eight miles, or spending two days blindfolded, had had to be concealed from her mother, and now any careless statement about activities at Burford could give rise to fresh waves of anxiety in Mary's mind. Therefore the picture of the daughter Kate who had perforce to escape from her mother could have had special significance for Katharine.

Even the sheep's head and the nuts, both part of the original tale, may be seen as fitting into the inner situation which Katharine and her sisters in their loyalty never seem to have put explicitly into words. In the story, the well-protected and cherished daughter was threatened by the sheep's head, symbol of ignorance and isolation from her own kind, while the nuts in which the other Kate delighted, and which in the end were the means by which she found a cure for her sister, might serve as a fitting symbol for the folk tales to which Katharine now devoted her energies: 'Folktales give the mind something to bite on', Margaret Hodges remembers her saying. More than one person who knew Katharine has recognised her likeness in old age to Mrs Dimbledy in *Hobberdy Dick,* but a different and no less essential side of her may also be seen in *Kate Crackernuts,* which I would claim as one of her major achievements. The reviews of the book emphasise the difficulties of the Scots dialect, which the critics felt made it unsuitable for a children's book, but it is a mistake to judge it from this angle: it is far more than an entertaining adventure story for children.

The picture of the two kinds of fairy, the white and the green, in this story indicates Katharine's interest in the various types of fairy people in folklore and literature, which was to become her main area of study. In *The Personnel of Fairyland* she had already found the key to the problem; the development and working out of this insight was to take many years, gradually winning her an international reputation and a wide reading public extending far beyond the narrow academic field. It would be helpful to know what Ethel Seaton said about her manuscript, but clearly she did not attempt to block Katharine's line of approach as many literary scholars might have done. A writer who quoted with approval in her introduction Purchas' remark, 'My Genius delights rather in by-wayes than high-wayes' was likely to be a good supervisor for Katharine. They quickly became friends, and Ethel Seaton used to visit the Barn House, while Katharine kept in touch with her after her retirement.

The little book which Katharine had feared Ethel Seaton might find unscholarly is unpretentious enough, with its sub-title: 'A short account of the Fairy People of Great Britain for those who tell Stories to children.' In the preface she emphasises the lamentable weaknesses of many fairy-tales in circulation, as she had discovered when looking for material for the Brownies:

> A good many of the stories which children are told are not folk stories, nor true to the robust tradition of folklore. They are full of careful and innocuous prettinesses, and offer food for the fancy

rather than for the imagination. For folklore the native story-tellers seem to go chiefly to foreign sources, and our native sources are curiously neglected.

Her intention, she declared, was 'to describe the characteristics of British Fairies', most of the book being taken up by actual tales. It is a collection of short but well-selected stories, such as 'Childe Roland', 'Cherry of Zannor', 'The Woman of Peace and the Kettle', with little gems like 'The Cauld Lad of Hilton', and includes a variety of rhymes linked with the old tales, like the Cauld Lad's song:

> Wae's me, wae's me!
> The acorn's not yet
> Fallen from the tree
> That's to grow the wood
> That's to make the cradle
> That's to rock the bairn
> That's to grow to the man
> That's to lay me!

There are brief comments on the existence of parallels to the various stories, and the material is taken from many different parts of the British Isles. More important, they are not put together at random or according to geographical distribution, but arranged under main headings, such as Heroic Fairies, Small Trooping Fairies, Tutelary Fairies, and Nature Fairies, with one section on Monsters, Demons, and Giants. In an article in *Folklore* in 1957 on 'The English Fairies',[7] Katharine states that she derived these divisions from Yeats' *Fairy and Folk Tales,* which had been in her father's library. However Yeats only singles out Trooping Fairies and Solitary Fairies, arranging his Irish tales accordingly. Much more concerning the general pattern of fairy lore and local variants already emerges from *The Personnel of Fairyland*.

Once settled in the Barn House, Katharine was prepared for hard work. The deprivation of reading and study in the war years no doubt spurred her on to concentrate joyfully on new exploration of the world of books, to spend many hours in libraries and later to accept the wearisome labour of checking references. Here Ethel Seaton's influence was of great value. She started Katharine off on books which opened new vistas to her:

Katharine after the war, probably at Burford.

I am still very excited about my reading; but it is an enormous subject, & I have so much to read. I hardly know what to do first. Still it's nice to have a big subject; it gives me a nice spacious feeling. I've finished St Augustine's City of God, but I'm only about a quarter through Johann Wayer, the Latin book.

There were entertaining sidelines, like the illustrations in the work of the Swede Olaus Magnus, which she commended to Winifred as possible embroidery designs, and later was to use in her own books. When Katharine published *The Anatomy of Puck,* she dedicated it to Ethel Seaton, referring to 'her advice and encouragement ... steady scholarship and unwearying enthusiasm' which 'have set a standard for many students as well as for the author.' Her letters record her working steadily through the chapters of her thesis, getting them typed, and adding references and bibliography, which she found the most trying part of the work. She relied on the help of several people for typing, and had a good deal of assistance over the finding and checking of references from the Reverend Fish Taylor, a priest and an excellent scholar, who came to Oxford late in life to work for a degree. It was undoubtedly the most sustained and disciplined piece of work she had ever embarked on. On Miss Seaton's advice, the thesis was finally submitted for a D.Phil. but it was not accepted immediately, but returned for various emendations and alterations. Some chapters were taken out (although Katharine was able to use them for her books later on), and part of the witchcraft section rewritten, before it was finally accepted in 1952 and Katharine granted her doctorate.

There were many distractions, of course, to tempt her from work during her time at Burford, and many pleasurable experiences and new friendships. First the house had to be made habitable. She had rented it to Evie Forbes during the war years when Evie was working in London and needed accommodation for her four children and their Danish nanny while her husband was in the army. But there had been no chance of improving it, and much work needed to be done. Katharine's letters refer to visits from the sweep, men working on the chimney, the installation of a new cooker, and the mending of burst pipes after the great freeze of 1947. She and Elspeth did some decorating, and there was the more enjoyable task of furnishing the house, bringing down much valuable old furniture from Dalbeathie, together with Dulcie and costumes for future play productions. She got bedrooms ready for her mother, sisters and guests, and planned that the big room in the centre was to be used for parties and activities. The kitchen had to be remodelled, but Katharine took little interest in this and the house was never really convenient to run, although an improvement on Dalbeathie.

Sometimes Katharine plunged into domestic jobs such as making marmalade, and she made some attempt to grow vegetables, but in the end was glad to leave this to Mr Cook, a local man who came to work in the garden and was finally installed in the cottage beside the house. He was rather a dour old man, but became devoted to Katharine and her sisters, and when he died after many years of faithful service his last word was 'Briggs'. Katharine found a good home help in Maude Peacock, who worked for her as long as she was in Burford. Katharine clearly enjoyed housekeeping, and on one occasion she gives her mother a detailed account of her meals for the day, to prove that she was looking after herself well: 'I think it would amuse you to see me sitting snugly by my nice cosy fire drinking peppermint tea & eating chocolate biscuits having finished the washing up.' She found a certain amount of cooking amusing, although she never had the patience to devote much time to it; if she prepared a meal, it had to be an interesting one, with sauces and trimmings. Faith Sharp, who knew her well during her time at Burford, came to realise this:

> All the Briggs were excellent cooks, but Katharine was also what I can only call a food-snob. When I told her proudly one day that after some practice I had managed to cook a delicious apple charlotte, she replied crushingly 'There is no such thing as a delicious apple charlotte.' So throughout our acquaintance I never dared to try to return her most generous hospitality in the food line, in case I committed some terrible gaffe.

However like a good north-country housewife, Katharine regularly made her own bread, baking a fresh batch whenever it was needed.

It was not long before Katharine was considering ways of getting dramatic work going again. Faith Sharp (then Faith Spachman) first met her in 1946, when Faith was working as sub-editor of *The Countryman* at Idbury Manor, under J.W. Robertson Scott. Faith was musical, played in the Burford Women's Orchestra, and also produced plays. She was asked if she could help the Briggs sisters in a play which they were producing for a Women's Institute Entertainment, since someone had let them down at the last moment. The play was Elspeth Briggs' little comedy, 'The Constant Gardener', and the part that needed filling that of the Baronet's young daughter. Faith went to the Barn House to discuss it with Katharine:

> I was impressed by Katharine's friendly but authorative, no-nonsense approach. 'How old *are* you?' she demanded, when I demurred at trying to take the part of a seventeen-year-old; and when I admitted to forty, 'Oh well, you don't look it; you can pass for seventeen with a bit of make-up. But can you learn the words in the time?' Yes, I was good at learning words; so without more ado I was enrolled as a member of the Summer Players.[8]

She describes all the sisters as good actors: 'they could all move beautifully and knew how to wear period costume with panache.' Winifred was excellent in a suitable character part, Elspeth could lose her shyness and be very amusing in comedy, while Katharine was good in male parts. They were delighted to discover Faith's abilities in playing and singing, and writing parts for various instruments, so that it was now possible to form a small group of musicians to augment performances. Faith sang folksongs and ballads, and used to play Dulcie until that rather frustrating instrument was taken over by Josephine Thompson.

Some of Katharine's productions were ambitious efforts, now that there was the possibility of obtaining men to play the male parts. Not that it was always easy to find them when needed; Katharine claimed that when producing Laurence Housman's play, *The Builders*, she visited as many as seventy men in Burford in an attempt to find a suitable St Francis. The Vicar was prepared to dragoon his reluctant curate into the part, but seeing his horror at the idea Katharine finally decided to take it herself. She did not find the unswerving loyalty and enthusiasm in Burford she had known with the Summer Players: Elspeth wrote in a letter to Winifred:

The Barn House at Burford.

Katharine has been having rather a time with rehearsals, because people just won't realise that it matters if they miss them, even the dress rehearsals. However, I think that it will turn out alright in the end. Considering that there were a lot of people not there at the dress rehearsal — some of them excusably, some of them quite inexcusably — it went quite well.

However, Katharine had become accustomed to dealing with such problems in her productions in the RAF, and was not easily put out. She was helped by some former Summer Players such as Barbara, Jean and Jane Kingshill (formerly Jane Moore), who came to Burford to help with special productions. *The Builders* was performed in the large and beautiful Burford church in 1947, when it was in great need of funds. Unhappily no one had warned them of the deplorable acoustics, and the speeches at the first performance were almost wholly inaudible. At the next they all spoke up manfully and matters were slightly better. Undeterred by this, Katharine produced another play the following year, *The Bells*, a chronicle play which brought in a vast number of actors, and produced problems as a result. Katharine remarked with unusual sharpness in a letter to Winnie: 'The singers are in a thoroughly disgruntled frame of mind, and won't take any part. They don't really deserve to have the money collected for their bells.' One happy event associated with this production was that Victor Sharp, who had played the Beggar the year previously and was now the Sacristan while Faith was the Witch, became engaged to Faith on the opening night.

Faith felt that Katharine was hardly an ideal producer and was apt to allot parts unwisely, to encourage individuals, rather than to think of the performance as a whole. Also her performances tended to be too slow. However the staging and costumes 'left nothing to be desired', and here Katharine benefited from the skills of her sisters as well as from her own considerable ingenuity. Her passion for play production is illustrated by a dream which she once recounted to Faith. She dreamed that she was a famous actor-manager who went to take a part in a Shakespearian play without knowing which play it was to be, and to her horror it was *Titus Andronicus,* which she had never even read. In real life she did not often attempt Shakespeare, but in June 1952 she produced an outstanding *Midsummer Night's Dream* in the garden at the Barn House, making full use of the slopes and terraces and creating a special bower for

Titania. The small orchestra, in Elizabethan costume, was on the balcony, and Faith had arranged music of the period for a mixed group of recorders, violins, viols, cello and singers. At one performance there was rain half-way through, but careful contingency plans had been made and the audience moved indoors. Katharine herself played Puck, and Evelyn Goshawk remembers the effect she created:

> While we waited for the show to start, I heard a voice behind me 'Good heavens, do you see Miss Briggs hiding up that tree?' There was Katharine, as Puck, lurking in complete absorption as the play opened ... no gauzy wings, no tinsel, a real earthy Elizabethan Robin Goodfellow, like the character she drew, so loved, Hobberdy Dick. ... As the last song 'Through the house give glimmering light' hung on the air the windows of the house came alive with twinkling light as the children ran with lighted candles in procession from room to room.[9]

The production had meant much work and planning and the tactful control of a huge cast, as Faith points out:

> I don't think anybody but Katharine would have attempted such a production entirely with amateurs, for it meant that the house and garden were invaded and turned upside down for months on end, bedrooms and all, by crowds of people of all ages from the tiny 'fairies' upwards; and on top of that she played Puck herself. It wasn't perfect, of course, but it gave enormous pleasure to a great many people for quite a long time, and was a typical Briggs achievement.

Katharine also revived the old Summer Players tradition, and organised performances of mimes and short plays in village halls under the title 'Commedia del Arte on the Road.' Barbara came down for some of the local performances, while Faith helped with the acting and singing. Elspeth also came for the first attempt, and her letters to Winnie at Dalbeathie chronicle its progress. She and Katharine set off in two cars, while Mr Pearman, a neighbour who ran a local garage and who was by now giving invaluable help with the staging, brought along the other actors. Elspeth writes after one of the last rehearsals:

> I do wish you could have seen The Gaoler's Daughter. Faith was perfect as the gaoler. We nearly burst with suppressed laughter when we were in the sleeping closet last night after we'd escaped. I am sure she ought to bring down the house. Barbara is singing

Sir Ryalas and working the boar stuck onto Harold & the Wild Woman & Katharine is Sir Ryalas, in spite of her lame leg. It is rather jolly, & it is nice to have the singing in. The Commedia del Arte on the Road is going well now, I think.

Another letter explains the boar as 'a head on a coat-hanger.' It seems that Katharine had hurt her leg moving the piano but refused to give up.

But the Burford way of life was less suited to this kind of entertainment than Dalbeathie, while Katharine was too engrossed in her writing to be able to give her undivided attention to a touring company. She had come to feel also, as a result of working with Faith, that something different was needed, and now longed to establish an Arts Centre, where the work done locally in music and drama groups could be brought together. She and Faith discussed this constantly, and searched for a suitable building:

> Faith and I have been diligently looking at possible places for a Little Theatre — or perhaps I should say impossible ones. The latest is a tiny little house in Witney Street, beyond the Methodist Chapel, with a longish garden at the back. But we could only afford to buy it very cheap & I expect dozens of people will be after it; though really to live between a graveyard and a fire station is not ideal.

In the end the meetings took place in the Barn House until Katharine was able to organise the rebuilding of the Parish Hall. They became enjoyable social functions rather than a part of the crusade for the Arts which Katharine had envisaged.

The years in Burford were marked by a succession of cats. There had always been cats at Dalbeathie, and during her time in the WAAF Katharine had discovered their possibilities as friends and lodgers, who would fit in with her way of life better than dogs. Blondie and George Moore, unhappily, did not survive long at Dalbeathie, but they had many successors. There is mention of Beaver, Little Ambrose, Jacky Fourpaws, Malkin, Tiddy and other temporary acquaintances in the letters. Beaver and Ambrose were taken from Burford to Dalbeathie; Beaver was Winnie's cat, a much loved animal with a short tail and an inveterate hunter. The sisters were always trying to persuade him to relinquish his captives, and a typical scene is described by Katharine in a letter:

> He chased rabbits like a dog, galloping after them. We saw him chasing one on the sunk lawn, & he almost caught it, & the poor little thing screamed — so we shouted at him, & he stopped & let it get away. He is very good humoured at being carried away. Yesterday he brought a little one into the hall, & it got into the dining room & behind the radiator, & Elspeth carried it out, quite unhurt, & Beaver was very sweet tempered about it. There are a lot of rabbits in the garden. I wish he would learn to kill them quickly, for it would really be the kindest way of getting rid of them.

Walker was a large cat whom one of the neighbours at Burford intended to have put down, and Katharine immediately took him over. He used to disappear for long periods, but was very affectionate, following her about like a dog, and could cram his large form into baskets and unbelievably small spaces. Little Ambrose was a playful Siamese, a great favourite, who was killed at Dalbeathie, while Jacky Fourpaws disappeared, much to Elspeth's grief. Katharine was devoted to Black Malkin, who kept her company at the Barn House in the early days, and who was remembered by Faith with affection:

> 'He likes you to take a real *interest* in his meals', she would assure me crouching on the floor opposite Malkin while he toyed with a saucer of milk. ... He was a large, thin ungainly animal but had beautiful manners, and I too was fond of him.

Afterwards Katharine was persuaded by her neighbours the Pearmans to keep Siamese cats, and she had two, Roland and Oliver, for many years, one of them accompanying her to Southolme in 1975. When Josephine Thompson conjured up a picture of the Barn House as she remembered it, the cats occupied a central position.[10]

> I can see the Barn House now: it is summer, the three sisters are there. Winnie is bustling about, laying the table at the top of the garden for breakfast. Winnie's beloved, short-tailed cat Beaver is still alive, and the Siamese brothers, Roland and Oliver, are looking their decorative best. Winnie takes great pains tenderly be remove caught birds from their jaws; and runs about with a ladder, standing it against a tree or wall in order to use it to rescue Roland or Oliver, who have a habit of isolating themselves on the roof and wailing for help. It is a beautiful morning, there is

a timeless atmosphere as if the family would always be in possession and enjoy stability and happiness.

From the beginning, Katharine had taken great delight in her garden and the Cotswold countryside. The first spring, when alone, she slept out on the balcony:

> These last three nights I have dragged my bed out on to the balcony & slept there, and it has been really lovely. There has been a warm, strong wind, & a cloudless sky. First thing in the morning, just at sunrise it is too lovely looking up into it. Yesterday morning a swan flew over, very high up, catching the sun before it had reached the lower sky, and this morning a cuckoo flew right over my head calling. I have all my meals outside.

She and Elspeth chronicle the beauty of the garden through the year when they write from Burford, noting the progress of the blossom and the flowering trees, while Katharine could see the countryside with the eye of an artist:

> Elspeth and I have just come back from an evening walk, & we did wish Winnie could have been with us. We went along Swan Lane & the apple trees are all out on that island in the river and the trees and grass were incredibly green & the river green below us and pale blue in the distance, & a soft glow over everything.

She began riding lessons again, sometimes joined by Elspeth. There were many country expeditions, picnics and visits to Oxford, to enjoy the singing early on May mornings, to go on the river, or to see plays or the ballet, and these the sisters could enjoy together. Their criticism of productions are trenchant and knowledgeable, as when Elspeth writes scathingly of a performance of *The Tempest* by a lake, in which the costumes were a bizarre mixture of sixteenth-, seventeenth- and eighteenth-century styles and the music provided by a gramophone. Something of the idyllic atmosphere of life in the early days at Dalbeathie was recaptured in a Cotswold setting.

Beside the hard work and the fun of her life at Burford, another element came in about which Katharine spoke little, but which clearly marked an important turning point in her life. She gave up her association with the Unitarian Church and became a member of the Church of England. Although the family tradition of the Briggs, including her father, had been with the Unitarians, there had never been any opposition to the Anglican Church, and many of the family had attended church services as well as those in the Unitarian Chapel. It seems that Katharine and her sisters had been baptized in an Anglican church in London. Ernest and Mary do not seem to have attended Unitarian services very often, except when on family visits. Katharine had clearly been going to church for some time, as letters during her time in the WAAF indicate, while her close friendship with Evelyn Goshawk and her husband Charles, who was Vicar of Hobling in Lincolnshire, meant that she was familiar with the Anglican tradition. The two elements missing in Unitarian services, the sacramental and the mystical, were those most likely to appeal to Katharine. Her study of religion in the seventeenth century must have caused her to give much thought to this, and she was attracted by various Anglican writers, particularly by Evelyn Underhill, according to Evelyn, as well as by the sermons of George MacDonald. She attended church at Burford from the time that she moved there, and in May 1947 took part in a Parochial Mission led by Fr Charles Preston and Fr Gilbert Elliot, two friars from the Society of St Francis, with two sisters from the Order. It was after this that she resolved to be confirmed, and after preparation she was received into the Church on 5 November 1947. On the second Sunday in Advent she was confirmed by the Bishop of Dorchester, Dr G.B. Allen, along with twenty-three other candidates.[11] The following year she was elected on to the Parochial Church Council, and from this time on her connection with the church was close. She became a quietly loyal member, attending early services and the special services of Holy Week with unfailing regularity, while she also organised plays to support the church and was generous in her giving. Elspeth also intended to join the Anglican Church after their mother's death, but she herself died before this could come about.

The constant need for Elspeth and Winifred to move to and fro, taking turns to keep their mother happy at Dalbeathie, must have been a strain on them all. Elspeth shows this when she wrote to her mother from Burford, asking if she might stay a little longer:

> I'm afraid it's leaving you & Winnie alone at Dalbeathie an awfully long time, but we have got so involved in things here, & it would mean leaving Katharine such a lot to do & finish off that I don't like to leave her alone to do it. ... I do hope this isn't leaving too much on you & Winnie at home. ... I wish I could be in both places at once.

All three daughters gave devoted service to their mother, but of them all it was Elspeth, the youngest and the delicate one in childhood, who was the closest to her. The letters show the cruel quandary in which she found herself, for she longed to be with Katharine and to help with the decorating of the Barn House, but knew that her mother needed her. There is not even a hint that she resented being placed in a position where her own wishes and interests always took second place. Katharine fully appreciated this side of Elspeth's character, and expresses this in a poem written for one of her sister's birthdays at Dalbeathie (*App. 4, viii*):

> She does her tasks and makes no stir.
> No kindly office is too low
> And no delight too dear to leave
> When kindness calls, she scarce will grieve
> To break imagination's flow
> In her own books, and rise and go
> On slightest errands.

Winnie, unfailingly loyal to Katharine and unselfish in her care for her mother, was less resigned, and still had fits of passionate anger and occasional breakdowns. She found it hard to come to any decision on her own, and worried constantly, and quite unnecessarily, about money. She had to go away for treatment from time to time, and at one point went to stay with Aunt Nell's daughter Dorothy, while Elspeth managed Dalbeathie with Katharine's help. Their mother came down to the Barn House several times, and Katharine evidently hoped at first that they could all settle down there together, but Mary could not be happy away from Dalbeathie. She always pined for her own home, and the doctor advised her return to Scotland. As the years went by, Mary Briggs' sight became less reliable, and her mind confused. Her life was complicated by imaginary experiences. Once they took her to Crieff shopping, and bought a book for her with photos of the royal children, for their mother had always taken a great interest in the Royal Family. When they came back, Katharine told Winnie that Mary was convinced that she had seen the children climbing in at a window in Crieff: 'But I don't think that one has stuck. On the whole she seems well, I think.' On another occasion her mother thought that the puppets at a show in Burford were real people, and was perplexed to hear one of them speaking in Winnie's voice. Barbara Innes who stayed for some time with the sisters at Dalbeathie, remembers how when she sometimes met Mrs Briggs in the house, she would ask anxiously 'I hope they are looking after you?' Mary was always aware of her responsibilities as hostess and mistress of the house. The strain of keeping her contented was considerable, as Katharine discovered when alone with her. When she went to church on Ash Wednesday, leaving someone sitting with her mother, 'Mother thought it a very long time.' She did her best to amuse her — 'I tossed up the pancakes on Shrove Tuesday for Mother's amusement & she enjoyed it very much' — but her own work had to be abandoned:

> I haven't got anything done in the way of work. I generally get a few letters written when Mother is resting in the afternoons. But I generally rest myself a little then & there is sometimes washing to do, and I sometimes go out for a little turn and do shopping I can't ask Mrs Bridgeman to do. I am well into the routine of the work, & could go on quite comfortably as we are, but, as I say, I don't get anything else done.

Mary Briggs died at Dalbeathie on 13 September 1956, at ninety years of age. Before the end came, it had taken the three sisters all their time to look after her, and the strain and sadness must have told on them all. Mary was buried in the little cemetery at Caputh beside Ernest.

All this time Katharine had been steadily extending her knowledge of the world of folklore. Her thesis completed, she gave occasional talks, and at the suggestion of one of her examiners, a paper on seventeenth-century books of magic was given to the London Folklore Society in 1953. Afterwards she was approached by Colin Franklin, of Routledge and Kegan Paul, with the suggestion that some of her material should be made into a book, and from this time on Katharine was working on a series of books on supernatural beings and the effects of popular beliefs on literature: *The Anatomy of Puck* (1959), *Pale Hecate's Team* (1962) and *The Fairies in Tradition and Literature* (1967).

Before these appeared, however, she had published *Hobberdy Dick,* a story for children, the first of her books to be accepted for publication without payment, which was brought out by Eyre and Spottiswood in 1955. She was already writing this in 1951, since she refers to it in a letter to Dalbeathie, sent from a private nursing home, Acland House, after she had gone in to be examined for possible appendicitis. After a week she was discharged, as nothing serious was wrong, but while temporarily immobilised she turned to imaginative writing as her father used to do.

The work done in the *Personnel of Fairyland,* and the years of reading and thinking at Oxford, come here to fruition in a joyous fashion. Having marshalled her fairy people in order with due academic seriousness, she now has fun with them, bringing them into humorous, imaginative life in her story. The roll-call of supernatural beings haunting Widford Manor and the country round is like an echo from one of her favourite authors, Aubrey or Burton or Reginald Scott, listing the beings with which 'in our childhood our mother's maids have so terrified us.'[12] Beside Dick, the Brownie or Hob who had been at Widford Manor 'time out of mind' there is the ghost of an unhappy child in the west attic, a miser's ghost in the bedroom, a 'shadowy Grim' in the ruined chapel, and another aged Grim in Old Stow Church, who sometimes appeared as a black dog. There is an Abbey Lubber at Swinbrook Manor, who 'since the Reformation ... had been a morbid creature, dedicated to the destruction of the house he inhabited', as well as Long George, a hob on a farm near the Windrush, with whom Dick used to play at ducks and drakes, and a small, good-humoured Taynton Lob with prick ears. Finally there are more sinister figures, a dubious company of black spirits and bogeys round the Rollright Stones, since 'the witch trials had raised up much mud lately, and the bogles and devils rose out of it like shrimps in a pond.' It is these engaging or sinister spirits of the Oxford countryside who determine much of the action, and react on the Puritan family which moves into the old Manor, until at last the desired end is brought about, Joel marries Anne, the rightful heir to the Manor, and they are left in possession. The chapter headings of the book are a selection of the spells and rhymes which Katharine used in her thesis, and out of her Oxford studies emerges the figure of Mother Drake, the witch who imprisoned little Martha (a childish version of the Maiden in Milton's 'Comus'), together with the picture of old Christmas customs condemned by the Puritans, and the link beween the Hobs and the fruitfulness of the land. Such however is the lightness of touch that there is no sense of heavy learning or whimsical antiquarianism to cumber the book. *Hobberdy Dick* is the only instance of a story by Katharine not derived from historical records or folktales, with the exception of 'The Witches' Ride' in 1938. *Hobberdy Dick* was illustrated by Jane

Kingshill, now living in London but still in touch with Katharine, and dedicated to her daughter Katharine, who was Katharine's godchild. It was reprinted by the Alden Press in 1938 and by Kestrel Books in 1976.

Among the characters is the unforgettable Mrs Dimbleby, the old grandmother able to free the house from the evil child-ghost, and give affection and understanding to the forlorn heroine. She had innate goodness and true Christian piety, and her gentle strength was sensed and feared by the Brownie, her champion and helper. He saw it as a luminous cloud surrounding her, which grew 'perilously bright' as she approached death, while her room in that troubled household was 'the only place where tranquility still dwelt.' The conflict between good and evil, as well as between two ways of thinking, which Neil Philip finds expressed in this tale, comes out with unforced clarity, as it had never done in the earlier novels. It is not expressed now through the arguments of human characters, but through the evocation of the characters from the Other World. To quote Neil Philip again, neither this book nor *Kate Crackernuts*[13]

> are simple-minded books, nor anti-rational ones, and both foresee a partnership of instinct and reason. The thematic basis of both books is the same: it is not the action of our brains which redeems us, but the 'goodwill of our hearts.'

There is naturally a close link between *Hobberdy Dick* and the two volumes published in 1959 and 1962, *The Anatomy of Puck* and *Pale Hecate's Team*. In these Katharine brings together a treasury of booklore and folklore on the supernatural world, and deals with the vexed question, of great interest to folklorists, of links between popular beliefs and literary tradition. The first is concerned with the fairies of Elizabethan and Jacobean literature, and evidence for popular beliefs from the countryside which have found their way into the work of many seventeenth-century poets. The second book deals with witch beliefs in the same way. If the reader hopes to find answers to such questions as 'What are the origins of fairies?' or 'What is the basis of the phenomenon of witchcraft?' he will be disappointed. Katharine's mind did not work in that way. But she has made an important and original contribution to the subject of fairy mythology, first discussed by Keightley and Hartland in the nineteenth century, by showing how dominant intellectual theories, the social climate, the influence of court fashions, church teaching and the interests of learned antiquarians merged with popular lore. She sought out traditions about fairies and witches among simple-minded countrymen and also among learned men, poets and dramatists, and she found an abundance of little known material both in the main works of the period and in neglected corners of literature. Thus her work is likely to be of value long after books of theorists like Lewis Spence and Margaret Murray have become out-of-date curiosities. She showed also the strength of the two-way traffic between the printed word and oral tales and rhymes, and how potent this can be in creating myths and perpetuating legends.

The books received good reviews, and awakened a wide interest in many readers. They appealed not only to those interested in the literature of the period, but also to those who longed to know more of the origin of Shakespeare's fairies, ghosts and witches, and the tradition lying behind such unforgettable figures as Puck and Ariel. Even W.J. Rose, that relentless spotter of inaccuracies, proved kind.[14] He found one footnote on Psellos which was 'sheer nonsense' and a few misleading references to the classics, but concluded: 'Alteration of perhaps a dozen lines would rid the next edition (which the book well deserves) of these and other trifling slips.' This from him was indeed an accolade. *Pale Hecate's Team* has less life and enthusiasm than the first book, possibly because Katharine basically disliked witchcraft, but is full of good and unusual material. 'Sad and grim though the subject is on the whole' she wrote of witchcraft, 'it is not wholly without its lighter aspects', and these she brings out, as well as exploring one little investigated aspect of the subject, the relationship between witches and fairies. Her instinctive sympathy with some of the supernatural beings in the literature is in keeping with *Hobberdy Dick,* and brings a new interest into some of the duller corners of Jacobean literature, while she can throw light upon their origins and relationships in a way perceptive and surprising:

> Pug in *The Divill is an Ass,* is an even less effectual agent of evil, though he is incompetent rather than friendly. It is difficult not to feel a certain affection for this sad and innocent little devil. ... This is no fallen angel, but a boggart, dobie or bwbach, a devil of the same kind as that tricked by the Shropshire farmer in *Tops and Bottoms,* with his innocent cry of 'When do we wiffle-waffle, mate?'
>
> *Anatomy of Puck,* p. 74

Katharine's strength in these books, then, is not in the working out of elaborate theories, but in her sensitive appreciation of literature, learned or popular, and of the links between the different types, her ability to seize on relevant material, often from very obscure sources, and her robust common sense, as when she points out that some folklorists tend to forget that things may be done purely for fun:

> I have heard someone say, for instance, that in the Basque Provinces when the young men black themselves and black the girls it is part of a fertility rite. Anyone who has seen a group of little boys who have blacked their hands on a pot will be sceptical about this. The boys run about blacking everyone they can catch; the girls scatter and scream, but if any one of them is not blacked she is secretly a little hurt, not because she thinks she is doomed to sterility but because she does not like to be ignored.
>
> *Pale Hecate's Team*, p. 7

The third book, *The Fairies in Tradition and Literature*, forms a bridge between *Personnel of Fairyland* and *The Anatomy of Puck*, for it was while she was working on the fairies of the seventeenth century, she explains in her preface,

> I found so many accounts of the fairies that belonged to later times that it seemed to me worth pursuing the subject and examining the survival of fairy beliefs and the various fashions in the literary treatment of fairies, from Shakespeare's time to the present day.

She also reiterates her attitude to fairy beliefs clearly and succinctly:

> As in my earlier books, I have no special axe to grind. This is not an attempt to prove that fairies are real. My intention has been to report objectively what people believed themselves to have seen. My standard has been truth to tradition rather than truth to fact.

In this book she moves a step away from the academic world of literary history, and nearer to the popular reading public. Many of these, of course, remained utterly unaware of such statements as that just quoted, and thought of her in later years as an old lady who believed in fairies, but such was the price of increasing fame. The book is a delightful one, the old patterns of *The Personnel of*

Fairyland worked out anew, elaborated under such chapter headings as 'Hobgoblins and Imps', 'Times and Seasons', 'Changelings and Midwives'. In the last section she treats such subjects as the moralizing fairy tales and the whimsy in modern fairy books, taking up her earlier crusade against the degenerate fairy world of children's literature in recent years.

The three fairy books all contain lists of fairy beings. In *The Personnel* there are 188 items, ranging from Afanc to Will o' the Wisp. There is a shorter list in *The Anatomy of Puck,* and a much longer one in *The Fairies in Tradition and Literature.* The lists overlap. but are not identical, as they were compiled to extend the material used in each book. It was these lists which paved the way to Katharine's later *Dictionary of Fairies,* produced by Penguin Books in 1976, which was a deservedly popular treasury of fairy lore. It was indeed as if Katharine had discovered a rare new world of inexhaustible riches. One cannot compare her books on the fairies with those of others working in the same field, for she was a pioneer and stands alone.

Meanwhile there had been momentous changes in Katharine's life, while she was occupied with the fairy books, some of them painful ones. After her mother's death, Dalbeathie House was finally sold, and this must have been a major uprooting. In the *Album on Dalbeathie* the departure from the house is recorded as taking place in June 1958, after the family had been there for forty-seven years. The same year, on 5 January, Katharine had a serious motor accident, from the effects of which she was never fully to recover. She and Winifred both drove, and were accustomed to long journeys by road, and Katharine had possessed a small Mini, a Renault, a Standard Estate, a Hillman Minx, an MG and a Jaguar at various times. However, though a careful driver, she was not free from faults, and had not been accepted as a driver in the WAAF because of sight defects. Her worst fault was driving too slowly, and crossing roads in top gear without changing down. This was what caused her accident, as she was hit by a fast car coming on her right as she drove across a main road and did not accelerate fast enough. When they cut her out of the smashed car, her first words were: 'I should be at a rehearsal. Please make my apologies.' Her leg was badly broken, and when it was set at the Radcliffe, the setting did not prove wholly satisfactory. There were further attempts to reset it, but these were not successful. The accident meant giving up many of the physical activities which she had greatly enjoyed, but she characteristically accepted this hard fact without self-pity or recriminations, and refused to let it prevent her leading an active life.

She was walking with a stick at Dalbeathie in the summer, when she was arranging for the selling of the house. Her fierce love for the place and for her father's memory comes out in Patricia Atkinson's description of her first meeting with Katharine, when her parents, Sir Fenton and Lady Atkinson, came to make an offer for the house.[15] Katharine had firmly rejected other prospective purchasers of whom she did not approve. 'It doesn't matter what they offered', she told the no doubt scandalised house-agent, 'they are *not* having our home.' The Atkinsons were clearly an ideal family, but Katharine was determined to be sure, and was more dictatorial than was her wont:

> I will never forget, Dr Katharine's first words to me were 'Are there more of you?' She was so keen to have a family home. And then 'Do you do anything?' — not my job, nursing, but i.e. did I act or do guides etc. Luckily the answers must have satisfied her and the fact that we attended the Episcopal Church.

They were ready to agree to keep Dalbeathie as nearly as possible as Ernest had left it. Several of his enormous pictures were left on the walls, together with some of Winnie's flower paintings. The decoration was to remain the blue which her father had chosen, now in a rather faded condition but fortunately not unattractive, while the bath, an outstanding period piece, was not to be replaced, and so on. Katharine sat there with her stick, a rather fierce figure like a beneficent but dangerous fairy godmother, as she interrogated them and made her conditions. Clearly the selling of Dalbeathie awoke powerful emotions in her which caused her to act contrary to her usual nature. She would have liked to have kept the house in the family, but no one would take on the responsibility. So what could be fitted in at Burford was taken there, and many fine items of furniture and pictures distributed to relatives, as had happened when Pull Wyke was sold. Katharine steadfastly refused to sell her father's pictures, but the enormous size of many of them made it increasingly difficult to find them suitable homes. She was indeed fortunate to find a family prepared to respect her wishes and love and cherish the beautiful house in its unforgettable setting. The faithful MacKillups, Jimmy and Janet, stayed on with the new owners,

Jimmy having worked for Mrs Briggs as a boy and returned to Dalbeathie after his war service.

Thus Katharine and her sisters were at least free from Dalbeathie and permanently established in Burford. By this time the neighbours were accustomed to them. They had at first found them surprising, alarming and a little comical, with their strange preoccupations about art and drama, their incredible energy and their mixture of princely hospitality and freedom from convention. They had, for instance, some unusual hats with the crowns made of soft material and large straw brims, which they would wear on hot days for shopping in the High Street, caring nothing for current fashions. 'There go the three Miss Briggs in their funny hats', commented the girl in the chemist's shop one day, in the hearing of Evelyn's daughter who was shopping in Burford.[16] Not surprisingly, there were garbled accounts of Katharine's researches. The daughter of a friend went to call on her, after describing her jokingly as the 'Witch Doctor', and was somewhat taken aback to find her with one of the Siamese cats perched on her shoulder. 'They just sit on the floor, eat honey and read poetry', was another summary of their activities.[17] Katharine herself seems sometimes to want to build up such a picture, as when she told the interviewer for *The Sunday Telegraph* about her life in Burford: 'We all painted and wrote. People came to stay. We made jam.'[18]

Most of Burford fell under her spell, even though individuals might criticize or find Katharine rather overpowering when she sought to impose the standards she desired at rehearsals. But people delighted to attend parties at the Barn House, always surprising and unusual. Katharine sometimes laid out beautiful illustrated volumes for her guests to see, or arranged little exhibitions of Winnie's paintings, or organised story-telling sessions. The Guild of Arts which Katharine and Faith had formed used to meet there, even if it did not prove the kind of powerhouse which Katharine had originally envisaged:

> 'Oh yes, I love to come and listen', was a typical comment from members, 'but don't ask me to DO anything.' So it remained a rather middle-class and middle-aged society, very useful as a centre where newcomers to Burford could meet and mix with like-minded neighbours, but not quite what Katharine and I had originally hoped for. However the Christmas parties (and sometimes the Hallowe'en ones) were hugely enjoyable, and these

did give scope for Guild members to entertain one another. There was such an atmosphere of old-time cordial hospitality about the Barn House that nobody wanted to think about an alternative meeting-place although we were beginning to realise that the family couldn't go on sacrificing their privacy for ever. They solved the problem themselves in the end by their gift of the re-built Church House, which was opened in December 1962 and has been an invaluable asset to the town ever since. (But for years we still flocked to the Barn on every possible excuse.)

Towards 1960 the sisters started a country dancing group, recalling the time when their house had really been a barn and Cecil Sharp himself had danced there. They had been experts in their Guiding days, and taught the steps while music was provided by a gramophone. This was very successful, but soon after a sudden blow fell. At the beginning of 1961 the sisters had influenza, and while they were apparently recovering Elspeth went down to fetch drinks for her sisters and suddenly collapsed in the kitchen with a severe coronary thrombosis. She was rushed to the Radcliffe, and it seemed at first as if she might recover, but she had a relapse and died within a few days, on 20 February 1961, at fifty-eight years of age. Winnie also collapsed with the shock and had to go away for treatment, so that when Elspeth died Katharine was alone, although her close friend Barbara Innes came down immediately from Scotland to be with her. Evelyn wrote:

> The loss of her sister was I think the major tragedy in Katharine's life, a shattering, almost overwhelming loss. Both emotionally and intellectually they were entirely at one, sharing outlook and interests in a near-unique way, as if they were twins. 'It was like being widowed', Katharine said to me.[19]

Beside this close sympathetic link with her sister, Katharine had intense admiration for Elspeth's abilities and character. Elspeth was educated at home, but she had considerable intellectual gifts, which her modesty and diffidence partially concealed from those who did not know her well. Her writing was kept up all her life, although often sacrificed to the demands of her family. While the historical novels are rather dull, they are scrupulously accurate, and she had a gift for feeling her way into the atmosphere of the past. Her lighter works have a sureness of touch which proves her to share Katharine's gifts for story-telling. She was somewhat overprotected by her family, especially in her girlhood, but she had a considerable strength of character which won great respect from Katharine. To her, Elspeth was a person of unselfishness, wisdom and complete integrity, and she accepted her judgement unquestioningly. To lose her sister meant therefore not only the end of happy companionship, shared creative projects and enjoyable discussions on literature and art, but the removal of the rudder which to some extent, strong individualist as she was, had guided her life.

The fact that Katharine survived the shock and pain without being broken by it was due to her strong religious faith, in which Elspeth had shared. She told her close friends, those to whom she could speak freely on such matters, that when Elspeth died it was as if God took her from her arms. Somehow she found the courage to go on living, helping Winnie, who was also shattered by the blow and had increasing periods of mental stress, making her difficult to deal with. Winnie, however, had also something to contribute; she looked after Katharine faithfully, with great efficiency. Always 'a Martha between two Maries', as Josephine Thompson called her, she cooked and ran the house with deft skill. Katharine was in need of her help in her increasing lameness, for she now knew that she would be lame for life. This too she accepted: ' "Oh well", she said ... "I shall just have to turn into an old lady a bit earlier than I expected." And she did, very gracefully, making the most of enforced physical inactivity by concentrating on her writing.' Katharine, according to Josephine, would declare that she was blessed with 'a zest for life', and that 'she consumed her own smoke'. Another favourite expression of hers, according to Katharine Law, was that in bleak periods of her life she would 'twiddle her mind.' Now once more all her courage and resolution were needed to accept suffering constructively instead of letting it destroy and embitter her. 'To consume one's own smoke' is a way of describing her capacity to turn painful experience into something positive.

As an imaginative memorial to Elspeth, Katharine and Winifred had the stone figures of the Virgin, St John the Baptist and St John the Evangelist over the south door of Burford Church restored. They had been mutilated at the time of the Reformation, and in view of the great interest which Katharine and Elspeth had taken in this period, it seemed a fitting memorial. Evie Forbes commented that although the sculptor had never seen Elspeth, the faces were exactly like her. Yet another gift to Burford was that of three cottages to be used as almshouses for old men. One was the cottage beside the Barn House, while the other two were designed by Winifred and built in Sweeps Lane. Katharine took a great interest in this project, and always tried to get to Burford in later years for meetings of the Trust. A third memorial to Elspeth was the publication by the Alden Press in 1962 of her novel, *Seven Bold Sons,* which she had considered to be the best of her books. It is the story of the family of Sir Thomas Brocas, who owned land in Hampshire, and the tragic effects of the Civil War on his sons and daughters.

Winifred lived on until 1966, when she fell in the garden, presumably from a stroke, and died after some days on 22 November. She too was a gifted woman, although continually unsatisfied with her work as a painter. She is the one of the three who remained sadly unfulfilled, but who gave loyal service to her mother and sisters, and whose organising powers and practical ability were outstanding. Loyal in her turn, Katharine said little of the problems associated with her sister in her later years.

Thus Katharine was left alone at the Barn House just when she was beginning to reap the harvest of years of hard work and creative ability, and was being recognised as a scholar and writer on fairies who had caught the attention of a wider public. Her gift for story-telling was now becoming known across the Atlantic. In 1959 she had attended the first Congress of the International Society for Folk-Narrative Research at Kiel and Copenhagen, and found herself welcomed as a recognised authority on folktales. In 1960 she had made her first visit to the United States, to Bloomington, Indiana and was an immediate success with the Americans, who admired her gifts as a story-teller and her energy and personality. She was asked to lecture at Bloomington and Columbus, and from that time onwards her links with America formed an important part of her intellectual and social life, while she also began to make closer contacts with the London Folklore Society.

Fame then, long sought after and desired, came to Katharine in her sixties. It only reached her when her links with her family were breaking; they had supported and believed in her, but to some extent held her back from wider achievements. With the deaths of her sisters, she lost much, but she was sustained by what might be seen as fairy gifts bestowed at birth: an ability to tell stories, and a gift for holding friends and making new ones. These lasting gifts were to make the final period of her life a rich and fruitful one.

6 Tales and Traditions : Work in Folklore

> *My contention is that any class of people, lettered or unlettered, may be a carrier of folklore. ... We are collecting not a cut stone but a water-rounded pebble.*
> *(K.M. Briggs, 'A Tentative Essay')*

One positive result of living alone was that it left Katharine free to form new friendships. It might well have been too late for a woman well into her sixties to do this, but the ebullient youthfulness of spirit and generosity of heart of the younger Katharine had not deserted her, and these are the qualities for which those who knew her in her last years remember her. The wisdom learnt during the War and in her years at Burford comes out in an essay written after Elspeth's death, published in *A Chaplet for Charlotte Yonge* in 1965. Katharine much enjoyed Charlotte Yonge's novels, and became an enthusiastic member of a group of twenty women scholars and writers founded in honour of the authoress by Margharita Laski and Georgina Battiscombe. Her essay is called 'Charlotte Yonge's Ethics; some Unfashionable Virtues.' One virtue which she finds emphasised in the novels is that of humility, and on this she comments:

> Humility is the crown of Christian graces, and those who are fortunate enough to be born with natural humility are not only a long step towards holiness but they are well equipped to taste happiness as well. Those of us who are cursed with a natural pride know that it is not only the greatest of spiritual sins but also the heaviest piece of baggage a man can carry through the world.[1]

This is an illuminating glimpse into Katharine's thinking at the time, and significant also is her comment on resignation, on which, she felt, Charlotte Yonge placed too much value:

> This is always the chief danger about resignation, that one can start resigning oneself too soon. It is as well to remember the homely proverb:

For every evil under the sun
There is a remedy or there is none;
If there is one, try to find it,
If there is none, never mind it.[2]

In one sense, there was no remedy for the death of her loved sisters and the end of a long companionship, but Katharine accepted this without bitterness. However, the three of them had not been inward-looking or desirous to keep out the rest of the world; they had always welcomed and needed their friends, and sought for communal activities to enrich their lives. In her loneliness Katharine at first turned to various familiar occupations, baking bread, for instance, in the bleak days following Elspeth's death. She then turned to work which stood ready to her hand, which would bring her more contacts with others. She was already committed to activities in Burford, and she now allowed herself to an increasing extent to become involved in the affairs of the London Folklore Society.

Katharine had joined the Society in 1927, when she wanted to find out more about fairies and folktales. After the War she kept in touch by means of the journal *Folklore*, occasional attendance at London meetings, and use of the Society's Library, a unique collection of books and periodicals on folklore lodged in University College. Katharine turned to it, as to many other collections, in search of anything relevant for her *Dictionary of Folk-Tales*, a project which she had proposed to Colin Franklin, and which Routledge agreed to publish. In 1958, she published a letter in *Folklore*:

> I am setting to work on a Dictionary of British Folktales, and have already received some valuable material from members of the Society. I should be most grateful if any members who know of unpublished tales, or variants of tales, would be so kind as to put me on the track of them.[3]

This was clearly an ambitious project, for no extensive collection of English folktales, including local legends and oral narratives of various kinds, had ever been attempted. Comparatively few *Märchen,* 'fairy tales' of the type collected by the Brothers Grimm and others, have survived in England, and little attempt had been made to treat the wealth of English local legends seriously. Katharine told her publishers that the work would take her ten years to complete. She outlined the principles on which she was to work in *Folklore* in 1960.[4] In her usual optimistic way, she had at first meant to include material from all over the British Isles, but had to recognise that this was impossible. The amount from Scotland, Wales and Ireland was enormous, and could not be studied without knowledge of the Celtic languages, and in any case it was already being collected and studied in Edinburgh, Cardiff and Dublin. Katharine therefore decided to limit herself to the English tales: 'I have therefore with deep regret abandoned this mass of beautiful material to be dealt with later, by a worthier scholar.'

Katharine realised that a collection of English tales was greatly needed, and knew that much excellent material existed in scattered sources little known to the general reader. In many books of tales, like those of Joseph Jacobs which had aroused her own interest in childhood, the stories were rewritten and presented in a way which the author felt at the time to be suitable, but which might be considerably removed from oral tradition. Ideally, each tale needed to be traced back as far as possible to establish its variants and local background, but when hundreds of tales were involved, such a task was hardly possible for one individual working alone. Katharine's method was to build up card indexes: one, of collections of tales already available; a second, of individual tales, with titles; a third, of Scottish, Irish and Welsh tales for comparison; and a fourth with texts of the tales or summaries of the longer ones. In summarising the tales and getting her material typed she depended greatly on her friend Margaret Nash-Williams, who had been with her at Lady Margaret Hall. When she finally retired from teaching, she was persuaded by Katharine to move to a small house in Burford, so that they were near neighbours. Margaret's assistance was particularly valuable to Katharine because of her knowledge of Latin and other languages.

The search for tales gave Katharine the opportunity to visit pleasant places and meet congenial people. She was working largely from books, and was not greatly concerned about the occasions on which the tales were told or how they were transmitted. However, as Stewart Sanderson points out in the first Katharine Briggs lecture of 1981,[5] she was also a very sociable person, who 'retained through life an enquiring mind which was receptive to new ideas.' Thus she did not confine herself to libraries, but went out to meet those interested in folk-tales and those who still practised story telling, whenever she could. She learned to use a tape-recorder to collect short tales and legends from various friends and acquaintances.

Her own library was considerably enhanced as the work grew, since she bought many of the books she used. She was helped here by her friend Katharine Watson, who ran an excellent small bookshop in Burford and found some of the rare volumes which Katharine needed. Through the generosity of Katharine Law, this section of her library has now been given to the University of Leeds and remains intact to benefit other workers in the field. Katharine now possessed the great advantage of being free to travel, and so could follow up new trails wherever they beckoned.

In spite of the recognition given to her earlier work on the seventeenth century, Katharine remained to a large extent a lone scholar outside the main academic stream, like many others working on folklore in England. She did not need to turn to any organisation for financial help, but the danger of such isolation and independence was lack of stimulation and criticism from other scholars. However she made many and varied contacts, and found friends to give her help and encouragement. One of these was Christina Hole, then Honorary Editor of the journal *Folklore,* who ran the Oxfordshire and District Folklore Society with Professor James. Christina, 'one of the last of the nineteenth-century cultivated ladies who never went to College', had proved that it was possible to collect folklore without elaborate organisation or fuss; as she herself describes it:

> I was often able to learn a great deal in the course of ordinary conversation without my informant realizing that I was doing so. I was struck then, as I have been constantly since in many other parts of England, by the vigorous survival of numerous ancient beliefs and customs that are usually thought to be dying or dead.[6]

This was very much Katharine's own approach. In 1959 Christina became joint editor of *European Folk Tales,*[7] responsible for selecting the English material for this. Thus she and Katharine had interests in common.

Katharine also came into contact with Stewart Sanderson, one of the few folklorists in England working in the academic field. As Director of the Institute of Dialect and Folk Life Studies in the University of Leeds, he inspired and helped many graduate students working on folklore and oral literature, and he became a member of the Council of the Folklore Society in 1963. Both Leeds and Edinburgh were familiar ground to Katharine. In Edinburgh she had the rich archives of the School of Scottish Studies, which included many recordings of oral tales, while at Leeds she could use the notebooks of T.W. Thompson, a collection of stories and lore collected from gypsies in northern England during the First World War. She was in touch also with Peter and Iona Opie, who were extending the whole range of folklore studies with their collection from schoolchildren, and with Theo Brown in Devon, who had collected material from the West Country for many years. In the 1960s Katharine met Ruth Michaelis Jena, who was working on the tales of the Brothers Grimm; Katharine selected English material to be translated into German in a book edited by Ruth and herself, *Englische Volkmärchen,* which was published in 1970. Ruth wrote a warm appreciation of Katharine's work in *The Witch Figure,* published as a tribute to Katharine on her seventy-fifth birthday in 1973.[8]

Katharine also had the benefit of the Norton collection of tales, written out in longhand in six large notebooks, and catalogued according to the Motif Index of Antii Aarne and Stith Thompson. The tales were taken from printed sources, carefully copied out and arranged in order by F.J. Norton of Cambridge. He generously passed these over to Katharine, and many of them were incorporated into the *Dictionary.* His collection is now part of the archives of the Folklore Society in University College.

Such contacts stimulated and inspired Katharine, and she encountered some vigorous characters outside the field of printed books. In Scotland she heard Jeannie Robertson sing traditional songs, and met some fine story-tellers among gypsies and travelling men, recorded by Hamish Henderson and others. Through contact with Enid Porter, curator of the Cambridge Folk Museum, she discovered the forceful old story-teller of the Fens, Jack Barrett, whose racy tales were being published with Enid Porter's help. An even more fruitful association was with Ruth Tongue, the daughter of an army chaplain in Taunton, who had collected songs, rhymes and tales in Somerset from childhood, and was herself a gifted singer and teller of stories.

Ruth had an apparently inexhaustible supply of unpublished material and Katharine was corresponding with her by the late 1950s, and invited her to stay at the Barn House. She put Ruth in touch with Faith Sharp, Assistant Editor of *The Countryman,* and sections of Ruth's book, *The Chime Child,* appeared in the magazine in 1965, and was published by Routledge two years later. Faith was impressed by Ruth's tunes, and with her permission made trio arrangements of them for the little local choir at Burford. 'Enchanting', one sophisticated listener declared, 'but surely not genuine folksong? It's too good to be true.'[9] This is an instinctive reaction to much of Ruth Tongue's material, because of what seems to be the deliberate artistry of her songs and tales. Nevertheless she clearly had an unsurpassed knowledge of Somerset traditions, riding round the countryside on her pony from her home in the Quantocks, and well-known as a singer and herb-doctor.[10] She herself claimed she was entrusted with much secret lore because she was a 'Chime Child', born between midnight on Friday and cockcrow on Saturday. Now most of her informants were dead, so she felt free to tell what she knew, and she rejoiced in the chance to broadcast and to speak at Women's Institute meetings, collecting fresh material from her audiences. Katharine was fascinated by her rich repertoire and made extensive use of her tales. She realised it was not easy to check Ruth's credentials:

> Ruth Tongue's method of reporting a story cannot pretend to scientific accuracy, though she is careful to record the narrator or narrators of each tale, and to make it clear when she has pieced the story together from fragments, but her long and intimate connection with the people of Somerset has made it possible for her to discover things carefully hidden from the 'foreign' collector.[11]

Feeling that this material should be recorded, Katharine was responsible for the publication of Ruth Tongue's *Somerset Folklore* by the Folklore Society in 1965. She edited the confused records, wrote an introduction, and saw the book through the press, as well as contributing £300 towards publishing costs. With characteristic generosity, she put Ruth Tongue's name alongside her own on the titlepage of *Folktales of England,* which also appeared in 1965 in a series edited by Richard Dorson and published by the University of Chicago, because she had used a number of Ruth's stories in the book. One further volume of Ruth's tales, *Forgotten Folklore of the English Counties,* was published by Routledge in 1970, also with an introduction by Katharine after much of Ruth's collected material had been destroyed in a fire at her cottage.

In 1961 Katharine was elected a member of the Council of the Folklore Society, when Professor Mary Williams, the elderly Celtic scholar, was President. Katharine had read a paper to the Society in 1953, the result of which had been the publication of *The Anatomy of Puck*, and made various contributions to the journal.[12] In 1960 she gave £200 to the Publication Fund, being shocked to discover that nothing except an Index to the journal had been published for many years. In fact, although there were gifted individuals like Peter Opie on the Council, the Society at this time was living on its past and going through a lean and depressing period. Once a dazzling array of scholars had attended its meetings, while a long line of books in the familiar brown and gold covers appeared from the time of the Society's formation in 1878.[13] But while subjects like anthropology and sociology won academic recognition, folklore studies in England remained in a kind of limbo, while the general image of the Society beame one of an oddly dressed group of individuals with an interest in magic. The fact that one Council Member had opened a popular witch museum on the Isle of Man and published books on practising witchcraft hardly improved matters.

When Katharine came on to the Council, affairs were largely in the hands of the Honorary Treasurer of the Society, who for many years had acted as Honorary Secretary also. She was a well-meaning but dominating elderly widow, who, together with her sister who was also on the Council, viewed the Society as a family concern. Their brother had been a devoted folklorist in the early days, and after his death the sisters gave the Society dedicated service and generous gifts of money to keep it afloat. During the bombing of London, the Honorary Treasurer had made heroic efforts to rescue the archives from University College, and they now gathered dust in her attic, while papers and correspondence, in a state of wild confusion, piled up in a small back room of her house in Highgate. She was apt to embark on a long history of the Society on any pretext, complaining of lack of support from the Council and of the misdeeds of many of its members. She wrote long and controversial letters, made interminable telephone calls to her colleagues, and had many strange prejudices, one of which was against anything originating in America. The monthly Council meeting became an extravaganza, leaving members exhausted and frustrated with no business done. The President, elected for two years at a time, was intended under this regime to be an elderly academic, who would add lustre to the

Society but never interfere unduly. After one had walked out during his first experience as Chairman, never to return, and Peter Opie, who had begun to instil new life into the Society, felt driven to give up after one year, the Folklore Society appeared to have no future. It was at this unpropitious moment that Katharine was elected on to the Council.

Katharine had two great advantages in this internecine struggle. First, she possessed a natural dignity and the control of a well-bred lady who never openly lost her temper. She never even raised her voice, however great the provocation. This control was the more impressive in view of her own statement towards the end of her life, that 'she was naturally quick-tempered, had a biting tongue and did not suffer fools gladly.'[14] But beneath this quiet courtesy she possessed steely resolution and never gave up. Secondly, she was in a position to counter the Honorary Treasurer's policy of spending her own money to get her own way; Katharine also had a reliable solicitor and other experts available, and could consult them at her own expense if this seeemed necessary. She gradually became the recognised leader of revolt, and in due course was invited to stand for President. By this time the Presidential Office had assumed something of the menace of the Dangerous Quest in the fairytale; few were bold enough to accept it. Douglas Kennedy of the Folk Dance and Folk Song Society had striven manfully in his term of office, but the term was now drawing to a close. As the AGM of 1967 approached, the Honorary Secretary did everything in her power (and in terms of letters and phone calls this was a good deal) to prevent the election going through. She tried hard to find convincing reasons for keeping Katharine out of office, claiming that 'she has had no business experience and has apparently always lived in small towns except for being at college in Oxford'.[15] She accused her of falsely claiming to be a Fellow of the Librarians' Association, this being based on a secretarial error over Katharine's qualification of FIAL (Fellow of the Institute of Art and Letters); she even implied that Katharine's judgement was not to be trusted because 'she had spent some years in the unwholesome study of popular witchcraft.' The Honorary Treasurer also did her best to oppose the election of Venetia Newall as Honorary Secretary, declaring that she wore unsuitable hats and was too young for the post. Finally she arranged that, should the election go through, the Assistant Secretary should threaten resignation, so that there would be no one to run the office.

However at the AGM the members stood firm, the resignation was calmly accepted, and Katharine duly became President in March 1967, with Venetia Newall as Honorary Secretary.

If there were any doubts as to Katharine's strength of character and powers of effective organisation, the transformation of the society under her leadership would be sufficient to dispel this. She had had to endure cruel and wounding attacks before the election, while she had undergone the painful experience of Winifred's death about six months earlier. But she remained in good heart, and indeed the crusade to free the Society may have helped her to recover from her losses and take up the business of living without her sisters. Once installed as President, she wasted no time on recriminations or complaints, but turned to action.

The written records scarcely do justice to her achievements during her three years as President from 1967 to 1970. Her three Presidential addresses, 'The Transmission of Folklore in Britain', 'Heywood's Hierarchie of the Blessed Angels', and 'The Fairies and the Realm of the Dead'[16] are based on earlier work and do not break new ground; they are adequate but not outstanding. It was the strength of her personality, and the energy, tact and enthusiasm with which she worked behind the scenes, with no attempt at self-advertisement, which made her so effective as President. To establish peace and efficiency in the everyday running of the Society's business proved no easy matter. The first four secretaries engaged left after very brief periods, unable to cope with the confusion in the books or alarmed and distressed by an encounter with the Honorary Treasurer. Katharine remained calm and undismayed, patiently coming up to interview fresh applicants, and encouraging them, until at last the office settled down. Venetia Newall, once she was permitted to get control of the records and left free to act, proved a capable and gifted organiser: 'She gives a constant dedication to the interests of the Society unrivalled even amongst the most devoted members in the past', Katharine wrote of her some years later.[17] At the AGM of 1968, after Katharine had been a year in office, the Honorary Treasurer retired, and the President graciously presented her with a brooch of gold and Tay pearls which she had had specially made after the design of the Society's emblem, a branch of mistletoe.

One of Katharine's first tasks was to revise the constitution of the Society. The original one was now out of date, and it seemed right to review it in the light of changed conditions. A small committee was appointed, and Katharine turned what could have been a dreary and controversial activity into a pleasant occasion. She invited the committee to the Sesame Club in Belgravia and provided delicious teas to cheer them in their labours. Her experience at Dalbeathie and Burford had made her realise how much more reasonable and creative people are likely to be if they are enjoying themselves in comfortable surroundings. Under her benign influence, it was decided to hold an annual dinner, and to replace the former Council by a committee, with an additional council of Officers and Honorary Members who were distinguished folklorists. The new constitution was carried through with the minimum of fuss, and has worked very satisfactorily ever since.

She also set about arranging an Anglo-American Conference at Ditchley Park in September 1969. This beautiful eighteenth-century house, built for the Earl of Lichfield, is now a conference centre, 'for study and discussion of matters of common concern to Britain and America.'[18] With the help of Richard Dorson of the Folklore Institute in Indiana, Katharine succeeded in holding a joint conference of eleven American and twelve British delegates, with Venetia Newall acting as Secretary, to discuss the future of folklore studies. The American participants obtained a grant for expenses, and Katharine contrived to pay the fees of the British group from the Society's funds, to which she herself generously contributed. She took great delight in planning this meeting of folklorists in beautiful, serene surroundings, with an open day in which others were invited to Ditchley Park for a crowded meeting. Those who stayed in the house will long remember one golden evening when the morris men danced on the black and white marble floor of the entrance hall. After the music and dancing had ended, Katharine stepped on to the centre of the floor and told the story of Mr Fox, one of her favourite English folk tales. She told it superbly, in that characteristic manner described by Katharine Lea, who knew her at Oxford:[19]

> She had a way with a story that put me in mind of the powers of story-tellers in earlier ages and simpler conditions. She wooed you with a tale. I can hear in my inner ear that purring tone with a tiny lisp, I think, that went on so softly that you daren't stir.

She was particularly happy when she could hold her audience spellbound in a memorable setting, in an atmosphere of gracious hospitality, and once more at Ditchley she achieved this, recalling earlier days at Dalbeathie. In such an atmosphere she was completely at home, a natural mistress of ceremonies, taking delight in the good fellowship, and bringing out the best in her companions.

It was also due largely to Katharine's support that a publishing scheme was at last brought to fruition, and a new series of publications by the Society, the Mistletoe Books, launched. She invited a small working party to stay at the Barn House to work out a list of possible titles and arrange to proceed with the first book. The series was to include new editions of rare source material, and Katharine immediately offered to set the ball rolling by lending her own 1715 edition of the *Autobiography of William Lilly,* the seventeenth-century astrologer, so that the text could be photographed, while she provided an introduction and notes. Although this did not appear until 1974, owing to the usual setbacks which affect publishing schemes, it was largely due to Katharine's loyal support and patience over the delay that the project ultimately succeeded.

Katharine held office for three years as President, and her successor, Stewart Sanderson, worked hard to get the publications and other plans forward, and to continue the Society's work on a firm and harmonious footing. Katharine continued to attend the meetings regularly, and was an excellent committee member, ready with sensible comments and generous offers of help, but never attempting to push her own views unduly. One of her excellent ideas had been for members to gather in a restaurant near University College for a meal after the meeting, and this meant that it was not very easy for her to get back to Burford the same night. Sometimes she stayed at the Sesame Club, and she sometimes arranged for a car to meet her at the nearest railway station to Burford, but it was a long and tiring journey for someone of her age after attending meetings in the afternoon and evening. One pouring wet night in winter the car failed to arrive, and she found the station deserted, with no telephone. Katharine, lame as she was, had to walk to the nearest house; she survived the misadventure, and made a good story out of it, but the long journey back to an empty house caused her friends some anxiety. Although she found walking slow and tiring, she refused to let this prevent her from travelling widely.

In 1968 her *Dictionary* was completed, and the story of how she delivered it to her publishers, to their incredulous surprise, on the appointed day fixed ten years earlier has become a legend. 'A publisher's dream', commented the *Telegraph:* 'Exactly ten years to the day she arrived at Routledge's offices with a trunkful of manuscripts' (others say it was a green suitcase). Katharine's own account of the episode was given to Margaret Hodges:

> I came struggling up to the publisher's office with a big box of manuscripts, which surprised them. If I had died leaving it incomplete, it would have burst like a bubble and all the work would have gone for nothing.[20]

The completed *Dictionary,* the first volume of which appeared in 1970, was indeed an impressive achievement. There were four massive volumes, with the material divided under the headings Folk Narrative and Folk Legends (i.e. stories once believed to be true), with further sub-divisions within each group: Fairy Tales, Jocular Tales, Local Legends, the Supernatural, and so on. She gave each tale its appropriate number according to the system used by Aarne and Thompson in their *Index of Tale-Types.*[21] The reviews were good, almost reverential in admiration and awe at the range of the material. *The Times* declared it to be 'a complete, authorative and seminal canon.' There were, inevitably, some limitations in so ambitious a project. The title — *British Folk-Tales* — Robin Gwyndaf felt was misleading;[22] while as Peter Opie pointed out in a review in *New Society,*[23] the history of various printed sources is often ignored. However the collection is so rich a treasure-trove to any one working on folk-tales that it might be claimed that Katharine was justified in not holding it back until she had followed up the history of individual tales more fully and produced adequate notes. Had she done so, it would almost certainly never have been completed. As she herself told Peter Opie: 'I've got to press on. I'm more up against Anno Domini than most people.'

It is possible, looking back on Katharine's early life, to see how her love of story-telling and her training in arranging confused source material prepared her for this daunting task to which few would have dared commit themselves.[24] We know that she hated to refuse a challenge, and this was one to which she responded triumphantly. Her delight in the tales themselves, since as a practised story-teller they meant far more to her than mere items in a theoretical scheme, enabled her to present them with love, enthusiasm and touches of humour in her brief, informal comments. The *Dictionary* appeared at a happy time for her. She was awarded the degree of Doctor of

Katharine at Burford in her doctor's gown, 1969.

Letters (D.Litt.) by the University of Oxford shortly before its publication, in recognition of her two books on seventeenth-century beliefs and her treatment of the supernatural in the literature of the period. This happened in October 1969, while she was still President of the Folklore Society, and was a great joy to her. She was photographed in her doctor's gown outside the Barn House, and was deeply happy to receive this recognition of her work as a scholar.

Meantime she was making visits abroad, discovering the possibilities of international conferences as a means of meeting folklorists from other countries, and new and appreciative audiences for her tales. She particularly enjoyed the company of Americans and their warm hospitality, which she reciprocated when they visited her in England, while they appreciated her story-telling gifts, her personality, and the glimpses which she offered them into an older, vanished world. Now that the *Dictionary* was completed, Katharine began to give an increasing number of papers at meetings and conferences. Indeed she gave so many that it was impossible for her to give much time and thought to the preparation of new subjects, and in general she re-used material collected earlier, relying on her skill in presentation to put the paper across. She often showed her special gifts more in discussion than in lecturing; she would produce a relevant source or tale to illustrate a point, and tell it unfalteringly from her place in the audience, to provide a telling parallel or suggest a different approach. Her memory for tales was amazing; like many famous story-tellers in oral tradition, she could draw on a huge number at will without hesitation or fumbling. She had, of course, one great advantage over other workers in the field of the folktale; she had told tales over many years and seen their effect on audiences, so that they were as familiar to her as work which she herself had composed. She continued to do some local collecting of traditions and stories, and her little book *The Folklore of the Cotswolds* published by Batsford in 1974, shows that much of the material in it was collected from neighbours and acquaintances.

Meanwhile her record of travel is an impressive one. In 1968 she was at a conference at Wurzburg and at the annual meeting of the American Folklore Society at Toronto. In spite of the responsibilities of the Ditchley Conference, she visited Los Angeles in 1969 and gave papers there, at Berkeley and at Bloomington, Indiana.[25] In 1970 she was made an Honorary Member of the American Folklore Society, and lectured to the University of Pennsylvania.[26] She was at the annual meeting again in 1971 and 1972, and in 1973 became Visiting Professor at the University of California, a demanding assignment for a woman of 74, and also guest of honour at the annual meeting at Tennessee.[27] In 1974 she was at Helsinki for the sixth congress of the International Society for Folk Narrative Research, and spoke on the tale of Kate Crackernuts. She made many new friends on her travels, and thus in old age she was able to satisfy her longing for new experiences, attempt impressive feats of energy and endurance, come into touch with a wider academic world, and use her gifts as a story-teller to entertain large audiences. She was able to try her hand at teaching students, who no doubt found her methods surprising. Faced with a class of untidy individuals who dropped ash and left chewing-gum everywhere, she provided them all with ashtrays and gave them practical suggestions on how to achieve more pleasant surroundings, while she divided them into two sections, those interested in fieldwork and those preferring to use books.

Margaret Hodges, Professor Emeritus of the University of Pittsburgh, never forgot Katharine's paper on Kate Crackernuts, which was never published. Katharine had taken the opportunity to tell the tale, and Margaret Hodges noted in her journal: 'Katharine Briggs is among the few who know and love the stories as stories.' In an article written after Katharine's death, she quoted the description of Mrs Dimbleby's voice in *Hobberdy Dick* as one which might be applied to Katharine herself when she told a story: 'The words dropped softly and slowly from the old lady, like the musing notes of a bird's evening song, seeming rather to belong to the silence than to break it.' Whilst American audiences appreciated her gifts, in English academic circles she made little headway. At one symposium in Cambridge, a distinguished anthropologist, who should have known better, was observed ostentatiously reading a book while she gave a talk on myths of origin in folk tales. Katharine was fully aware of this attitude of hostility, although she made light of it: 'I thought a few stories might cheer them up a little', she observed afterwards. She steadfastly, almost wilfully, refused to join in the academic exercises of analysing material, establishing theories, and demolishing those of other people; her method of pursuing truth was of a different kind, and had its limitations, but she followed it with integrity and singlemindedness.

She was becoming a successful broadcaster at this period, interviewed in Woman's Hour in 1973, and in a television programme on fairies in 1974, as well as taking part in a thirty-minute radio programme, The Realm of Fairyland. Her abilities as talker and story-teller, excellent memory and quiet compelling voice made her well-suited to the medium. In the winter of 1973, when she reached her seventy-fifth birthday, Venetia Newall organised a splendid reception in her honour, with the backing of the chairman and director of Routledge, at the Belfry Club in Belgrave Square. Venetia had edited a collection of papers by folklore scholars to present to Katharine, under the title of *The Witch Figure,* in recognition of her work on wizards and magicians. It was a happy occasion, in which Katharine held the centre of the group with dignity and charm, and enjoyed herself greatly. 'What a delightful party and what a wonderful presentation', she wrote afterwards; 'it is the kind of thing that I can never imagine really happening to myself.'[28] There was a kind of innocent delight in the way in which Katharine greeted such events, enjoying the compliments and the affectionate enthusiasm of her friends without a trace of self-confidence or arrogance.

In looking back over Katharine's work in folklore, it is not easy to define her special contribution. She was never a conventional, scholarly folklorist, limiting her activities to detailed, thorough studies of particular subjects, or tracing individual tales and traditions back through printed sources and defining their local background. Looking over her many papers published in the journal *Folklore* or given at various conferences, one searches in vain for clear statements about what she believed to be the work of the folklorist, or for any theoretical answer to such questions as that of the origin of fairy beliefs or of the practice of witchcraft. One brief exception is what she calls 'a tentative essay' published in 1962,[29] which begins with some basic questions to which we long to find an answer: 'What constitutes Folklore as a study? What are the objects towards which it is directed? What human activities are legitimately to be included in its scope?' She had heard these questions debated in America and on the Continent, for at that time they were felt to be very relevant to the development of folklore studies, and because of this, she says, she is now advancing some 'rather vague and tentative ideas' in the hope of awakening a response from other English folklorists.

This essay is typical of Katharine in its mixture of apparent naivety and good common sense, in its impatience with theoretical approaches, and its reluctance to follow up important questions. What might have developed into a valuable appraisal of the situation is suddenly abandoned just as our interest is aroused; she refuses to think the questions through. All that finally emerges is her appreciation that oral tradition and written literature are so closely intertwined that neither can exist without the other, and that folklore cannot be isolated as a 'pure' phenomenon. Yet this in itself is a valuable truth, brought out ably in the detailed studies included in her books on seventeenth century ideas of the supernatural world for which she received her doctorate. The appreciation of the two-way traffic between oral and written sources, between tales deliberately and artistically shaped by the writer and those told orally to a particular audience, was one of the important contributions which she made to folklore studies. Another was her revelation of the rich abundance of English tradition about the fairy world, and in *The Vanishing People* and elsewhere she was able to establish some of the laws and patterns governing it. In the books written at Burford she showed how different strands in literature, including scholarly theories about spirits, have joined with the oral tradition to build up the picture of the fairy world we know, literary masters as well as unsophisticated tellers of tales contributing their shares. Again in the later *Dictionary of Fairies* she establishes herself as a tradition-bearer, making this extensive collection of fairy lore available once more, not only for children but for older readers who retain their delight in the Other World conjured up by man's imagination and deepest instincts throughout the centuries.

In her collection of folktales there is again what feels like a deliberate withdrawal at times from scholarly investigation of the material. While producing a wealth of tales for future investigators, she made no serious attempt to arrange and index them conveniently. Norton had arranged his tales according to the internationally accepted index of tale types, and Katharine classified each tale individually according to this system, but to find any individual story one has to know what title she has given it. Many would disagree with her allocation of a particular tale into the rather vague category chosen for it. It is not fully clear which of the tales are summarized, or what the previous history of a number of tales in print has been. One reason for this was limitation of time, but it seems as if she was unwilling to do further investigation. The little paper on Kate Crackernuts given at Helsinki shows no attempt to make a serious study even of this one tale which she loved; a glance at its first appearance in *Longman's Magazine* would have made it evident that it could not have come from Orkney. Katharine's uncritical acceptance of Ruth Tongue's tales as examples of genuine oral tradition, so that she included a number of them in the collection of English folktales published in 1965, is another example of the instincts of the story-teller proving stronger than those of the scholar. Nor, as Robin Gwyndaf pointed out, did she ever attempt to tackle the vexed problem of the relationship between folk belief, memories, local or migratory legends and folktales proper.

It is not difficult to make such criticisms, but it must always be remembered that had the *Dictionary* not appeared it is highly unlikely that any other scholar would have attempted to bring together so large a body of existing English tales. There could indeed have been few people who had her long training in collecting stories enabling her to build up so extensive a body of material, or who possessed the means and energy to work independently for ten years on such a publication. In his review, Robin Gwyndaf calls attention to the lamentable lack of any institute of folklore in England such as exists in most other European countries, and more than a decade after he wrote, the need is as great as ever. Katharine's sincere hope, like that expressed in the 'Tentative Essay', was that she might stimulate others to carry on the work which she had begun. In some ways she seems to have possessed the uncritical innocence of the true tradition-bearer, who passed on the old tales and beliefs, enriching them by story-telling skills, but not tampering too much with them or attempting to analyse. As I have claimed elsewhere, she was much more than a collector of folktales:

> She might be called a tradition-bearer and an active one at that, gathering tales from multiple sources and retelling them to many different audiences, in a world where story-telling no longer forms a major part of our culture.

Her other great contribution to folklore studies should not be ignored: the forging of new links between scholars and the building up of the Folklore Society. She had a firm belief that the work of folklorists was worthwhile, and that there was a future for such studies, both for professionals and amateurs. She brought together many of the friends made both in the British Isles and in the United States and further afield, and so formed new contacts for other workers without her opportunities. While she herself was not prepared to meet the exacting demands of specialised scholarship in her collecting of tales and traditions, she had full and generous appreciation of others who were doing such work and did a great deal to bring them together and give them support. It would be a sad thing if in a period of increasing specialization we came to reject the work of the gifted amateur and of such a scholar as Katharine, who refused to make a sharp dividing line between creative intuition and critical analysis or to confine herself to one particular field. In her story-telling she was, in fact, working within the very tradition which she took as a field of study, and her hesitation about treating the tales as a wholly academic subject no doubt arose from an inner conviction that in so doing she might lose the power to pass them on creatively to a wider world.

It is noteworthy also that the work on folktales was done comparatively late in her life. She never lost the sense of wonder and delight in her work which some scholars of the analytical school never experience at all, or lose in their early years. Nor did she ever surrender the joy felt in exploration of new fields. It is not surprising that one of her favourite poems, recited to Margaret Hodges when they met at Helsinki in 1974, was Tennyson's *Ulysses,* for this sums up many of her own ideals as the years piled up for her:

> How dull it is to pause, to make an end,
> To rust unburnish'd, not to shine in use!
> As tho' to breathe were life. Life piled on life
> Were all too little, and of one to me
> Little remains: but every hour is saved
> From that eternal silence, something more,
> A bringer of new things.

It might seem odd to declaim a long poem to a new acquaintance, but Margaret had asked her to record some poetry for her, and also to tell her more about herself and her interest in folklore and folktales.[30] The choice of that poem must have been an instinctive one, since it expresses so much of Katharine's own hopes and beliefs. In the mid-seventies it seemed that her strength and energies were failing, but as things turned out, there was still much for her to experience and enjoy before her death.

7 Golden Harvest: The Last Years

If you rise up at morning and roam the whole world round
You'll see that lovely, joyful things throughout the world abound.
But of all the lovely, joyful things the best thing that I know
Is to sit rejoicing with my friends while the winter breezes blow.
                                    (K.M. Briggs, *Manuscript Book of Poems*)

In spite of all the pleasures and excitements which came to Katharine in the pursuit of folklore, life for her was becoming difficult — to an extent that even some of her close friends hardly realised — because she would never complain or ask for help. She remained very lame, and in 1971 had a second accident at Oxford when she was knocked down by a motor-cyclist. She was still recovering from the effects of this when she went to the first mini-conference of the Folklore Society at the University of Exeter, bringing Ruth Tongue with her and working hard to make it a success. But alone at the Barn House it was not so easy. She was determined to keep active, and with her usual resolute stance of never owning herself beaten, had a shower installed downstairs and organised her life on the ground floor. But the house was not conveniently arranged for a handicapped person, and the long path up to the garage was difficult and dangerous, particularly in winter. She had now no adequate permanent help, and various attempts to find someone to live upstairs and assist her never came to anything. Katharine was apt to offer accommodation impulsively to those whom she liked, and then find they had their own commitments and were not there when she needed them.

For many years she had depended on her loving and capable sisters for a background of domestic efficiency, only taking part when she felt inclined, and yet she still wanted to have visitors, for she was longing to talk and entertain and offer warm hospitality. She delighted to show them her library, as one visitor from the United States, Margaret Hodges, records in her journal:

> Katharine has a spacious and lovely old house with a garden of velvety lawn and beds of glorious roses. She gave us cream sherry by an open fire in her drawing-room, after which we had lunch at the Lamb Inn and returned to the Barn House to see Katharine's

library. It is lined to the ceiling with books, including many treasures of folklore and one whole alcove of rare books in fine bindings. Katharine gave us her afternoon, climbing nimbly up and down a ladder, in spite of her lameness, to put the precious volumes in our hands.

There were constant visitors in the 1970s. Kaye Webb came to discuss a new Kestrel edition of *Hobberdy Dick,* and was fascinated by Katharine's wartime reminiscences over lunch. One winter day Jeanine MacMullen came to interview her for a possible radio programme. She wrote years later:

> I am still your devoted fan and spend many hours listening to those tapes which I insisted on keeping in their original, unedited version before I allowed anyone to approach them with editing machines.[1]

To all her visitors Katharine gave of her best, and put all her energies into welcoming and entertaining them.

There was also dramatic work still continuing in the summer. A group of children had taken part in Katharine's production of *A Midsummer Night's Dream,* and some of these later formed themselves into a group known as The Young Visitors. The leaders were Jane Kingshill's children, Katie, Dannie and Sophie. One year Katharine made 'Childe Roland' into a play for them to act, and this was a delightful production, with the children tossing a golden ball in the picturesque setting of the Barn House garden. Another time they did *The Rose and the Ring,* with Katharine playing Bilbo. It became customary for the young people to come and camp at the Barn House in the summer, while Katharine rented the Church Hall for a fortnight and they gave a performance there at the end of their stay. As they grew older and wanted to produce their own entertainments, these summer periods became an additional strain on Katharine; some of their efforts were successful, like one excellent Variety Show they produced, but others, like the miming of the *Beggars' Opera,* were not well received by a Burford audience.

The last elaborate production in which Katharine herself took part was that of *The Tempest* in 1972, in which she played Prospero. The scenery was designed by Jane Kingshill, and the music composed by Jane's son Dannie, but the performance was very uneven. There were some fine moments, and the shipwreck scene was superbly done, but

Katharine was unable to remember her words, and the whole production was far too slow. She was no longer capable of such a sustained effort as that of producing a full-length Shakespearian play and also taking the main role. But indeed the choice of *The Tempest* and the words of renunciation and farewell by the old magician had clearly been deliberately made to mark Katharine's retirement from dramatic work, which had meant so much to her.

In December 1974 she had her third accident. She was coming into the committee room in University College when she suddenly slipped and fell awkwardly as her leg gave way under her. She was wheeled across the road to University College Hospital, where the new fracture was reset. She insisted on going home by Christmas, and was taken in an ambulance to the cottage hospital, to be near her friends. There she had to go through the process of learning to walk again on crutches. Movement was slow and difficult, and she must have endured a great deal of pain.

Katharine acting for the last time, as Prospero in *The Tempest*, Burford 1972.

It became essential that she should go somewhere where she could be looked after for a while, for her health was failing generally. Early in 1975 she went down to St Margaret's Bay near Dover to stay with Jean Melhuish, a daughter of Donald Briggs, married to a local doctor. Katharine had always kept in touch with Donald's family, and she and her sisters had each chosen one of his three daughters to whom to leave a share of the family money. Once arrived, Katharine was incapable of moving out of the house. She was confined to an upstairs room, still manfully trying to deal with the proofs of her *Dictionary of Fairies*, without her secretary or her books. She was alone a good deal during the day, and it was at this point that she was visited by Katharine Law, who lived not far away. The meeting between the two Katharines led to a friendship which was utterly to transform the last five years of Katharine's life.

Katharine Law lived at Southolme, a beautiful house built in the early years of the century, slightly reminiscent of Dalbeathie in style, although in a very different setting. The windows on one side looked over the English Channel, and the lights of the French coast could be seen on clear nights. Like Dalbeathie, the house seemed bathed in sunshine on summer days, and was surrounded by lawns and trees and a peaceful, half-wild garden, with a pond where toads assembled in the spring, a fox's earth, and many pleasant secluded corners in which to sit and talk. Katharine Law was an active, energetic Irishwoman who always seemed to have time for her many friends. For years she had done the kind of work which meant dealing with people, many of them people in trouble. After her husband was killed in the War, she joined the YMCA National Women's Auxiliary, helped to start the first Officers' Club in Rome, worked in soldiers' clubs elsewhere in Italy, and was about to transfer to the Far East when the war ended. Then she trained as a probation officer, and after retirement still kept busy as Joint Chairman of the East and West Kent Supplementary Benefit Appeals, and worked with the Community Help Council. She had given a home at Southolme to her sister's children after their mother died, and in 1975 was sharing the house with a friend, Dr Carol Duff, who came from the Highlands and ran a busy medical practice in Dover. There were always dogs and visitors at Southolme, and warm hospitality for their many friends without ostentation or fuss. Every room was filled with beautiful and unusual treasures, fine china and porcelain figures, books and paintings. Morning Glory shimmered blue in the sun-soaked conservatory, and there was coffee on the terrace or in the bright welcoming kitchen for all comers.

The two Katharines immediately and instinctively recognised one another as kindred spirits, and before long Katharine had been invited to Southolme, and installed in a peaceful bedroom overlooking the sea to be nursed back to health and cosetted with loving care. Katharine Law threw herself with understanding and enthusiasm into discussions on *The Dictionary of Fairies* and other current projects, and Katharine Briggs once more had listeners on which to try out her stories. To find someone endlessly willing to talk and listen was something for which Katharine must have hungered since Elspeth died. It was like a breath of inspiration to her. Her general health and walking improved, and before long, almost without a recognisable moment of decision, it was accepted by all three that she would give up the Barn House and move down to Southolme for good. Katharine Law was even willing to embark on the task of building a new library on to the house to hold Katharine's cherished books. Katharine had been somewhat uneasy at first at the thought of moving Roly, her beloved Siamese cat, who had survived his brother Oliver, but on visits to Southolme it was clear that he accepted the friendly house and the garden filled with exciting scents wholeheartedly, and there was no hostility between him and the dogs. A later book by Katharine on the folklore of cats was to bear the dedication: 'To Katharine Law, who taught my Roly to live with dogs.' In between visits to Southolme and plans for the future, Katharine returned to Burford to sort out her papers and belongings.

Once back at the Barn House, however, she was overcome by the difficulties of the uprooting. She sorted out a few papers with the help of Josephine Thompson, and continued to entertain guests, while the Young Visitors came in the summer as usual. Katharine Law came to see her, found her exhausted amid general chaos, and put her in the car to take her away from it all, leaving confusion behind and much lamentation among the Young Visitors. Katharine would willingly have offered the Barn House to anyone who would take it, but, as with Pull Wyke and Dalbeathie, no one was prepared to step in. Many of the beautiful and valuable pieces of furniture were distributed around the family, and the house finally sold. However the new library was built in record time, under Katharine Law's supervision, and when Katharine finally moved in December 1975, her books came with her. The rich friendship and fun of

Southolme, and the opportunity of continuing work with her books around her, made the change not only possible, but irresistible.

She could not have regretted the loss of the Barn House unduly, since she was now back in a setting which recalled that of early days with her sisters. Once more she was one of a trio, with a new and widening circle of friends, while able to keep in touch with friends of the past. With publishers pressing for more work, and constant help and encouragement from Katharine and Carol, she blossomed in a way which few would have believed possible. Katharine Law was an intuitive person with a zest for life and a gift for unobtrusive organisation. She encouraged Katharine to meet new people, to buy new clothes, have her hair done becomingly, and think about her appearance. Katharine had always enjoyed wearing beautiful things, but in Burford she had come to care little about her looks or what she wore as her health deteriorated, and she had to struggle to survive. Evie Forbes, who lived not far away in Brighton, was delighted at the change in Katharine:

> I was sad when she gave up Burford, but I needn't have been. At St. Margaret's Bay she, who blossomed late, came to full flower. Her work, which of late years had become more and more significant, began to achieve the credit it had always merited. She became beautiful, really beautiful. She relaxed, thoroughly enjoyed life and was full of fun and gaiety. I was so happy for her.[2]

Many old friends visited Southolme, Barbara and Pelican Snelson from Scotland, friends from Burford, Brian, who now lived in Sussex, and others from the Folklore Society, publishing firms and the BBC. Indeed so constant was the flow of visitors that Katharine Law had to impose some kind of restriction: only genuine friends of Katharine, or those on serious business, could be entertained, and not chance acquaintances, or people just trying to get something out of her for themselves. Katharine, well-known for her books and broadcasts and believed to be rich, had to some extent to be protected; she was apt to fall into conversation with total strangers and invite them in to see her library. But this was not through loneliness, for now the days passed quickly and happily, while she read and wrote, sketched in the garden, visited friends, and walked as her leg grew stronger, getting down to church regularly on Sunday mornings. She amused herself by composing little verses for various occasions, like one to her doctor, whose name was Nick; Katharine herself was still known by that nickname to some of her friends from Dalbeathie days:

> When I was young they called me Nick
> Because in mimes I played the devil.
> My dear physician's now named Nick
> As one pre-eminent in revel.
> Young Nick I was, old Nick am now
> And proud to have a grand successor.
> To my young heir I make my bow
> Of my old title the possessor.

These were the kind of ploys in which she had delighted at Dalbeathie, and it seemed that sometimes she thought herself back there. She still took pleasure in new experiences, in having her ears pierced, for instance, for her eightieth birthday, so that she could wear a new pair of pearl ear-rings. Her absent-mindedness, indeed, often got her into trouble, but she used her considerable ingenuity to get herself out of it again. It was only after she died that it was discovered that a mysterious broken tile beneath an upstairs window had been caused by the postman climbing into the house for her when, not for the first time, she had left her key inside. He kept the secret loyally as long as she lived. Another time she arrived back from the United States a day early; she had persuaded the airline that she was due back the day before the date on her ticket. Back at Southolme, she would greet her friends with the words 'Now we are all together again.' Above all, she revelled in the opportunity to sit and talk. When once Katharine Law expostulated at the weekend breakfast table that she really must stop talking so that they could get on, Katharine was unrepentant: 'But talking is so much more fun!' she declared. In her desire to play a full part in the household, she used to get down early to sit with Carol over breakfast. Carol liked to breakfast peacefully without the need to talk, and began rising earlier and earlier, whereupon Katharine did the same, until at last she realised the truth of the situation, and used to tell the story against herself.

Katharine could, at times, be maddening, but it was never difficult to forgive her because of her humility, that rare quality which she praised in her essay on Charlotte Yonge, together with her sense of humour and enjoyment of living. She took delight in little things; she modelled small clay animals for the Christmas crib, and painted eggs to roll down the lawn at Easter; when she had bought a new dress, she would wear it at breakfast for her friends to admire. A friend at Sandwich who first met her about a year before her death, has summed up the impression she made on him:

> Katharine had, like all of us, virtues and faults. But her faults were loveable weaknesses. She was a strange mixture of the childlike and the adult (I didn't say childish). Perhaps that was why children liked her. She didn't talk down to them but she would talk at their level — at anyone's level ...
>
> In conversation with a group she was often silent and then when one had almost forgotten her existence she would come out with, in the gentlest voice, some cogent or even shattering remark. But I don't remember her being uncharitable.[3]

He remembered her as a story-teller ('I can hear the cadence of her voice still as I read her books') and also how she would quote 'chunks of prose, ballads, poetry and scripture.' For Katharine was still entertaining those around her. While at Southolme she inspired and captivated three little girls, aged eight, nine and ten. They used to slip in and visit her whenever they could, sometimes warded off by the watchful Carol in case they tired Katharine. 'She was a wonderful person. I would like to follow in her footsteps as long as I live.' wrote Lindsay in a letter published in the Parish News after Katharine's death: 'Every time I went up there she was always cheerful, and when I came home again I was always happy. She was always willing to help anyone who was in need but chose her friends carefully.'[4] They acted little plays for her and read her poems they had written, and made up their minds to be folklorists one day. Marguerita remembered her telling her that if she had faith she 'would do well and be famous', while Rebecca, the youngest of the three, commented:

> She had great faith in God, and kept a little Prayer Book by her bedside. I once wrote a prayer for her and she kept it in her book. She was really jolly and I loved her a lot ... I will always remember her.

After a time the two Katharines decided to buy a cottage in Sandwich, the picturesque 'Long Cottage' in Milwall Place. This was in case Katharine Law had to be away at any time, since it was near the station and post office, and Katharine Briggs could get help from neighbours if she were there alone. They enjoyed finding it and planning improvements, which must have taken Katharine back to the early days of the Barn House, although this time there was Katharine Law to insist on a convenient kitchen. Katharine made many new friends in Sandwich and often used to spend part of the day in the cottage. But she did not stay the whole time in Kent; she went up to Burford several times a year, and sometimes up to Scotland to stay with Barbara Innes and other friends. She attended Folklore Society conferences; she told some of her folktales at one at Reading in 1976 and afterwards wrote an introduction 'The Folklore Society and its Beginnings' to a volume of conference papers published for the Society's centenary in 1978. She met many old friends at an International Conference at Royal Holloway College to celebrate this, organised by Venetia Newall, and gave a lively paper on 'Some Unpleasant Characters among British Fairies.[6] In 1980 she gave her last paper, 'Tradition and Invention in Ghost Stories', at a small Folklore Society conference at York.[7] Her friends at Southolme had wondered if this would be too much for her, but she had a very happy time there, and her short paper was full of good sense and presented with her customary vigour and charm. She enjoyed herself greatly: 'The nicest I've ever been to', she declared in a letter, 'and I always enjoy conferences'.[8] In spite of her lameness she gamely insisted on taking part in a 'Ghost Walk' through York one evening, and later characteristically apologised for having perhaps held up the party by her slowness.

There were even visits to the United States, where American publishers were taking considerable interest now in her work. She was at Philadelphia in 1976, and next year at Detroit, and gave lectures at the Universities of North Carolina, Tennessee, Alabama and Pittsburgh. In 1978 she was at Pittsburgh again, and gave a paper at a conference at Okaha University, Nebraska.[9] Such efforts meant considerable expenditure of energy and exposure to risk. Margaret Hodges remembers her falling in the street in Pittsburgh and cutting her leg, while at Philadelphia she had to be brought down from her room when a fire broke out in her hotel. Several of her books appeared in America, revealing the new access of energy which came to her at Southolme. In 1977 Routledge published a selection of tales from her big *Dictionary,* under the title *British Folk Tales and Legends: a Sampler,* and this was brought out by Pantheon Books in New York as *British Folktales.* It was dedicated to Katharine Law, thanking her for 'the help and advice she has given me in the selection of the tales'. New editions of *Hobberdy Dick* and *Kate Crackernuts* came out in Kestrel Books, with new and attractive illustrations, and the *Encyclopedia of Fairies,* the American edition of the *Penguin Dictionary,* appeared in 1977. The *Dictionary of Fairies* was the book which won the widest fame for Katharine, and it was well deserved. In its richness and informality, and its appeal to those of different ages and backgrounds, it may well be the work for which she will be longest remembered. Various published interviews in America include some lively comments by Katharine on fairies and fairy tales. She told Israel Shenker, who interviewed her for the *New York Times* (31 October 1977):

> If I saw a fairy I wouldn't stare. I'd say 'You're welcome here. Is there anything I can do for you?' When the fairy leaves, you wouldn't say 'Have a good day.' Fairies are night creatures. You might say 'Have a good night', though it would be more appropriate to say 'Merry dancing to you'. ... I think children are quite realistic about life, and if they're not going to learn the facts of life from fairy stories they'll have to learn them in a much more unpleasant way later. I don't think you should be mimmy-minded.

The first new book written at Southolme was *The Vanishing People: a book of Fairy Lore and Legends,* based on material from the earlier books on fairies; it came out in 1978 with a dedication to Katharine Law and Carol, 'whose kindness and enthusiasm made it possible.' In 1979 this was followed by *Abbey Lubbers, Banshees and Boggarts,* described as 'an illustrated Encyclopedia of Fairies', with vigorous illustrations by Yvonne Gilbert of robust fairies of the type approved of by Katharine, published by Kestrel and Pantheon Books in London and New York. Katharine was delighted about this time to be consulted over the planning of a Festival Exhibition in Brighton planned for 1980, a collection of fairy paintings and photographs, with an excellent catalogue. She is mentioned there as one of three consultants 'without whose cooperation this exhibition would have been impossible ... tireless and endlessly patient.' Another book which gave her pleasure to write was *Nine Lives,* on the folklore of cats, brilliantly illustrated by the artist John Ward, which appeared shortly before her death, so that she was able to enjoy a publishing party. A review by Jan Morris in *The Times* describes it as 'a somewhat random, not to say ramshackle, collection of tales, beliefs, prejudices and superstitions about cats, assembled with artless charm', a fair enough description, and added the comment that the 'eminent folklorist ... could not have asked for a more endearing memorial'. One can only regret that she never included the long procession of cats in her own life, observed with such affection and delight.

Katharine had met the artist, John Ward, some time earlier, and he declared one day that he would like to paint her. Katharine much enjoyed the visits to his studio, which brought back memories of Hampstead and her life as an artist's daughter, and it was he who suggested that she should recall some of these in writing. The portrait of Katharine was exhibited at the Royal Academy in 1980, and it is an arresting one, showing Katharine alert and serious, as if about to speak.

After leaving the York conference in July of 1980, Katharine went up to Edinburgh to visit friends; she had a happy stay at Comrie with her old friend Barbara, 'doing nothing but what we wanted to', and visiting the theatre at Perth once more. Then she went to Oxford, to work on references for her latest book on Lilith. It had been suggested by her American publishers because of the current interest in Lilith as a symbol of women's rights, and the idea was that Katharine should present some folklore about women. Katharine was always unwilling to refuse a challenge, although this meant a departure from previous lines of work, and so spent some time collecting suitable tales and reading about the original Lilith of Babylonian and Hebrew belief. She had hoped to take the manuscript to New York in October, but Carol judged that her heart was showing signs of strain, and advised her not to travel. Katharine wrote to Margaret Hodges in Pittsburgh that she had been 'overdoing things a bit' and needed a few weeks rest. She wrote a second time on 9 October:

> Sense is a thing I am going to have to learn. ... At the moment I am only writing short articles retelling the Khoja (Naar-el-Deen) stories which were popular with us as children. The next festivity I look forward to is my 82nd birthday. Quite a venerable age. I shall begin to respect myself.

Birthdays at Southolme had once more become joyful, festive occasions, as in the early days of the Briggs family, when not only the one whose birthday it was but the rest of the family received

Katharine in her last years at Southolme.

gifts. Katharine Law organised wonderful birthday lunches every year at the Wife of Bath at Wye, famed for its superb cooking. The people who ran it were friends of hers and they welcomed Katharine royally, while she looked forward to any excuse for a party there with real excitement and delight. It was a wonderful place for old and new friends to meet, and she could welcome people she respected and liked from many different backgrounds, recalling past associations. There were old friends like Evie from her schooldays, Brian from her time in the WAAF, scholars and folklorists, the artist John Ward, who designed some delightful menu cards for her, and others from the publishing world and from the area round St Margaret's Bay and Sandwich. The outstanding feature of these lunches was the way in which Katharine drew the very varied guests together; all were struck by the warmth, friendliness and joy of the occasion. Carmen Blacker wrote to Katharine after the lunch of 1978, celebrating Katharine's eightieth birthday:

It was a marvellous day in every way, in which golden sunshine, delicious food, delightful company all combined in an auspicious whole greater than themselves which was the celebration of your birthday. ... And how lovely it was to come back to your house to the cake cutting ceremony afterwards.

That year another lunch party was organised for her by Carmen Blacker at the University Women's Club in London, when members of the Folklore Society gathered to do honour to Katharine.

In 1980 there was to be another party, but that year it was never held. Katharine had never feared death; she faced its coming with equanimity and courage, and once told one of her friends that she did not want to miss dying; it was something she wanted to experience. She had nevertheless some apprehension lest she should be made increasingly helpless by a series of strokes, as had happened to others in her family. In 1975 she remarked, with a characteristic facing up to realities: 'I shall have to get on as fast as I can before I become absolutely senile, which may happen to any of us at any time when we get into our seventies.'[10] A short while before she died she stayed the night with Evie Forbes, her old schoolfellow, at Brighton. They sat up until one, drinking gin together ('She would never have done this at one time', Evie observed, 'she used to be very abstemious'). As they talked, she showed Katharine a poem written at a time of depression, expressing a fear of death:

> It was there she gave me the best sermon I have ever heard, and I am an expert on sermons. My father was a great preacher; I have heard most of the great preachers of these times. ... This made her speak about death, Christ and the life to come. I shall always remember it. It makes me happy about Katharine's death. It will make me happy at my death.

Katharine's own death, on 15 October 1980, came to her suddenly in a contented, relaxed moment, typical of her life at Southolme. She had spent the morning writing, working on an account of her childhood; the few pages she completed are as lively and vivid as anything she wrote, and the memory of those early days was evidently crystal clear as she recaptured the fun and happiness of her life with her adored parents and little sisters. She came in to have lunch with Katharine Law and pressed her to have a gin and tonic, but there was no gin left. 'Have some wine then', said Katharine. As Katharine

Law poured some out for her, Katharine dropped the biscuit she had taken. Her friend bent to pick it up for her, and as she did so Katharine fell back in her chair and was gone.

Like Evie, Katharine's friends could not but be happy about her death, which came to her quickly and painlessly, at a time of fulfillment and happiness: the grief came in the acute sense of loss experienced even by those who had known her slightly. In the pile of letters Katharine Law received, there were many tributes and vivid memories of Katharine at different stages of her life. Two notes constantly sounded were the extent of her influence on others, and the amount of affection she had inspired. One Oxford friend wrote:

> She was demanding both of herself and on those who worked for her, but fair enough. I was aware of her devotion to her sisters and the depths of her caring. To my view she exercised a kind of despotic benevolence in some areas. ... I found her both amiable and loveable. There was a solid bone of real goodness to support the individual quirks.[11]

Katharine herself was aware of her power over others, both to inspire and to demand; this awareness lies behind her wise utterances on the importance of humility and the grievous burden of pride. She was aware too of the power which her wealth brought her, and like her father and earlier members of the Briggs family, felt acutely that she was under an obligation to use it for others. Letters received over the years from relatives, friends and neighbours testify to the amazing generosity, indeed munificence, of her gifts, and these were never offered ostentatiously or in a dreary spirit of duty, but with warmhearted readiness and careful thought for the recipient. There were countless gifts of small things, always distinctive and chosen with care — books, pictures, scarves, brooches and the like, and practical presents offered where needed, such as a room-heater, or a car passed on to a friend; loans were made interest-free to make it possible to purchase a house at the right moment, school-fees paid for her friends' children. She gave generous support to the musical festivals held by Noel Currer-Briggs and his wife in the Cotswolds, and made many gifts to the church and town at Burford, to the Folklore Society, and to charities in which she had a special interest. It was sometimes necessary for old friends to refuse Katharine's impulsive offers gently but firmly, but there were many occasions when the sensitive perception of a need made a tremendous difference to the life of someone she knew. Her friends' children and grandchildren were remembered constantly by Katharine, and her many godchildren received kind and generous gifts. Those out of her vast circle of friends able to attend the funeral at Southolme remember it as an almost happy occasion, when Noel Currer-Briggs, whom Katharine had regarded as the head of the family, read one of her early letters, and the organist suddenly broke into 'An English Country Garden.' It was almost as if Katharine herself were once more the centre of the group, welcoming her friends around her. There was a memorial service in the church at Burford on her birthday in November, and her ashes were laid in a simple grave in the little cemetery there, beside the graves of her two sisters.

Katharine indeed was born into a goodly heritage. She had behind her a family which produced not only abundance of wealth, but also many characters of great energy and ability, capable of hard work and innovation, a series of strong individualists who were at the same time conscious of their responsibility towards others. She grew up in a loving home, with parents of unusual innocence and warmheartedness, where there was an atmosphere of goodness without sentimentality. Her father was a man of rare gifts and ideals, and his influence remained with Katharine all her life. From him she learned to enjoy living, to discover the excitements and importance of art and literature, the fun of good company and stimulating conversation, and the beauties of the countryside. With her opportunities, she might easily have lived a life of cultured self-indulgence, playing at the things which amused her, but she was saved from this by her sound good sense, her inherited ability to work hard, her sense of humour and capacity for growth. One of her favourite prayers in old age was 'Lord, I pray that I may learn from the experiences of today the lessons that Thou meanest them to teach me'.[12] To look back over her life is to see that prayer answered, for hers is a story of continual growth and development, and a continual search for new challenges and experiences. She was conscious from the first of a capacity for something above the ordinary, and felt the need for appreciation and achievement. In an obituary in *The Brown Book,* a friend who had known her at Lady Margaret Hall wrote: 'She was at the same time completely humble and confidently ambitious ... "Wouldn't it be dreadful", she once said to me with disarming simplicity, "if we were not famous by the time that we were old?" '[13] This was not merely the naive vanity of the talented undergraduate. Part of Katharine's power and drive came from a desire to open windows for others, showing them undreamed-of possibilities and the untapped riches of life. Her effect, for instance, on Catherine Hollingsworth, who in turn was to have immense influence on others in her work on speech and drama in Scotland, cannot be fully assessed; she herself declared that Katharine could never have known how much she revealed to her in those early days at Dalbeathie. We cannot know the extent of Katharine's influence on those who met her in her work on Guides and Brownies, or took part in the Summer Players, worked with her during the war, or simply listened to her telling stories, reciting ballads and giving counsel to those in trouble. So many people, young and old, came into contact with Katharine and never wholly forgot the experience. She was one of those radiant spirits with a true zest for life, a delight in the created world and in people, and yet wholly free from humbug and sentimentality. This side of her character did not fade with age, but grew stronger as she neared the end of her life.

Privileged as she was in many ways, she was by no means immune from disappointments, failures and suffering. But when painful experiences came to her, like the death of her father, the sudden loss of Elspeth, and her increasing lameness and physical weakness, they were faced with that true resignation which arises from inner strength. Those who knew her well realised how much power she derived from her steadfast Christian faith, which she never paraded on tried to force on others. As a writer and scholar, she was unconventional in her approach and uneven in quality. It was many years before at last she found her true medium of expression, and this was as a story-teller in the old traditional sense rather than as academic writer, novelist or poet. She had exceptional power over the spoken word, giving her an immediate appeal to those of all ages and backgrounds who knew how to listen, but her gifts went beyond this; she recaptured in her books much of the wealth of the imaginative world which men have created since the time when tales were first told. She brought back to us much that had been forgotten, and left a treasury of tales and legends in our hands, so that we might not neglect to our peril the dreams and visions beyond the range of ordinary human experience.

Perhaps the final word on Katharine's personality and influence on others had been said by a humble friend, 'Coops', who for a while came to clean in the new cottage in Sandwich, and used to talk to

Katharine there.[14] The two became close friends, chatting together and quoting poetry to each other. 'Come and sit down and talk to me', Katharine would say, and Coops would reply 'I've only got half an hour.' To which Katharine would retort 'What's time?' They talked about many things. 'She almost knew what you were thinking', Coops declared, and she described Katharine as a 'one-of, for there was no one like her', 'she could draw anybody out, whether it was a duke or a dustman.' When she heard of Katharine's death, Coops declared that she could not write anything about her, but nevertheless she left a memorable tribute in a few lines which she put on paper:

> To be loved as she was loved is a wonderful thing. Her whole life was a dedication to all whose life she touched. And she touched so *very* many.
>
> I envy Eternity, cos' that's where she is.

Appendix 1 Her Account of Her Career

Katharine Briggs was born in November 1898 in Hampstead, the daughter of Ernest Briggs, an eminent water-colourist, who had been early elected a member of the Royal Institute of Painters in Water-colours and was an active member of the St John's Wood Arts Club. He specialized in Highland scenery and particularly in running water, and with his wife and his three young daughters he spent his time between the Highlands of Scotland and his London studio. The three children keenly enjoyed both aspects of life, felt themselves country children in Scotland and enjoyed the social winters in London. Katharine in particular loved to listen to discussions of art and politics in her father's studio, and to squeeze into a corner on billiard nights and postpone her bedtime as long as possible. All her grandmother's family was interested in private theatricals, and Ernest Briggs read aloud and told stories extremely well. His children loved to listen to him. He had some interest too in folk traditions, an interest developed and carried on by his eldest daughter. In 1909 a legacy from his mother enabled Ernest Briggs to build a house in Scotland, and the family moved up to Perthshire in the spring of 1911. An idyllic year passed, filled with the visits of friends, in the hot delightful Summer which marked George V's Coronation; but in 1912 Ernest Briggs, who had suffered from heart disease from his youth, and whose health had been deteriorating for several years, was taken seriously ill. The devoted nursing of his wife saved his life for the time, but in September of 1913 he died, and his wife was left in charge of three growing girls to face the isolation of the War Years of 1914-18.

She was a brave woman, and the whole family was a devoted one, and manufactured their own interests. Katharine, who was an out-looking person, chose to go to boarding school in Edinburgh, and, though the environment was alien to her, she made some lasting friendships and was enabled to go up from school to Oxford. She was admitted to Lady Margaret Hall in the Michaelmas Term of 1918. She was blissfully happy there. During her time at Oxford degrees were granted to women. She took her B.A. in 1922 and her M.A. in 1926. She read English at Oxford and became interested in the seventeenth century, and particularly in the period of the Great Civil War.

After taking her degree Katharine returned to Perthshire, where she and her youngest sister collected a considerable library, particularly of seventeenth-century history. Both wrote historical novels, some of which were published. The years between the Wars were filled with many activities. The two younger sisters had studied at the Byam Shaw Vicat Cole School of Art. The middle sister, Winifred, became an artist, and also served apprenticeship as a printer, and set up her own private press, Capricornus, Dunkeld. Elspeth illustrated some of her own books with masterly woodcuts, but otherwise pursued literature; all three sisters were active in organising and participating in an amateur touring company, The Summer Players, for which Elspeth and Katharine wrote plays, printed by Winifred, who made the costumes, printed the programmes and organised the tours. Both Winifred and Katharine were enthusiastic Girl Guides, and Katharine was awarded her Brown Cord Diploma in 1926, and travelled as far afield as Newfoundland, giving training to guiders, doing some public propaganda and founding companies and packs.

The family home, Dalbeathie House, Dunkeld, was a happy centre of hospitality, rehearsals and various activities. In January of 1939, however, the three sisters, feeling that their mother had all the hard work of this way of life and not much of the fun, bought a small house in the Cotswolds, which would be more available for Oxford friends and where they themselves could take their fair share of the work. However, before the house was put into full use the Second World War broke out, and they returned hastily to look after the thirteen evacuees who were allotted to them. The next two years were spent on evacuees, the establishment of hostels, an acceleration of Guide Training Work, teaching in a Polish Refugee School in Lanarkshire, and so on. At the end of 1941 Katharine volunteered for the WAAF and was put into the medical branch. Elspeth went up to London to train in draughtsmanship, and was finally posted back to the Admiralty Stores at Almondbank to work as a draughtsman. Winifred grappled with the multifarious activities of country life in wartime Britain, and worked harder than anyone.

For Katharine Briggs life in the ranks was in many ways a valuable experience, for her fellow-workers represented a cross-section of the population. When she was finally posted to RAF Errol she was fortunate in being appointed the dramatic producer for the Station. She was also in charge of the Station Sick Quarters. Both offices required a good deal of resilience but were full of interest. She was fortunate in never rising beyond the rank of corporal.

When the war ended and she was demobilised in 1945, she decided to fit herself for the academic life again by training for her D. Phil, Oxon. Residence was not necessary, so she returned to the Barn House at Burford in term time and rejoined the family in the vacations, except when they came south to Burford. Here the Summer Players were revived. Whilst she was near London she had the opportunity of attending meetings of the Folklore Society, of which she had long been a member. After she had been awarded her D. Phil, she was invited to read occasional papers to the Society, and she made more general international contacts after attending the first Congress of the International Society for Folk-Narrative Research in Kiel and Copenhagen in 1959. By that time *The Anatomy of Puck* had been published and she found herself greeted as a recognised authority. The next year she visited the USA to attend a summer session in Bloomington, Indiana, where lectures were given by several distinguished American Folklorists, such as Archer Taylor and Edward MacLeach, and was in her turn invited to give lectures in Bloomington and in Columbus, Ohio. At this time she was on the Council of the Folklore Society and taking an active interest in its affairs. In 1967 she was appointed President and led a strenuous three years. She was now alone in the Barn House. After their mother's death in 1957 the three sisters sold the house in Scotland and moved down to Burford. Elspeth died in 1961 and Winifred in 1966. The last joint performance in which the three acted was in the summer of 1960.

Katharine continued to work hard at her writing, and had many pleasant contacts in the United States. In 1970 she taught at an été term in Pennsylvania University, Philadelphia, and she was visiting professor in Berkeley, California, for the winter term of 1973, January to March. Many of her American friends and correspondents visited her in Burford, and continue to keep in touch with her in the new home at St Margaret's Bay, to which she moved, with her library, in December 1975. She has plenty to do, for she has two books forthcoming and is at work on a third.

She has always been lucky in her friends, and perhaps specially so in being able to count many of the children and grandchildren of her oldest friends among them.

(Written by K.M. Briggs after 1975)

Appendix 2 An Artist's Daughter

We were three sisters — Molly, Winnie and Elsie were our short names. I was a year and a half older than Winnie and Winnie was nearly two years older than Elsie. Before Winnie was born I was my Father's playfellow, and we were playfellows and companions for all the rest of his life. For the first twelve years of my life our home was in London, in the last corner house of Fellows Road, a pretty little house, smaller than any of the others, although it was bigger than it had been, for a dining room had been added to the basement, with a day and night nursery and a bathroom on the first floor. It had a splendid big studio with a separate door for models and a corner where Mother's writing desk and work-table stood. The billiard room was in the basement, and there were lovely, safe banisters to slide down leading to the bottom floor. We loved our house and it was a great pleasure to come back to it in Autumn. But we loved the summer too, for that was spent in different parts of Scotland, generally in Galloway, Perthshire or Argyllshire where my father sketched and fished, carrying his sketches back to be worked up in the studio ready for the Royal Academy and the Royal Institute in May.

It was an exciting time as May drew nearer. Show Sunday, the Sunday before entry day, was a most interesting time, for the studios were open to friends and everyone went from house to house, drinking cups of tea and eating tiny sandwiches and looking at the pictures that were going to be adventured. In those days only painters in oils were eligible as Royal Academicians but my father's pictures were always accepted and generally hung 'on the line'. If any of the artists were away their friends wrote and told them how they were hung, 'on the line', that is, with the eye-level of the picture at the spectator's eye-level, 'skied' so that people had to crane their necks to see them, or 'sunk' so that one had to bend down to look at them, and they were only visible to the front row of the spectators. It was exciting to come in and see a red spot on one's picture, but often the artist knew already for the agent or patron would get directly in touch with him. Some artists tried to prevent themselves from being skied by painting an unusually tall picture, but if it was too awkward a shape it ran a risk of never being hung at all.

I knew myself to be very lucky to have an artist as a father. There were, I knew, some little girls whose fathers went to offices in the morning and came back tired and cross at night; while I could always go quietly into the

APPENDIX 2

studio and sit down in a far corner with a book, while Daddy went backwards and forwards to look at his picture and then put a few strokes on it. Sometimes he'd call me to see how it was getting on, and when we'd looked and talked about it perhaps he would lie on the sofa and we'd talk for a bit. He had a weak heart and sometimes he could not stand too long. Often other artists would come in, and hold long discussions on art and politics, and I'd look up from my book and listen. One didn't in those days join in with grown-ups' conversation, but when they'd gone I'd say things like: 'I don't know what all this fuss is about composition. Isn't Nature good enough for you?' My Father would try to explain to me that every scene is complex and in depth and that an artist had to take out of it the aspect which he wanted people to dwell upon. But I still thought that there was something artificial about it.

From 1906 to 1914 was a great time for illustrated books, and our circle was very much interested in Rackham and Dulac's early illustrations, *The Arabian Nights* and *The Tempest* in particular. So were all three of us, and for years our birthday and Christmas presents to each other was the latest illustrated book.

The conversation among the artists was not only earnest but full of jokes and merriment, so that I used to say in a grandmotherly way that artists never grew up. But we all three thought it very entertaining. There were some touches of human nature, too. There was one man who was famous for getting fellow-artists to touch in any part of a picture he couldn't manage himself: 'I'm in rather a puzzle about those hands, old fellow. I wonder if you'd put in a touch or two to them.' So that his pictures were a kind of mosaic, and people visiting him on a Show Sunday would know who'd looked into his studio lately. Phil May must have known him, for he put a joke into Punch about that.

Norman Wilkinson, who loved the sea and painted almost exclusively sea pictures, was a great humourist and could make himself look like almost anything from a scarecrow to a lunatic or an agile gibbon. He was very clever at keeping a carriage clear for his friends by sitting in a corner pretending to have a fit. But the man whose company we enjoyed most was Oswald Moseley, who was very impetuous and merry with a bit of a stammer. I remember him one billiard night when he was newly engaged to be married. Everyone was teasing him and he was so excited that he kept making ridiculous mistakes, so that the billiard cloth was a little endangered. He painted rather solemn religious pictures which I did not think good as a child. I did not care for Norman Wilkinson's naval pictures, though I liked his later water-colour landscapes.

We had one visitor who was not an artist but a musician. He wrote the music for 'Pinkie and the Fairies', a very popular children's play with an all-star cast. It was not till years later when I was looking at a copy of the play that I realised that I had seen Ellen Terry in it. We thought her very amusing, but had no idea that she was anyone special. Mr Norton was a humourist, and I said to Daddy once that it would be fun to see him and Mr Wilkinson together, but he said that they were very quiet when they were together.

Some time in 1909 my Father had a bout of heart trouble and couldn't stand at the easel, so he set to work on writing and produced *Angling and Art in Scotland*. He told me afterwards that he found he was getting very depressed and decided that he must do something.

It is a lively, merry book, full of zest for fishing and for landscape. It begins with their boyhood expeditions in Galloway, anecdotes which we used to hear as children, and goes on to various other fishing experiences. The illustrations to the book were reproductions of his pictures with black and white tailpieces by Hugh Radcliffe Wilson, a connection. The proofs of the pictures were corrected with great care and delicacy.

Our back garden consisted of two lawns with a straight pink-tiled path between leading from the tool house to the billiard-room door, up and down which Sir James Stevenson rode many miles on his tricycle carrying private despatches from King Bruce Rutherford of Dash. Sir James was the head of the royal guard of Dash — a picked body of twelve knights, all mounted on tricycles. Winnie was the proud owner of a tricycle — a real one with bicycle type wheels — on which Winnie used to go rides with Daddy on his bicycle along Adelaide Road, and up and down King Henry's Road.

The back garden was a very good place for playing. There was a high wall between it and the road, over which you could only see the tops of people's heads, but there was one solid wooden gate rather lower than the road, and ill-bred people used to stand and look over the wall to watch us playing. I used to stop and stare at them furiously, but they never took any notice, and I often wondered what kind of insensitive creatures they were.

(Written by K.M. Briggs in 1980)

Appendix 3 Eric Notes

I suppose the first beginnings of 'Eric' were somewhere about 1907 when Elspeth would be five (June 8th), Winnie would be seven (July 14th) and I would be nine (November 8th). They always gained on me in this way, and nothing would prevent it, but they never quite caught up. Elspeth had no wish to join in the competition. She agreed with Humpty Dumpty who thought it a pity that Alice hadn't stopped at seven. Seven seemed to her the best age to be.

We had played of course a number of imaginary games before we were swept into the big net of 'Eric'. Elspeth, when she was three or four, had a game of her own about two children called Biddy and Widdy. We didn't know anything of the incidents, but we used to hear her crooning to herself: 'I am Biddy and Widdy', and once we saw her sitting on the stairs with a doll on each arm, rocking herself from side to side, and singing 'Go to seep, Biddy and Widdy'. The only thing that we never heard about Biddy and Widdy afterwards is that they had a goat that they were very devoted to.

Elspeth must have had more heroic and imaginative games than this, for one evening, when she and Winnie were in the night nursery, she stood up on her bed and with stiff, dramatic gestures she recited the lament of an exiled man:

> Loch Donna, Loch Donna,
> I love thee not.
> By thy waters I suffer
> By thy waters I'll die.
> With no friends around me
> But a waste of black water
> Between my loved ones and me.
> Loch Donna, Loch Donna,
> I love thy black waters not!

Unfortunately Winnie burst into a peal of laughter, really, I think, of admiration, and Elspeth darted down under the bedclothes in tears, but Winnie coaxed her out and persuaded her to say the poem again. Then we wrote it out and both admired it intensely. I personally felt that I could never write anything as impressive. We never heard who the exile was.

I am not quite sure when my sisters' separate fantasy worlds were fused in fully fledged imaginary games. They had some idle bedtime games that they used to play together between milk and biscuits and being settled for the night. There was Mr E. Gray and Mr A. Gray, for instance, who lived underground to save taxes. Mr A. Gray's garden path was down the parting of Winifred's hair and Mr E. Gray, down the parting of Elspeth's; but these were pure amusement games, like Miss MacTowel's Bathing Establishment, kept by our dear Nursery Governess, Kathleen Godfrey, and attended by all kinds of eccentric characters, such as Prince Ensor, who insisted on wearing a wide gray hat in the bath, with an ostrich feather in it. I think Sir Arthur O'Bower, one of Winnie's knights, attended her sessions too.

While the other two were still rather young to play complicated imaginary games my father was my great playfellow. The games were generally taken from literary sources. The first, I believe, was founded on *The Water Babies*, the game of a little boy who dived into a river and turned into a water-baby. My father told me once that this was our first game together, but I was only about three at the time, he said, and I soon forgot it. One that I remember very clearly is the story of *As You Like It*. I loved all the bits about the wrestling with Charles. I was rather embarrassed at having to enter rudely into the polite exiled company and demand food which they were perfectly ready to give to me, but I very much liked killing the lion and the serpent. What I could not condone was Orlando's conduct in carving names on trees and sticking up bad rhymes about Rosalind all over the place. I remember the Duke coming up to me one day, when I was Orlando, and saying: 'Orlando who do you think can have been writing all those poems and sticking them on the trees?' And I blushed hotly and said, 'Oh Daddy — out of the game — can we cross all that out? It's so silly.'

It was obediently crossed out, and Orlando's follies were forgotten. Even more popular were the heroes of *Coral Island,* Jack, Ralph and Peterkin. I was Jack and my father was the rest of the cast. These were very early games.

The background of all this, as may be presumed, was literature and the books my father read to me. When I was eight I was promoted to an eight o'clock bedtime, and the hours between six and eight were always the reading time unless anything special was on, like the billiard night on Thursdays. Elspeth went to bed at six, and Winnie would wedge herself into the sofa between my father and the back and listen with eyes as big as saucers. *Ivanhoe* and *Quentin Durward* and *Guy Mannering* were read to me from six onwards, with some of the longer descriptions left out. Then there was *Treasure Island* and *Kidnapped* and the *New Arabian Nights,* but Winnie's special favourite was *Lorna Doone;* and Ensor and Charlesworth were the names of two of her Princes.

APPENDIX 3

I was first introduced into what was later to be called *Eric* to play in a part about two little princes called Charlie and Ernest, who, for reasons which were never quite clear to me, were living in the care of two footmen in a large capital city of which neither was a native. The footmen were rather harsh and given to spanking them as a form of discipline. A pleasant young King Robert, made by me, took pity on this forlorn pair, and persuaded their parents to let them come and stay in his Palace — he was King of the country afterwards called Astgal — where they were in the care of a cousin of King Robert — Eric was his name. He was an eccentric character, a tremendous reader and book-lover, never without a large tome in hand, who was nevertheless a splendid athlete, who could leap straight up from the floor of the Hall on to one of the rafters. Here Charlie and Ernest were very happy for several years until King Robert was assassinated by one of the Colour Stripes, a nihilist gang who crossed over from Asia and behaved with meaningless malignity. It was the first death in Eric, and we were quite subdued for three days after it.

Before this tragedy happened the game had expanded quite a lot. At this time it was generally called *The Three Kings*. For reasons of policy every country that came in was called Dash because it was felt that everyone would want to lay claim to England. So it was decided that the names of all the countries should be wrapped in decent obscurity. And about this time too we decided that the period of our game should be set a thousand years in the future. The present was no good, for we were dealing with the fates of kingdoms and as things happened in the real world they would always be falsifying us. If you played about the past you had the depressing knowledge of the things that were going to happen hanging over you all the time. Besides one didn't know in enough detail what had happened and if one had to stop and do research it would hopelessly limit the freedom of play. No one would be alive in a thousand years to prove us wrong and the whole world was ours to play with.

Europe was a wild world to live in in those days. All the towns were tunnelled under by secret passages and trap-doors. A few of them belonged to do-gooders, like The Quicksilvers and The Rosebudders, but most of them were inhabited by particularly nasty villains such as The Colour Stripes or 'They'. Our villains had to do double work as criminals and comics. One did not call people 'good' or 'bad' but 'silly' or 'sensible'. Elspeth specialised in comic villains. One of our favourites was 'Carrots Sawdust, Henry Jack', pronounced 'Keeruts, Seerdust, Hinry Dick', for he had a dialect of his own. He was small and enormously fat, no taller than Elsie in height but as broad as my arms at full stretch. He had large flat feet and ran at a tremendous speed. One could hear his flat footfalls approaching at a great rate along the sandy floors of his passages. You could always tell his trap-doors because they were so large to let him in and out. He was a great robber, and money was always to be found down his trap-door. So if you were in need of money and of a daring disposition you could always lift the large square trap-doors you found and explore along until you found a cache. But though he was a successful thief his chief hobby and delight was to ill-use little girls. He would shuffle up to them with a wide ingratiating smile, saying 'Heed ye die today mi dare?' Which was his pronunciation of 'How do you do today my dear?'

(Unfinished)

Appendix 4 Selected Poems

1. A handsome sailor came to woo me
   And thus said he:
   'Let's love, my pretty, for a season
   Till I go to sea.

   'And we will break a ring between us,
   Give half to each,
   And I'll remember where to find you
   When I touch this beach.'

   'Oh pretty sailor, that's well spoken,
   And like the free.
   Come let us part this golden token,
   Give half to me.

   'For I've a box banded with silver
   And locked with gold,
   Full of my pretty sailors' tokens,
   Full as 'twill hold.'

   He looked at me with brown cheek flushing
   And tossed his head;
   'Oh wanton woman past all blushing!'
   He sighed and said.

   He left me then alone to ponder
   Why he was sure
   That a man's love might freely wander
   But woman's must endure.

   (from 'Whispers', 1940)

2. If you eat of Fairy fruit or drink of Fairy wine
   You will pass outside the World for seven years or nine;
   Or seven days or seven hours or minutes it may be.
   You will not know how long it's been until once more you're free.

   Oh up among the Standing Stones, the Standing Stones bare,
   I once laid down an apple and I picked up a pear.
   I set my teeth against the rind, I bit the soft rind through.
   Oh, had I that to do again I know not what I'd do.

   For as the sweet juice touched my tongue the world flowed all
       away,
   And I was light as thistledown with which the breezes play.
   I saw the world outside me, I saw it through and through;
   And I cared no more what happened, as mortal people do.

   And oh, to live outside the world is lonely, sweet and grand.
   For a mountain is no greater than the shadow of your hand,
   And a dewdrop is no smaller than the basin of the sea.
   It was strange to be inside again when the spell was loosed from
       me.
                  (from Manuscript Book, written during the War)

3. I met a fairy on the hill,
   More pale than moonlight, and as still.
   She stood like mist between two rocks,
   But a cool mind looked from her eyes —
   An alien mind, whose strangeness mocks
   The thought that human beings call wise.
   She did not move, but looked and stood,
   Something that knew not ill nor good.

   And I stood startled on my track —
   Dared not advance, nor yet turn back,
   While mind struck mind with harsh, cold blows,
   Creatures from two creations drawn.
   Over the rocks a thin moon rose
   And paled before the spreading dawn.
   Then before night could turn to day,
   Hostile and slow, each drew away.
                                  (Manuscript Book)

4. I waked or slept, I knew not which,
   And waked in sleep to such a dawn,
   So sweet, so glowing and so rich
   As comes not once in many years.
   I knelt upon my window seat
   And looked out on the terraced lawn,
   Upon the road was tramp of feet,
   And on the terrace stood my dears.

   They glowed with joy, and I leant out
   And called to them, they made reply
   Clear, sweet and distant to my shout,
   I heard gay music in my head,
   The feet marched on the road behind,
   I was afraid, I knew not why.
   The truth came sudden to my mind —
   All those I saw outside were dead.

   (Manuscript Book)

5. The sun shines warm upon my limbs,
   But my dead eyes
   Cannot be dazzled by his light,
   Nor know earth from skies.

   Although I hold my memory fast
   It fades away;
   I have half forgot the thousand shades
   Between night and day.

   On my dark screen I still can see
   All the sweet sights
   That once gave glory to the day,
   Joy to the nights.

   I see the silver birches swing
   Their tasselled leaves,
   And the bright moon on harvest fields
   Touching the sheaves.

Though a mist is breathing on the screen
I can see them yet.
Oh hold the details clear, my heart!
Do not forget.

(Manuscript Book)

6. Triolet

What a lively piece of clay
Bears my drowsy soul about!
Watching angels well may say:
'What a lively piece of clay!
Pity 'tis, without a doubt,
Such a lively piece of clay
Bears that drowsy soul about.'

(from a Notebook)

7. Occupied Territory

I heard one say,
Outside in the cobbled street,
Where the booths shone gay
And the clatter of hard-shod feet
Livened the air, and the children's voices rang,
I heard one say
'They are killing my brother today.'
Then the clatter and clang
Of the wagons over the stones, and the casks rolled down
From the draymen's carts, and the merry noise of the town
Stifled the voice, and now I shall never know
The beginning or end of that half-suggested woe.
A voice so casual and light I could hardly believe
That it sprang from a heart that had desperate reason to grieve.
Surely so deep a woe would call for a heavier word.

And yet in my heart I knew that I had not misheard,
So casual and light are the sorrows we do not know,
Striking the heart with a touch like a butterfly's blow;
Yet my tossing mind will not lightly forget today
What I heard one say.

(from 'Poets Now in the Forces', No. 1)

8. Elspeth

>A little apple tree in flower,
>The distant sound of silver bells,
>A still, clear spring, from which there wells
>A sparkling stream, all quiet power
>Rings in my mind at thought of her;
>Moving in her own crystal air,
>True-minded, clear-eyed, kind and fair,
>She does her tasks and makes no stir.
>No kindly office is too low,
>And no delight too dear to leave
>When kindness calls, she scarce will grieve
>To break imagination's flow
>In her own books, and rise and go
>On slightest errands, yet we know
>How clear a mind dwells there apart
>Unfettered by her tender heart.
>
>*(written for one of Elspeth's birthdays)*

Chapter Notes

1 Yorkshire Heritage: The Family Background

1. 'An Artist's Daughter', Appendix 2.

2. *A History: Henry Briggs Son & Company Ltd: adapted from some historical notes* by Miss K.M. Briggs, Great-Grand-daughter of the Founder, n.d., privately printed.

3. Kathleen Lea in a letter to Katharine Law.

4. *English Homes of the Early Renaissance,* ed. H.A. Tipping, vol. 1 (n.d.) p. 278f. The Currers form a tenuous link with the Brontës, since Miss Currer of Eshdon Hall was the patron of the two schools which Charlotte Brontë attended. Charlotte must have seen memorials of the Currer family in Kildwick Church, and chose Currer Bell as a nom-de-plume with the same initials as her own.

5. I am most grateful to Noel Currer-Briggs for allowing me to use this information.

6. University College School Register 1860-1931 (London 1931) p. 13.

7. John Briggs (III) married Mary Rawdon, daughter of Christopher Rawdon of Bilborough, in 1755, and they had eight surviving children. Their granddaughter, Charlotte Briggs, married another Christopher Rawdon (the sixth to bear that name) in 1821. For an account of the adventurous and successful Rawdon family, see H. Armitage, 'The Rawdon Family', *Trans. Halifax Antiq. Soc.* 1967, p. 37f.

8. Detailed accounts of the Briggs' banking ventures and of their partners and associates are found in G. Chandler, *Four Centuries of Banking,* vol. II (London 1968) p. 207f. and H. Ling Roth, *The Genesis of Banking in Halifax* (Halifax, 1914).

CHAPTER NOTES

9. John Crabtree, *Concise History of the Parish and Vicarage of Halifax* (Halifax, 1836) p. 534.

10. Richard Milnes was a timber merchant who died in 1770. His four sons all lived in or near Flockton, the eldest in Flockton Hall, and James, the father of Margaret and Marianne, at the Manor House. The brothers worked the Flockton Mine, making use of rails laid down to transport timber to the River Calder to move the coal. James Milnes died in 1803.

11. A brief history of the Company is given by D.H.C. Briggs, *A Merchant, a Banker and the Coal Trade, 1693-1971* (Denis Weaver, Dover, n.d.).

12. First Report of the Commissioners on the Employment of Children: Children's Employment (Mines) vol. XI, 1842, p. 52f.

13. Ibid. p. 53.

14. Ibid. p. 272, par. 171.

15. Ibid. p. 201, par. 258, 259.

16. Ibid. p. 203, par. 262f.

17. Henry Briggs, 'On the Use of Gypsum ...' read before Wakefield Farmers' Club, 25 April 1844; 'On Lime and its uses in Agriculture' (substance of a paper read before the Yorkshire Geological and Polytechnic Society, Halifax) 12 March 1845.

18. Part of a letter in the possession of the family.

19. See M. le Comte de Paris, *The Trades' Unions of England*, trans. N.J. Senior, ed. Thomas Hughes (London, 1869) pp. xii and 214f.

20. This is implied in an address to Henry Currer Briggs when he was presented with an epergne in Leeds Town Hall in 1866: 'By being the first to initiate and also to practically carry out the new system of partnership between employer and employed, you have become the pioneer in the endeavour to bridge over the gulf that has so long separated capital and labour.'

21. From an unpublished family history, 'Family Notes Past and Present' by Edith M. Jackson (Madge), the daughter of Marion Jackson. I am most grateful to the daughter of Edith Jackson, Mrs Catherine Laurie, for allowing me to make use of this.

22. Catherine's father was Edward Shepherd, and her mother Hélène O'Dwyer. Edward's brother, Thomas, was the Governor of York Castle, and other members of the family held the position of Governor in various Yorkshire prisons.

23. Walter Geoffrey Jackson had trained as an engineer in South America. He met Marion when the Briggs were living at Saltburn, and when they became engaged he worked as engineer at the Collieries.

24. It is clear that Donald was devoted to his father, who used to play imaginative games and read to the children when he was at home, and who taught Donald to fish. He has left a pleasant picture of Arthur in a little book, *Victorian Memories,* by D.H.C. Briggs, Buckland Press, Dover, n.d. Arthur had three children, Reginald Martin (Mark), Donald Henry and Dorothy.

25. Alice Steward was the daughter of James Steward of Llandudno. The story most frequently told of Alice, and said to come from her diary, was that when she heard that Archibald, the son of a wealthy mine-owner, was to call next day to propose to her, she resolved to refuse him, on condition that her maid brought up her hot water as usual next morning. The maid however was ill, and the cook came up instead, so Alice accepted Archibald. A good deal of information about Alice Steward is given in Winifred Briggs' notebook kept when she was working on the family history. Before they moved to Italy, Archibald and Alice lived at Stanley Hall, Wakefield, and some posters and programmes of plays and light opera performed there are among the family papers. Their son Christopher played first violin in the Hallé Orchestra, and their daughter Olga married James Scott, son of C.P. Scott of *The Manchester Guardian.*

2 An Artist's Daughter: Parents and Childhood

1. 'Life and Background of Katharine Briggs, a Memoir', Appendix 1.

2. 'An Artist's Daughter', Appendix 2.

3. Ibid.

4. E.E. Briggs, *Angling and Art in Scotland,* (London, 1908), p. 6.

5. Ibid, p. 90.

6. Ibid, p. 11.

7. Ibid, p. 20.

8. E.E. Briggs, *The Two Rivers,* (London, 1912), p. 59.

9. *Angling and Art* (note 4 above) pp. 3-4.

10. Introduction to the catalogue of the Centenary Memorial Exhibition of Ernest Briggs' paintings, 15 July — 6 August 1966, at the galleries of the Federation of British Artists, Suffolk St., Pall Mall East, London.

11. D.H.C. Briggs, *Victorian Memories,* (Buckland Press, Dover, n.d.), p. 9.

12. Ibid. p. 11.

13. *The Two Rivers,* (note 8 above) p. 151f.

14. Ibid. p. 310, cf. a remark made to Andrew, p. 203: 'I suppose the girl was just some common farmer's daughter.'

15. Beatrice Barmby suffered from childhood from an injured back. She was a gifted writer of historical stories, and some of these, with one

novel, *The Gods are Just,* were published after her death in 1900. She studied Old Icelandic, and composed a play and a number of poems on themes from Norse poems and sagas. A small notebook written when she was 12 years old gives a delightful picture of her father and mother, to whom she was devoted.

16. From Winifred Briggs, unfinished history of the family.

17. E. Cholmondeley, *The Story of Charlotte Mason 1824-1923* (London, 1960) p. 32f.

18. K.M. Briggs, 'Christina Hole: an Appreciation', *Folklore* 90 (1979) p. 6. She wrote out some of the tales in 1980, under the title 'Tales of the Khoja.'

19. 'Eric Notes', Appendix 3.

20. *The Two Rivers* (note 8 above) p. 160.

21. E.M. Briggs, 'Thomasina's Kittens', MS written at Dalbeathie, date unknown.

22. Evelyn Goshawk, 'Katharine Briggs: an Appreciation', sent to Katharine Law.

23. K.M. Briggs, *British Folktales,* (New York, 1977), p. 1.

3 Growing Up and Making Out: The Imaginary World of the Briggs Sisters

1. W. Gérin, *Charlotte Brontë* (Oxford 1967) p. 25.

2. M. Gaskell, *Life of Charlotte Brontë* (Everyman, 1971) p. 68.

3. W. Gérin, *Anne Brontë* (London 1959) p. 87.

4. C.S. Lewis, *Surprised by Joy* (London 1955) pp. 21-2.

5. E. Farjeon, *A Nursery in the Nineties* (Oxford 1960) p. 31.

6. H. Hartman, *Hartley Coleridge* (London 1931) p. 36f.

7. E. Farjeon (note 5 above) p. 322.

8. From an account of the conversation sent to Katharine Law.

9. K.M. Briggs, 'Eric Notes', Appendix 3.

10. E. Forbes, 'Memories of Katharine', sent to Katharine Law.

11. E. Goshawk, 'Katharine Briggs: an Appreciation', sent to Katharine Law.

12. Originally included in the paper 'Tradition and Invention in Ghost Stories', published in *The Folklore of Ghosts* (1981) but omitted from the printed version. (Note 18 below).

13. Information from Isabel Hale.

14. Vera Brittain, *Women at Oxford* (London 1960) p. 152.

15. Information from Karen Hardcastle.

16. Rose Kerr, *The Story of the Girl Guides* (Girl Guide Association 1932) p. 62.

17. *Traditional Singing Games from Scotland and the Border*, collected by R. Cowan Douglas and K.M. Briggs (Girl Guides Association 1936, revised 1955). It bears the note: 'These games were collected from children in the Lowland Counties of Scotland and are all traditional.'

18. *Tradition and Invention in Ghost Stories*, ed. H.R.E. Davidson and W.M. Russell (Woodbridge 1981) p. 3.

19. K.M. Briggs, *Welshill School* (Centaur Press, London, n.d.).

20. K.M. Briggs, *Mime for Guides and Brownies* (Girl Guides Association 2nd edition 1955) pp. 4-5.

21. Some idea of Catherine Hollingworth's work is given in a special edition of *Spotlight,* the magazine of the Aberdeen Children's Theatre, published June 1968.

22. Barbara Innes wrote an account of the Game as she remembered it for Katharine Law, and afterwards found a letter to her brother written shortly after it took place, which she kindly allowed me to read. Evelyn Goshawk also recorded her own memories of the Game (note 11 above).

4 Feats and Quests: The War Years

1. Information from Evelyn Goshawk.

2. Evelyn Forbes, 'Memories of Katharine', sent to Katharine Law.

3. *The Sunday Telegraph* Colour Supplement, October 1976.

4. Evelyn Goshawk, 'Katharine Briggs: an Appreciation', sent to Katharine Law.

5. 'Occupied Territory', *Poets Now in the Forces, No. 1,* (Favil Press, n.d.).

5 Search for the Hidden People: The Barn House, Burford

1. Printed 'Capricornus, Dunkeld, Perthshire', probably in the 1930s, and illustrated by black and white silhouettes.

2. *Longman's Magazine* XIII (1889) pp. 661-3; *Folklore* 1 (1890) pp. 299-301. When Andrew Lang published the story in *Folklore,* he gave the name of Duncan J. Robertson as his informant, but in the earlier publication he stated that it was sent to him by a lady. Duncan Robertson sent him another story published in vol. XIV of *Longman's Magazine,* and Lang may have confused the two.

3. J. Jacobs, *English Fairy Tales* (London 1890) p.

4. K.M. Briggs, *The Anatomy of Puck* (London 1959) p. 216f.

5. K.M. Briggs, *Dictionary of Folk Tales* I, (London 1970) p. 344f.

6. Margaret Hodges, 'Katharine M. Briggs, a memoir', *Children's Literature in Education* XII (1981) p. 209.

7. *Folklore* 68 (1957) p. 270.

8. Faith Sharp, 'Katharine Briggs', sent to Katharine Law.

9. Evelyn Goshawk, 'Katharine Briggs: an Appreciation', sent to Katharine Law.

10. Josephine Thompson, 'Some Memories of Katharine', sent to Katharine Law.

11. Information from the Burford and Fulbrook Parish Magazine, supplied by the Revd V.D. Rogers and the Revd T. Fish Taylor.

12. Reginald Scott, 'The Discovery of Witchcraft', quoted K.M. Briggs, *The Anatomy of Puck* (Oxford 1959) p. 20.

13. N. Philip, 'The Goodwill of our Hearts: K.M. Briggs as Novelist', *Folklore* 92 (1981) p. 155.

14. W.J. Rose, Review, *Folklore* 69 (1959) p. 558.

15. Information from Miss Tricia Atkinson, to whom I am much indebted for allowing me to visit Dalbeathie and for answering many questions.

16. Information from Evelyn Goshawk.

17. Information from David Ayerst.

18. *The Sunday Telegraph* Colour Supplement, October 1976.

19. Evelyn Forbes, 'Memories of Katharine', sent to Katharine Law.

6 Tales and Traditions: Work in Folklore

1. *A Chaplet for Charlotte Yonge,* ed. G. Battiscombe and M. Laski (London 1965), p. 23.

2. Ibid. p. 24.

3. *Folklore* 69 (1958) p. 52.

4. *Folklore* 71 (1960) pp. 300-5.

5. Stewart F. Sanderson, 'The Modern Urban Legend', Katharine Briggs Lecture No. 1 (Folklore Society, 1981).

6. K.M Briggs, 'Christina Hole: an Appreciation', *Folklore* 90 (1979) p. 6, the quotation is taken from C. Hole, 'Popular Modern Ideas on Folklore', *Folklore* 66 (1955) p. 321.

7. *European Folk Tales,* ed. L. Bodker, Christina Hole and G. D'Aronco, *European Folklore Series I,* for the Council of Europe, (Copenhagen, 1963).

8. R. Michaelis-Jena, 'Katharine M. Briggs. An Appreciation', *The Witch Figure,* ed. V. Newall, (London, 1973), pp. xi-xxi.

9. Foreword to R. Tongue, *The Chime Child* (London 1967), p. viii.

10. Theo Brown, 'Ruth Lyndon Tongue', *Folklore* 94 (1983) pp. 118-9.

11. Preface to Ruth Tongue, *Somerset Folklore,* (Folklore Society, 1965).

12. 'Some Seventeenth Century Books of Magic', *Folklore* 64 (1953), pp. 445-62; a letter on Human Fairy Marriages, ibid. 67 (1956), pp. 53-4; 'The Fairy Economy', ibid. 70 (1959), pp. 533-42; 'On making a Dictionary of Folktales' (note 3 above).

13. For the early days of the Society, see H.R. Ellis Davidson, 'Folklore and Myth', *Folklore* 87, (1976), p. 132f. and K.M. Briggs, 'The Folklore Society and its Beginnings', *Animals in Folklore,* Mistletoe Books IX (Woodbridge 1978) p. 3f.

14. Sister Mary Healey, 'Katharine M. Briggs', sent to Katharine Law.

15. Letter from Mrs Lake Barnett to members of the Council, March 1967.

16. *Folklore* 79, (1968), pp. 81-91; 80 (1969), pp. 89-106; 81, (1970), pp. 81-96.

17. 'The Folklore Society ...' (note 13 above) p. 19.

18. 'The Ditchley Foundation, for those attending conferences at Ditchley Park' (University Press, Oxford).

19. Kathleen Lea, in a letter to Katharine Law.

20. Margaret Hodges, 'Katharine Briggs, a memoir', *Children's Literature in Education* 12 (1981), p. 210.

21. A. Aarne, *The types of the folktale: a classification and bibliography*, trans. and enlarged by S. Thompson (2nd revision, *Folklore Fellows Communication* 184, Helsinki, 1961); *Motif-Index of Folk-Literature*, revised and enlarged by Stith Thompson, 6 vols, (Copenhagen 1955-8).

22. Robin Gwyndaf, 'A Standard Dictionary of English Folktales', *Journ. Soc. Folk-Life Studies* 10 (1972), p. 108.

23. *New Society*, April 1970.

24. I have treated this in detail in 'Katharine Briggs: The Growth of a Folklorist', Katharine Briggs Lecture No. 3, (Folklore Society, 1984).

25. At Los Angeles, a paper on 'Legend, True or False'; at Berkeley, one on 'The Folklore of Charles Dickens', and at Bloomington, one on 'Fairies and the Realm of the Dead', her Presidential address in 1970.

26. A paper on 'The Necessity of Scepticism'.

27. Here she gave a paper on 'Some Aspects of Fairy Tradition'.

28. In a letter to the author.

29. 'A Tentative Essay', *Folklore* 73, (1962), pp. 145-8.

30. I am grateful to Margaret Hodges for letting me have a recording of this conversation.

7 Golden Harvest: The Last Years

1. In a letter to Katharine Briggs, 26 September 1980.

2. Evelyn Forbes, 'Memories of Katharine', sent to Katharine Law.

CHAPTER NOTES

3. Letter from Jim Rositter to Katharine Law.

4. Three letters from Lindsay Morris (ten), Rebecca Morris (eight) and Marguerita Newton (nine) which appeared in the *Parish News* for St Margaret's-at-Cliffe and St Peter's, Westcliffe, January 1981.

5. 'The Folklore Society and its Beginnings', *Animals in Folklore,* Mistletoe Books IX (Woodbridge 1978).

6. *Folklore Studies in the Twentieth Century,* ed. Venetia Newall (Woodbridge 1980), pp. 143-6.

7. *The Folklore of Ghosts,* ed. H.R.E. Davidson and W.M.S. Russell, Mistletoe Books XV (Woodbridge 1981), pp. 3-11.

8. In a letter to the author.

9. The title of the paper was 'Creatures of Legend'.

10. Margaret Hodges, 'Katharine Briggs, a memoir', *Children's Literature in Education* 12 (1981), p. 210.

11. Kathleen Lea in a letter to Katharine Law.

12. Sister Mary Healey, 'Katharine M. Briggs', sent to Katharine Law.

13. Una Moore, who collaborated with Margaret Nash-Williams to write the obituary.

14. Information given to the author by Mrs Peg Cooper, who wrote the lines quoted in a letter to Katharine Law.

Published Work

The following list of the publications of Katharine Briggs is as full as I have been able to make it. A number of the books printed at Dalbeathie are undated. She also left several notebooks containing poems, two collections of poems, *Lost Country* and *The Halfcut Wood*, various unpublished papers delivered at meetings and conferences and one almost complete book, *Double Your Numbers*, a story of childhood and youth in the seventeenth century probably written just before the war.

1915	*The Legend of Maidenhair* (Arthur H. Stockwell, London).
1931	*The Garrulous Lady*, a play in one act (Golden Vista Press, London).
1935?	*A History 1860-1935, Henry Briggs Son & Co Ltd: adapted from some historical notes* (Privately printed, n.d.).
1935	*The Lisles of Ellingham* (Alden Press, Oxford).
1936	*Traditional singing games from Scotland and the Border,* collected with R. Cowan Douglas (Girl Guides Association), Revised edition, 1955.
1936-8	*The Fugitive,* a play in one act. *The Peacemaker,* a play in one act. *Lady in the Dark,* a play in one act. *The Prince, the Fox and the Dragon.* All privately printed, Capricornus Press, Dunkeld. Undated.
1937-9	*Stories arranged for Mime:* 1. 'The Golden Goose' (1937) 2. 'Whuppity Stoorie' (1938) 3. 'Jesper who herded Hares' (1939) Privately printed, Capricornus Press, Dunkeld.
1939	*Mime for Guides and Brownies* (Girl Guides Association), Revised edition 1956.
1940	*Whispers: an experiment in lino cuts,* with Winifred and Elspeth Briggs. *The Twelve Days of Christmas,* with Winifred and Elspeth Briggs. Both privately printed (Capricornus Press, Dunkeld).
1944?	'Occupied Territory', *Poets Now in the Forces,* ed. A.E. Lowy (Favil Press, London, n.d.).

PUBLISHED WORK

1953 *The Personnel of Fairyland* (Alden Press, Oxford).
'Some seventeenth century books of magic', *Folklore* 64, pp. 445-62.
1955 *Hobberdy Dick,* (Eyre and Spottiswood, London). Re-issued Puffin Books, 1972, Kestrel Books, Harmondsworth 1978; Greenwillow Books, New York, 1977.
1956 Letter on Human-Fairy Marriages, *Folklore* 67, p. 310. Review of *The Well at the World's End, Folklore* 67, p. 310.
1957 'The English Fairies', *Folklore* 68, pp. 270-87. Review of *Grimm's Other Tales, Folklore* 68, pp. 375-6.
1958 Letter announcing work on dictionary of folktales, *Folklore* 69, p. 52.
Reviews in *Folklore* 69: *The Silver Bough, vol. 1,* pp. 56-7; *Folklore of Other Lands,* p. 277.
1959 *The Anatomy of Puck: an examination of fairy beliefs among Shakespeare's contemporaries and successors* (Routledge & Kegan Paul, London).
'The fairy economy', *Folklore* 70, pp. 533-42.
Review of *Tales from Cloud Walking Country, Folklore* 70, p. 495.
1961 'Making a dictionary of folk-tales', *Folklore* 72, pp. 300-5.
'Some late accounts of the fairies', *Folklore* 72, pp. 509-19.
Reviews in *Folklore* 72: *Ancient Ballads traditionally sung in New England,* p. 268; *Hans Andersen's Fairy Tales,* pp. 268-9; *The Tiger's Whisper,* pp. 418-9.
1962 *Pale Hecate's Team.* (Routledge & Kegan Paul, London).
'A tentative essay on the area and scope of folklore', *Folklore* 73, pp. 145-8.
Reviews in *Folklore* 73: *The Silver Bough, vols. 2 and 3,* pp. 68-9; *Burmese Law Tales;* pp. 70-1; *International Dictionary of Regional Ethnology and Folklore,* pp. 202-3; *The Science of Folklore,* pp. 284-5.
1963 *Kate Crackernuts* (Alden Press, Oxford). Slightly revised, Kestrel Books, Harmondsworth, 1979; Greenwillow Books, New York, 1980.
'Influence of the Brothers Grimm in England', *Brüder Grimms Gedenken,* Marburg.
Reviews in *Folklore* 74: *Hungarian Folktales,* pp. 349-50; *A Razor for a Goat,* pp. 420-21; *The Witchcult in Western Europe,* p. 571.
1964 'Historical traditions in English folk-tales', *Folklore* 75, pp. 225-42.
'The folds of folklore', *Shakespeare in his own Age,* ed. Allardyce Nicoll. (Cambridge University Press), pp. 167-79.

Reviews in *Folklore 75*: *Songs of the Civil War*, p. 141; *The Traditional Tunes of the Child Ballads*, p. 218; *The Folktales of Israel*, pp. 212-3; *Round the World Fairy Tales*, pp. 218-9; *World Tales for Dramatics and Story-Telling*, p. 285; *Norwegian Fairy Tales*, p. 289; *Tree and Leaf*, pp. 293-4; *Fundamentals of Folk Literature*, p. 296.

1965   *Folktales of England* (Folktales of the World), edited, with R.L. Tongue, (Routledge & Kegan Paul, London).

'Charlotte Yonge's Ethics: some unfashionable virtues', *A Chaplet for Charlotte Yonge*, ed. M. Laski and G. Battiscombe for the Charlotte Yonge Society, (London), pp. 20-30.

'The Three Bears', *Lectures and Reports from the International Congress of Folk-Narrative Research*, (Athens, 1964). *Laographia*, pp. 53-7.

Edited, R.L. Tongue, *Somerset Folklore* (Country Folklore VIII) (The Folklore Society, London).

Reviews in *Folklore 76*: *Maori Myths and Tribal Legend*, p. 167; *A Book of Myths*, pp. 235-6; *A Handbook of Witches*, pp. 317-8.

1966   Reviews in *Folklore 77*: *The Morphology of North American Indian Folktales*, pp. 151-3; *The Magical Arts*, p. 293; *Tales of the North American Indians*, pp. 307-8.

1967   *The Fairies in Tradition and Literature* (Routledge & Kegan Paul, London).

Obituary: Professor Macedward Leach, *Folklore 78*, p. 305.

Reviews in *Folklore 78*: *100 Armenian Tales*, p. 76; *Type and Motif Index of the Folktales of England and North America*, p. 317.

1968   'The transmission of folk-tales in Britain', First Presidential Address, *Folklore 79*, pp. 81-91.

Reviews, in *Folklore 79*: *Witchcraft in England*, pp. 72-3; *Scottish Studies vol. 11*, pp. 315-6.

1969   'Heywood's Hierarchie of the Blessed Angells', 2nd Presidential Address, *Folklore 80*, pp. 89-106.

Reviews in *Folklore 80*: *The Study of American Folklore*, p. 62; *The British Folklorists*, p. 151; *Folktales and Society*, p. 228; *Cinderella Dressed in Yeller*, p. 229.

1970   'The Fairies and the realms of the dead', 3rd Presidential Address, *Folklore 81*, pp 81-96.

Englische Volkmärchen (Die Märchen der Weltlitteratur), edited, with Ruth Michaelis-Jena, Diederich, Dusseldorf-Köln.

Review of *Positively Black*, *Folklore 81*, p. 227.

PUBLISHED WORK

1970-71 *A Dictionary of British Folk-Tales in the English Language* (4 vols.). (Routledge & Kegan Paul, London).
1971 Reviews in *Folklore* 82: *An Egg at Easter*, p. 73; *Green Hills of Magic*, p. 81; *Religion and the Decline of Magic*, pp. 168-9.
1972 'Folklore in nineteenth century English literature', *Folklore* 83, pp. 194-209.
'Possible mythological motifs in English folk-tales', *Folklore* 83, pp. 265-71.
Review in *Folklore* 83: *American Folk Legend*, p. 72; *Leading Folklorists of the North*, pp. 162-3; *John Aubrey, Three Prose Works*, p. 163; *Dickens and the Fairy Tale*, p. 258.
1973 'Medieval survivals in seventeenth century English medicine', *CMA Journal* (Toronto), 20 Oct, pp. 765-71.
Reviews in *Folklore* 84: *The Cult of the Sun in the Ancient Middle East*, pp. 79-80; *The Sports of Cruelty*, p. 80; *The Folklore of Stanton Drew*, p. 259.
1974 *The Folklore of the Cotswolds* (Folklore in the British Isles) (Batsford, London).
The Last of the Astrologers: Mr William Lilly's *History of his Life and Times*, reprinted from the second edition of 1715, with introduction and notes (Mistletoe Books No. 1), (Folklore Society, London).
Reviews in *Folklore* 85: A Scottish Ballad Book, p. 68; *Tradition and Folk Belief*, p. 139.
1975 Reviews in *Folklore* 86: *The Classic Fairy Tales*, p. 62; *A Forgotten Heritage*, p. 143; *Remains concerning Britain*, p. 213.
1976 *A Dictionary of Fairies: Hobgoblins, Brownies, Bogies and other Supernatural Creatures*. (Penguin Books, Harmondsworth). Re-issued as *An Encyclopedia of Fairies,* Pantheon Books, New York, 1977.
A Sampler of British Folk-Tales (compiled from the Dictionary of British Folk-Tales) (Routledge & Kegan Paul, London). Re-issued as *British Folktales,* Pantheon Books, New York, 1977.
1977 'Symbols in Fairy Tales', *Symbols of Power,* ed. H.R.E. Davidson (Mistletoe Books No. 7). D.S. Brewer and Rowman and Littlefield for the Folklore Society (Ipswich and Toronto), pp. 131-55.
Reviews in *Folklore* 88: *Scottish Folktales*, p. 119; *Folktales told around the World*, pp. 119-20; *The Disciplina Clericalis of Petrus Alfonsi*, p. 241.

1978 *The Vanishing People: a study of traditional fairy beliefs* (Folklore of the British Isles) (Batsford, London). Re-issued as '*Fairy Lore and Legends*'. Pantheon Books, New York, and by Random House of Canada Ltd, Toronto.
'The Folklore Society and its beginnings', *Animals in Folklore*, ed. J.R. Porter and W.M.S. Russell (Mistletoe Books No. 9), D.S. Brewer and Rowman and Littlefield for the Folklore Society (Ipswich and Toronto), pp. 3-20.

1979 *Abbey Lubbers, Banshees and Boggarts: a Who's Who of Fairies* (Kestrel Books, Harmondsworth), and as 'an illustrated encyclopedia of fairies', Pantheon Books, New York. Illustrated by Yvonne Gilbert.
'Some unpleasant characters among British Fairies', *Folklore Studies in the Twentieth Century*, ed. V.J. Newall (Boydell and Brewer, Ipswich), pp. 143-6.
'Christina Hole: an Appreciation', *Folklore* 90, pp. 4-8.
Review of *The Faber Book of North American Legends*, *Folklore* 90, pp. 118-9.

1980 Review of *The Past We Share*, *Folklore* 91, p. 250.
'Brownie into Boggart', *Folklore on Two Continents: Essays in Honour of Linda Dégh*, eds. Burtakoff, N. and Lindahl, C., (Trickster Press, Bloomington, Indiana) pp. 79-85.

1981 *Nine Lives: Cats in Folklore* (Pantheon Books, New York). Illustrated by John Ward.
'Tradition and invention in ghost stories', *The Folklore of Ghosts* ed. H.R.E. Davidson and W.M.S. Russell (Mistletoe Books No. 15) D.S. Brewer, Ipswich, pp. 3-11.
'The Legends of Lilith and the Wandering Jew in nineteenth-century literature', *Folklore* 92, pp. 132-40.
Undated. *Welshill School* (Centaur Press, London).

Index

Abbey Lubbers, Banshees and Boggarts, 165
Aberdeen Children's Theatre, 70
acting, Katharine's love of, 58, 61, 117-8, 119; production of plays, 100-2, 119-20, 157-8
Alden Press, 79, 80, 81, 108, 128, 136
American Folklore Society, 150
Anatomy of Puck, The, 109, 115, 126, 128, 131, 143
Anglican Church, Katharine's change to, 123-4, 161
Angling and Art in Scotland, 35-6, quotations from, 14-7
Arts League of Service, 69
Atkinson, Tricia, 132
Autobiography of William Lilly, 147
Ayerst, David, 133

Barmby, Ada, 20, 25, 35; Mabel, 20, 24, 35, 43, 101
Barn House, 70, 83, 147, 156-7, 160; life at, 106, 116-23; picture, 118
Bells, The, production of, 119
Belvidere Gazette, 16-7
Birnham, 4, 45, 56
Blacker, Carmen x, 167-8
Blake, Sister Ursula x, 48, 50, 52
Briggs, Alice (née Steward) 11, 12, 190, Table 2 (p.3)
Briggs, Archibald, 11, 16, 190, Table 2 (p.3)
Briggs, Arthur, 9-11, 14-8, 34, 190, Table 3 (p.12)
Briggs, Catharine (née Shepherd), 9-10, 20, 23, 24, 35, Tables 2 (p.3), 3 (p.12) picture, 10
Briggs, Donald, 11, 17-8, 61, 159, 190
Briggs, Dorothy, (later Barren), 34-5, 125, 190
Briggs, Elspeth, activities, 49, 53, 72, 117, 120, 123, 134; as a child, 11-2, 24-5, 27-32, 48-9, 179-81; as artist, 61, 64, 81; as writer, 60, 64, 70, 72, 74, 79, 80-2, 117, 134-5; cat-lover, 40, 122; character, 125, 135; death, 134; memorials to, 135-6; relationship with mother, 124-5; warwork, 89, 93-4; pictures, 44, 87; Table 4 (p.14)
Briggs, Elizabeth (Biddy) (née Deniston), 61
Briggs, Ernest, 13-45; as artist, 2, 16-7, 19, 32, 36, 42, 173, 191; family, 2, 9, 11; fisherman, 2, 17, 36; games with Katharine, 1, 25-7, 190; influence on Katharine, 33, 43-4, 60, 84, 107, 170; pictures, 15, 22; Tables 3 (p.12), 4 (p.14)
Briggs, Evelyn Marion, 23, Table 4 (p.14)
Briggs, Gerald, 14-6, 35, 36, 37, 41, picture, 15; Tables 3 (p.12), 4 (p.14)
Briggs, Gilbert, 14, 15, 27, 41; picture, 15; Tables 3 (p.12), 4 (p.14)
Briggs, Helen (Aunt Nell) (née Jones), 10-1, 34, 35, 61, 81, 83; Table 3 (p.12)
Briggs, Henry, 5-9, 11; letters of, 8, 12; Table 2 (p.3)
Briggs, Henry Currer, 9, 16, 17; Tables 2 (p.3), 3 (p.12)
Briggs, Marianne (née Milnes), 6, 8, 9, 12; picture, 10; Table 2 (p.3)
Briggs, Marion: see Marion Jackson
Briggs, Mary (née Cooper), 19-25, 29, 30, 34, 37, 40, 42-5, 126; old age, 124-6; relations with Katharine, 55-6, 60, 61, 73, 83, 88, 93-5, 99, 106, 112; pictures, 24, 26, 44, 87; Table 4 (p.14)
Briggs, Noel Currer, 4, 169, 170, 188
Briggs, Rawdon, 5, Table 1 (p.3)
Briggs, Winifred, as a child, 24, 25, 27, 30-32, 34, 48-50, 179-81; as artist, 61, 64, 79, 83, 132, 133, 136; character, 82-3, 136; contribution to Summer

Players, 70, 117; to Companions, 85-6; mental breakdowns, 82, 125, 134, 135; printing skills, 67, 72, 80, 81; running Dalbeathie, 88, 89, 93, 174; work on family history, 11, 12, 27-8, 64; work with Guides, 88; pictures, 44, 87; Table 4 (p.14)
Briggs family, characters of, xi, 5, 8
Brittain, Vera, 61, 62
broadcasting, by Katharine, 151
British Folk Tales, 39
Broad Leys, 11
Brontë sisters, 46-7, 48, 53
Brown, Theo x, 141
Brownies, Katharine's work with, 64-7, 108, 113, 171
Builders, The, production of, 119
Burford, 116-24, 133-4, 164, 169, 170; church at, 119, 124, 135, 136; Church House, 121, 134: see also Barn House
Buttrey, Sarah, 4
Byam School of Art, 61, 174

Capricornus Press, 67, 72, 80, 103, 108, 174
Caputh, 44-5, 69, 88, 126
Castlemains, Douglas, Polish School at, 87, 88, 89, 174
Castilians, The, 76, 79, 80
Cats, at Burford, 121-2; at Dalbeathie, 73, 121; book on, 160, 165-6; death of Shookie, 98-9, 103; Thomasina, 34, 40
Civil War, the Great, 61, 74, 76
Coddington Hall, 95, 100
Coleridge, Hartley, 48
Commedia del Arte, 69, 120-1
Constant Gardener, The, 82, 117
Cook, Mr, 116
Cooper, Thomas, 19
Cooper, Mrs Peg (Coops),171-2
Currer family, 4
Dalbeathie House, x, 20-1, 34, 37-42, 64, 83, 106, 159, 162, 174; activities at, 69, 71-4; evacuees at, 87-9; pets at, 73-4, 99; poem on, 104; sale of, 131-2; picture, 41
Dalgleish, Jean, 71, 75, 84, 110

Dictionary of Fairies, 131, 153, 159, 160, 165
Dictionary of Folktales, 109, 138-40, 147-8, 153, 164
Ditchley Park Conference, 146
Dixon, Mr, 27-8, 64
Doctorate, awarded to Katharine, 148-9
Dorson, Richard, 146
Duff, Dr Carol, 159, 161, 162
Duff, 'Peter', 75, 84; 'Jim', 85
Dundee, 9, 13

Englische Volmärchen, 141
Eric Game, 48-54, 62, 74, 76, 80, 179-82
Errol, Perthshire, 100-101, 174

Fairies in Tradition and Literature, The, 126, 130-1
fairy lore, 39, 72-5, 105; Brighton Exhibition on, 165; in Shakespeare, 129; thesis on, 107, 110, 112-4
Farjeon, Eleanor, 47
Fellows Road, house in, 1, 13, 22, 40, 176
Fenton, charlotte, 56-60
Flockton Colliery, 6, 7
Florence, honeymoon in, 21
Folk-Lore/Folklore, journal of Folklore Society, 108, 114, 138, 140, 152, Presidental Addresses in, 145
folklore, Katharine's interest in, 39, 66, 107-8, 126, 128-9; work in, 152
Folklore of the Cotswolds, The, 150
Folklore Society, 66, 126, 136, 138, 143-7, 168, 169, 175; Ditchley Park Conference, 164; mini-conferences, 156, 164; new constitution of, 145-6; publications of, 147, 164
Folk-Narrative Research, International Conference of, 136, 150-1, 175
Folktales of England, 55, 142, 153
Forbes, Evelyn (née Hill),50, 57-60, 89-94, 116, 135, 161, 167-8
Franklin, Colin, 126, 138
Fugitive, The, 82

Galloway, 14, 36, 74-6, 109, 176, 178
Garrulous Lady, The, 81, 97

INDEX

Gérin, Winifred, 46
Ghyll Head, 35, 36
Girl Guides, Katharine's work with, 64, 67, 68, 71, 74, 83, 103, 107, 171, 174; Winifred's work with, 88
Godfrey, Kathleen (Gee), 29, 31, 92
Goshawk, Evelyn, 37, 52-3, 68, 71-3, 75-6, 84, 96, 100, 120, 124, 134
Grimm Brothers, 138, 141
Gwyndaf, Robin, 148, 153-4

Hale, Ellen Mary, 56-60
Hale, Isabel, x, 57-9
Henderson, Hamish, 141
Hobberdy Dick, 81, 105, 108, 113, 126-8, 129, 151, 157, 165
Hodges, Prof. Margaret, ix, 113, 151, 155, 156, 164, 166
Hole, Christina, 140
Hollingsworth, Catherine (Pelican Snelson), x, 70-1, 171, 194

Innes, Barbara, ix, 70, 74-6, 119, 120, 125-6, 134, 161, 164, 166

Jackson, Edith (Madge), x, 18, 20, 25, 29, 55; her daughter Edith, 75
Jackson, Georgina, 70
Jackson, Geoffrey, 9-10, 190, Table 3 (p.12)
Jackson, Marion (née Briggs), 18, 20, 21, 35, 41, Table 3 (p.12)
Jackson, Margery (Wilson), 18, 20, 36, 42
Jacobs, Joseph, 108-9, 139
Jena, Ruth Michaelis, 141
Jones, Helen (see Helen Briggs)

Kate Crackernuts, 100, 105, 107-13, 165; the folktale, 150, 151, 153, 195
Keith, Richard, 88-9; Rena, 88
Kennedy, Douglas, 144
Khoja Tales, 18, 166, 192
Kildwick Manor, 4
Kingshill, Jane (née Moore), 70, 93, 119, 128, 157

Lady in the Dark, 82

Lady Margaret Hall, 61-4, 107, 139, 173
Lake-Barnett, Mrs. H.A., 143-5
Lang, Andrew, 108-9, 195
Lansdowne House School, 59-60, 93, 173
Laurie, Catherine (Kitty), (née Jackson), 75, 84, 190
Law, Katharine, 135, 140, 159-69
Lea, Kathleen, 3, 146, 169
Leak Pasha, 16
Leeds, University of, 2, 18, 140
Legend of Maidenhair, The, 60
Lewis, C.S., 47, 48
Lilith, projected book on, 166
Lund, Niels, 33, 44

MacDonald, George, 124
MacKillup, Jimmy, 40, 132-3
MacMullen, Jeanine, 157
Mason, Charlotte, 28, 51; College, 28, 64
Melhuish, Jean, 159
Middleton, 38-9
Midsummer Night's Dream, A, production of, 119-20, 157
Milnes family, 12, Table 2 (p.6)
Mime, books on, 67; for Guides and Brownies, 66-9; used by Summer Players, 69-70
Mines in West Riding, 5-7; nationalisation of, 11
Mistletoe Books, 147
Moore, Una, 70, 170, 199; Jane, see Jane Kingshill
Morris, Jan, 165-6
Morris, Lindsay and Rebecca, 163

Nash-Williams, Margaret, 139
Newall, Venetia, 144, 145, 146, 151, 164
Newfoundland, Katharine's visit to, 65-6, 174
Newton, Marguerita, 163
Nine Lives, 165
Norton, F.J. 141, 153

O'Dwyer, Hélène, 12, 190
Olaus Magnus, 115
Opie, Peter and Iona, 141; Peter, 144, 148
oral tradition, 152
Order of the Rose, 83-7
Outwood Hall, 8
Oxford, doctorate from, 148-9; research at, 107, 114-6; student at, 55, 61-4

Padgate, 90, 91, 93, 94
Pale Hecate's Team, 126, 129, 130
Peacemakers, The, 71, 81-2
Pearmans, 120, 122
Personnel of Fairyland, The, 107, 113, 114, 127, 130-1
Perth, Repertory Theatre at, 70, 100, 166
Philip, Neil, 128
Pittsburg, 151, 164
Poems, quotations from, 34, 38-9, 53, 61, 72-3, 77, 84, 86, 97, 102, 103-5, 125; Tennyson's *Ulysses,* 155; Appendix 4, 183f
Porter, Enid, 141
Profit-sharing experiment, 9
Puck, acted by Katharine, 120; study of, 129
Pull Wyke, 9, 11, 18, 19, 21, 23, 24, 25, 28, 132

Rawdon family, 5, Table 1 (p.3)
Rogers, Byron, 64, 99
Rositter, Jim, 163
Routledge and Kegan Paul, 126, 138, 142, 148, 151, 164

Sach, Sylvia, 100
Sanderson, Stewart, x, 139, 140, 147
School of Scotish Studies, 141
Sandwich, Long Cottage at, 163, 171-2
Seaton, Ethel, 107, 113-6
Shakespeare, *As You Like It* game, 26-7, 180; productions, 119-20, 157-8
Shepherd family, 9, 37, 101, 190; Violet, 83, 93; Walter, 37
Schroeder, Revd Lawrence 10; Mary, x
Silvey, Robert, 47

Sharp, Faith (née Sprachman), 117-22, 133-4, 141-2
Shenker, Israel, 165
Slade School of Art, 17, 19
Smith, Alex Dalrymple, 85
Somerset Folklore, 142
Spens, Janet, 61-2
Stansfeld, William, 6; Miles, 7
story-telling, 56, 66, 108, 136, 146, 148, 150, 154, 163; in the Forces, 99-100, 171
Summer Players, 69-72, 82-3, 107, 117, 120, 171, 174, 175
Sunday Telegraph interview, 64, 90, 99, 133; see Byron Rogers
Syerston, 92, 93, 97, 98-100

Taylor, Revd T. Fish, 116
Templeton, Isabel, 65
Ternhill, Shropshire, 101
Thompson, Josephine, 118, 122-3, 135, 160
Thompson, T.W., 141
Thomson, Margaret, 88-9
Tongue, Ruth, 141-2, 153, 156
Traditional Singing Games 66, 193
Two Rivers, The, 17, 19, 20, 33, 41-2, 81

Unitarians, x, 4-5, 8, 10, 57, 123-4
United States, visits to 136, 150, 164, 175
University College, London 138, 143, 147, 158; school, 5, 14, 17

Vanishing People, The, 152, 165

WAAF, Katharine's time in the, 89-103, 174
War, 1914-18, 60; 1939-45, 83, 86-103
Ward, John, 165-6
Watson, Katharine, 140
Welshill School, 69
Whitwood Collieries, 2, 18
Webb, Kaye, 157
Widford Manor, 127

INDEX

Wilkinson, Norman, 33
Wilson, Hugh Radcliffe, 36, 178
Winthorpe, 92, 95-7
Witchcraft, 107, 110, 128, 129, 144
Witches' Ride, The, 108
Witch Figure, The, 141, 151
Wood, Brian, 95-9, 161, 167

Woodland House, Leeds, 9

Yeats, W.B. 39, 114
Yewell, A.T., 42
Young Visitors, 157, 160
Yonge, Charlotte, 137, 162